Legal
Writing

ASPEN COURSEBOOK SERIES

Legal Writing

Second Edition

Richard K. Neumann, Jr.
Professor of Law
Hofstra University

Sheila Simon
Lieutenant Governor of Illinois

Wolters Kluwer
Law & Business

AUSTIN   BOSTON   CHICAGO   NEW YORK   THE NETHERLANDS

Aspen Publishers
Attn: Permissions Department
76 Ninth Avenue, 7th Floor
New York, NY   10011-5201

To contact Customer Care, e-mail customer.care@aspenpublishers.com,
call 1-800-234-1660, fax 1-800-901-9075, or mail correspondence to:

Aspen Publishers
Attn: Order Department
PO Box 990
Frederick, MD 21705

Printed in the United States of America.

3 4 5 6 7 8 9 0

ISBN 978-0-7355-9994-9

Library of Congress Cataloging-in-Publication Data

Neumann, Richard K., 1947-
    Legal writing / Richard K. Neumann, Jr., Sheila Simon.—2nd ed.
        p. cm.
    Includes index.
    ISBN 978-0-7355-9994-9
1. Legal composition. I. Simon, Sheila J., 1961- II. Title.

    KF250.N484 2011
    808'.06634—dc22

2010052090

About Wolters Kluwer Law & Business

Wolters Kluwer Law & Business is a leading provider of research information and workflow solutions in key specialty areas. The strengths of the individual brands of Aspen Publishers, CCH, Kluwer Law International and Loislaw are aligned within Wolters Kluwer Law & Business to provide comprehensive, in-depth solutions and expert-authored content for the legal, professional and education markets.

CCH was founded in 1913 and has served more than four generations of business professionals and their clients. The CCH products in the Wolters Kluwer Law & Business group are highly regarded electronic and print resources for legal, securities, antitrust and trade regulation, government contracting, banking, pension, payroll, employment and labor, and healthcare reimbursement and compliance professionals.

Aspen Publishers is a leading information provider for attorneys, business professionals and law students. Written by preeminent authorities, Aspen products offer analytical and practical information in a range of specialty practice areas from securities law and intellectual property to mergers and acquisitions and pension/benefits. Aspen's trusted legal education resources provide professors and students with high-quality, up-to-date and effective resources for successful instruction and study in all areas of the law.

Kluwer Law International supplies the global business community with comprehensive English-language international legal information. Legal practitioners, corporate counsel and business executives around the world rely on the Kluwer Law International journals, loose-leafs, books and electronic products for authoritative information in many areas of international legal practice.

Loislaw is a premier provider of digitized legal content to small law firm practitioners of various specializations. Loislaw provides attorneys with the ability to quickly and efficiently find the necessary legal information they need, when and where they need it, by facilitating access to primary law as well as state-specific law, records, forms and treatises.

Wolters Kluwer Law & Business, a unit of Wolters Kluwer, is headquartered in New York and Riverwoods, Illinois. Wolters Kluwer is a leading multinational publisher and information services company.

for Lillianna and Alexander
RKN Jr

for Reilly and Brennan
SS

Summary of Contents

Contents

Contents

Chapter 10: Working with Statutes

Part II: The Process of Writing

Chapter 11: Getting to Know Yourself as a Writer

Chapter 12: Inside the Process of Writing

Chapter 13: How Professional Writers Plan Their Writing

Part III: Office Memoranda

Chapter 14: Office Memorandum Format   103

Chapter 15: Predictive Writing in an Office   107
Memorandum

Part IV: Organizing Analysis

Chapter 16: CREAC: A Formula for
Structuring Proof of a Conclusion of Law   117

Part V: Working Effectively with Details

Chapter 20: Paragraphing   151

Chapter 21: Writing an Effective Sentence   **155**

Chapter 22: Effective Style: Clarity, Vividness, and Conciseness   **161**

Chapter 23: Citing Authority   **173**

Chapter 24: Quoting Effectively   **181**

Contents

Part VI: Informal Analytical Writing

Chapter 25: Client Advice Letters   189

Chapter 26: Email Memoranda   193

Part VII: The Shift to Persuasion

Chapter 27: What Persuades a Court?   199

Chapter 28: Writing a Motion Memorandum   207

Part VIII: Telling the Client's Story

Chapter 29: The Statement of the Case in a Motion Memo or Appellate Brief   217

Chapter 30: Developing a Persuasive Story   221

Chapter 31: Telling the Story Persuasively   227

Contents

Part IX: Making the Client's Arguments

Chapter 32: The Argument in a Motion Memo or Appellate Brief   237

Chapter 33: Point Headings and Subheadings   247

Part X: Appellate Briefs and Oral Argument

Chapter 34: Appellate Practice   255

Chapter 35: Writing the Appellate Brief   259

Chapter 36: Handling Standards of Review 265

Chapter 37: Making Policy Arguments 271

Chapter 38: Questions Presented 277

Chapter 39: Oral Argument 285

Appendices

Contents

In this book our goals have been to explain analytical writing in ways that are concise, accessible, and occasionally conducive to provoking the type of smile that enhances learning. We have included special coverage on the process of writing, the use of policy, storytelling techniques, and the CREAC formula (also known as the paradigm).

Chapter 1 provides an overview of the book and how to use it. Here is how the rest of the book is organized:

Part	Chapters	Coverage
Part I	Chs. 2 through 10	analysis of legal rules, policy, and authority
Part II	Chs. 11 through 13	the process of writing and the value of students' own individuality as writers
Part III	Chs. 14 and 15	office memos and predictive writing
Part IV	Chs. 16 through 19	the CREAC formula and how to use it
Part V	Chs. 20 through 24	paragraphing, sentences, style, citations, and quoting
Part VI	Chs. 25 and 26	client letters (Ch. 25) and email memos (Ch. 26)
Part VII	Chs. 27 and 28	how lawyers persuade (Ch. 27) plus motion memos (Ch. 28)
Part VIII	Chs. 29 through 31	storytelling and fact statements
Part IX	Chs. 32 and 33	argumentation and point headings
Part X	Chs. 34 through 39	appellate briefs, standards of review, policy arguments on appeal, questions presented, and oral argument

Acknowledgments

From Richard K. Neumann, Jr:
Thank you to Elizabeth Brehm, Jennifer Garber, Rachael Ringer, Michelle Gordon, Samuel Lui, Laura Schaefer, Matt Weinick, and Frances Zemel for their research and valuable suggestions and to Barbara Dillon, Alex Fiore, Francis Forde, Angelina Ibragimov, Felicia Leo, Alex Leonard, Danielle Manor, Gariel Nahoum, Jody-Ann Tyrell, and Jason Weber for their many suggestions as well. Thanks to Anne Kringel, J. Lyn Entrikin Goering, Ruth Anne Robbins, Robin Boyle, Amy Langenfeld, Terry Pollman, and Judy Stinson for their advice. I'm especially grateful to Sheila Simon for her creativity and her perceptiveness about how to make both learning and coauthoring fun.

Thanks to Alex, Lill, and Deb. Lill and Alex have taught me enormously about how to learn and about how textbooks can become both lighter *and* deeper. At the keyboard I often wondered what kind of book they might want to learn from in future years, whatever they study.

From Sheila Simon:
Thank you to Susan Williams and Ramon Escapa, who contributed long and often tedious hours to this book. Jayne McCarroll and Linda Kalloran are the stars who turned scripts into moving images for the book's website. Thanks to many people who gave ideas and energy, including Peter Alexander, Levi Burkett, Delio Calzolari, Amy Campbell, Bruce Ching, Laura Cox, Brannon Denning, Andrea Jones, Elizabeth Kee, Hannah Kelley, Sue Liemer, Melissa Marlow, Matt Rokusek, Hollee Temple, Tim Ting, and Melissa Werish. Thanks also to the many students who allowed me to consider using their writing, particularly Elizabeth Gastélum, Nate Bailey, Joanne Olson, and Caroline Borden. I am grateful to Richard Neumann for the opportunity to work with him. I have learned from Richard far more than I have contributed to this book.

Thanks to my husband, Perry Knop, for his constant encouragement. And our daughters, Reilly and Brennan Knop, are my best source of learning about teaching. We were on to something with Barbie Math Bath!

From both Richard and Sheila:
At Aspen, thank you to George Serafin for suggesting the concept of this book; Carol McGeehan, Richard Mixter, Mark Scalise, and Mike Gregory for their help in brainstorming its possibilities and those of its website; and Betsy Kenny, Kaesmene Banks, and Julie Nahil for their editorial assistance. We are also grateful to the

Acknowledgments

anonymous reviewers who read drafts of the manuscript for Aspen and made many valuable suggestions. (It really is anonymous; you know who you are, but we don't.)

Copyright Acknowledgments

Legal Writing

Writing and Professional Work

§1.1 Memos and Briefs

In a writing course, "audience" means the people who will read a given document. A document communicates better if the writer considers the needs and sensibilities of the audience while writing.

An *office memorandum* analyzes a legal issue objectively. It answers a question about how the law treats certain facts. Its audience is usually a senior lawyer, such as a partner in a law firm.

A lawyer writes a *motion memorandum* (also called a *trial brief*) to persuade a trial court to decide an issue in favor of the lawyer's client. A lawsuit starts in a trial court, and the memo's audience is the trial judge. (Nearly all the courts you see on television and in movies are trial courts.)

A lawyer writes an *appellate brief* to persuade an appellate court to affirm or reverse the decision of a lower court. A brief's audience is the judges who will decide the appeal.

§1.2 Predictive Writing and Persuasive Writing

In an office memo, you *predict* objectively how a court would decide the issue on which you are writing. In a motion memo or appellate brief, you try to *persuade* the court to make a decision favorable to your client.

1

Here is an example of predicting: Suppose your client runs a website from which ringtones can be downloaded into cell phones. Your client asks, "If we copy the ringtones the telephone company sells and if we then sell them for a lower price, will we get into trouble?" Because you will think precisely about the law, your mind will translate "will we get into trouble?" into questions like these:

- Does the phone company own a copyright on its ringtones or have some other property interest in them?
- If the answer to that is yes, would a court order the client to pay damages if the client copies the phone company's ringtones?

Other issues could grow out of these facts, but these two illustrate predictive thinking.

Suppose the client does copy the phone company's ringtones and the phone company sues. In the trial court, you might make a motion to compel the phone company to respond in discovery or a motion for summary judgment. If you lose at trial, you might appeal to a higher court. In all these situations, you will try to persuade a judge or judges in a memo or brief to decide in favor of your client. You will do so by telling the client's story in a compelling way and by making logical arguments to support your position. Lawyers persuade primarily through storytelling and argumentation.

§1.3 Writing and a Lawyer's Career

In college, students write mostly to satisfy requirements, such as the requirement to write a term paper or to demonstrate knowledge in an exam. But clients pay lawyers to *get results*. Lawyers write to *cause things to happen*—such as a court deciding in the client's favor. In a lawyer's career, "good writing pays well and bad writing pays badly."[1]

The American Bar Foundation has done surveys to identify the skills hiring partners look for in making hiring decisions as well as the skills young lawyers find most important in their early years of practice.[2] The hiring partners surveyed consider the quality of a job applicant's writing sample to be one of the top factors in deciding whether to make a job offer.[3] (Employers ask job applicants to submit writing samples.) The young lawyers said that they had found written and oral communication to be the most valuable skills in law practice.[4] An ability to write well thus can help a new lawyer looking for a job. When you scan employment

---

[1] Donald N. McCloskey, *The Writing of Economics* 2 (Macmillan 1987).
[2] Bryant Garth & Joanne Martin, *Law Schools and the Construction of Competence*, 43 J. Legal Educ. 469 (1993).
[3] *Id.* at 489.
[4] *Id.* at 473.

announcements looking for your first job, you will see phrases like the following over and over: "seeks attorney with proven writing ability," "excellent research and writing skills required," or "recruiting for associate with superb writing skills."

Once you have a job, "excellent writing skills are a form of future job security."[5] A person who has supervised 400 lawyers at a major corporation says that if you write well, "you are more likely to get good grades in law school [and] become a partner in your law firm, or receive comparable promotions in your law department or government law office."[6] When you start work as a lawyer, "you will not be asked to give a talk on torts or property law. You will be given a set of facts and a legal issue about which you know almost nothing. You will be expected to find the law . . . and write a memo. . . . The finished product will be read by the person who signs your paycheck and who may rely upon your work to argue the issue in front of a judge."[7]

§1.4 Professional Writing and a Professional Audience

In law, what counts is what *works*. Legal writing is put to practical tests in the real world. Office memos must provide everything needed to advise a client or plan litigation. Motion memos and appellate briefs must persuade judges to decide in the client's favor. If these documents are to do their jobs, they must be able to withstand attack from what has been called the "reader in bad faith"—the opposing attorney who would like to distort an ambiguous phrase into something the writer never meant, the unsympathetic judge looking for a misstatement on which to base an adverse ruling, "and all the others who will want to twist the meaning of words for their own ends."[8] In law, good writing is strength. If you are a better writer than other lawyers, your clients will have an advantage.

What will your readers—your audience—be like? Whether a judge or a senior lawyer, your audience will typically share three characteristics. First, the reader must make a decision and wants from you exactly the material needed for the decision—not less and not more. Second, most readers are busy people, must read quickly, and do not have time to read twice. Third, many readers will be skeptical and will look for gaps or weaknesses in your analysis. For many lawyers, skepticism leads to better decisions.

This does *not* mean that all lawyers must write in the same way or in the same style. Most legal writing tasks can be done effectively in a variety of ways. While learning legal writing, it's important for you to assess your strengths and

---

[5] Mark E. Wojcik, Perspectives, Fall 1994, at 7.
[6] Richard S. Lombard (formerly general counsel at Exxon), remarks reprinted in *Lost Words: The Economical, Ethical and Professional Effects of Bad Legal Writing*, Occasional Paper 7 of the ABA Section of Legal Education Admissions to the Bar, at 54 (1993).
[7] John McNeill, Perspectives, Fall 1994, at 7.
[8] Henry Weihofen, *Legal Writing Style* 8 (2d ed., West 1980).

weaknesses—so that you can develop a method of writing that takes advantage of your strengths and minimizes the effect of your weaknesses. It's not unusual to hear students say that in the legal writing course they learn a lot about themselves.

§1.5 How to Use This Book and Its Website

The sticker on the shrinkwrapping of this book tells you how to get access to the text's website. The website contains valuable material that supplements the book.

Different people learn differently, and we have designed the book and the website to accommodate as many learning styles as possible. The book alone explains everything you need to know, but the website provides some enhancements.

Although we can't sit with you individually and talk, we try to come as close to that as we can in a book. We've also written this book in an informal, almost conversational style. We try to explain the things you need to know without creating a distance between you and the book.

When you write memoranda and briefs in this course, **please do *not* imitate the informality of this book.** Memoranda and briefs are formal documents. For example, in this book we use contractions (two words merged into one with an apostrophe), but **contractions do not belong in formal documents.** And we use italics and dashes a lot more than you should. In formal memoranda and briefs, italics and dashes have a place, for emphasis—but not frequently. (The dash in the preceding sentence would be fine in both formal writing and informal writing.)

On the other hand, we have tried to write the book in a style that illustrates some of the most important features of legal writing—clarity, precision, conciseness, and vividness. When you find those characteristics in any writing, they are worth imitating.

§1.5.1 What's in the Book

The book contains chapters that explain writing skills and the analytical skills that support them; exercises at or near the end of several chapters; checklists at the end of some chapters to help you write and rewrite; and sample memos and briefs in appendices at the end of the book.

§1.5.2 What's on the Website

The card inside this book has instructions for redeeming your access code and getting into the website.

On the website are

- videos that help explain (with a touch of humor) some of the most fundamental aspects of legal writing
- checklists from several chapters that you can print from the website to help you improve your writing throughout the course
- articles on Writing Exam Answers, Interviewing the Client, and other subjects

Legal Rules
and Their
Sources

Inside a Rule of Law

§2.1 The Inner Structure of a Rule

A rule is a formula for making a decision. For example: "A person who drives a motor vehicle at a speed greater than a posted speed limit is guilty of speeding." Here's how this rule would look as a formula:

$$\text{drives} + \text{motor vehicle} + \text{faster than} + \text{posted speed limit} = \text{guilty of speeding}$$

How do you know if you are guilty? Compare the phrases to the left of and above the equals sign to the facts. If you're behind the wheel and operating the controls *(drives)*, if the thing you're driving is a car *(motor vehicle)*, if a sign by the side of the road says "Speed Limit 45" *(posted speed limit)*, and if you're driving 60 miles an hour *(faster than)*, you're guilty of speeding. But if you're in the passenger seat *(not driving)*, one of the ingredients is missing, and you're not guilty, regardless of how fast the car travels.

Most rules have three components:

1. **A set of elements (the test):** In the example above, the elements are *driving, motor vehicle, faster than*, and *posted speed limit*. Some rules have criteria instead of elements (see pages 18–19).
2. **A result** that occurs when all the elements are present (and the test is thus satisfied). In the example above, the result is *guilty of speeding*.

9

3. A **causal term** that determines whether the result is mandatory, prohibitory, discretionary or declaratory (more about this in a moment).

Some rules also have:

4. One or more **exceptions** that, if satisfied would prevent the result, even if all the elements are present. If the rule above contained the words "unless the motorist reasonably believes it necessary to exceed the speed limit in order to prevent injury to a person or substantial damage to property"— that would be an exception.

§2.2 Four Types of Rules

Nearly all legal rules fit into one of the following four categories.

A *mandatory* rule requires someone to act and might be expressed in words like "shall" or "must" in the causal term. "Shall" means "has a legal duty to." "The court shall grant the motion" means the court has a legal duty to grant it.

A *prohibitory* rule is the opposite. It forbids someone to act and is expressed by "may not" or "shall not" in the causal term.

A *discretionary* rule gives someone the power or authority to do something. That person has discretion to act but is not required to do so. You might see words like "may" or "has the authority to" in the causal term.

A *declaratory* rule simply states (declares) that something is true. That might not seem like much of a rule, but the consequences of the declaration can be serious. The rule at the beginning of this section is declaratory: "A person who drives faster than the posted speed limit is guilty of speeding." Because of that declaration, a police officer can give you a ticket if you speed, a court can sentence you to a fine, and your state's motor vehicle department can impose points on your driver's license. A declaratory rule places a label on a set of facts (the elements). The rule's power is what that label permits people to do (the police officer to give you a ticket, and so on). Often the declaration is expressed by the word "is" in the causal term. But other words could be used there instead. And some rules with "is" in the causal term are not declaratory. You have to look at what the rule *does*. If it simply states that something is true, it's declaratory. If it does more than that, it's another kind of rule.

Here are examples of all four of these types of rules.

mandatory: A person driving a motor vehicle *shall* stop at a stop sign or a red traffic light. *(Do it.)*

prohibitory: A person *shall not* drive a motor vehicle in this state unless licensed to do so by the Department of Motor Vehicles. *(Don't do it.)*

discretionary: A person driving a motor vehicle *may* turn right after coming to a complete stop at a red traffic signal and yielding the right-of-way to pedestrians and other motor vehicles unless a sign erected by the highway department prohibits doing so. *(You are permitted to turn right but are not required to do so.)*

declaratory: A person who violates any section of the Vehicle Code is guilty of an infraction. *(If you do that, you are declared to be guilty. Other rules will give certain people, such as police officers and judges, permission to do things like issue a traffic ticket or impose a punishment on you.)*

§2.3 Digesting a Rule to Figure Out What It Means

There are three steps in digesting a rule to figure out what it means.

§2.3.1 *Step 1*: Break Down the Rule into Its Parts

List and number the elements in the test. (An element in a test is something that must be present for the rule to operate.) Identify the causal term and the result. If there's an exception, identify it, and if the exception has more than one element, list and number them as well. (Exceptions can have elements, too; an exception's element is something that must be present for the exception to operate.) In Step 1, *you do not care what the words mean.* You only want to know the structure of the rule. You are breaking down the rule into parts small enough to understand when you do Step 2. Let's take the discretionary rule above and run it through Step 1. Here is the rule diagrammed:

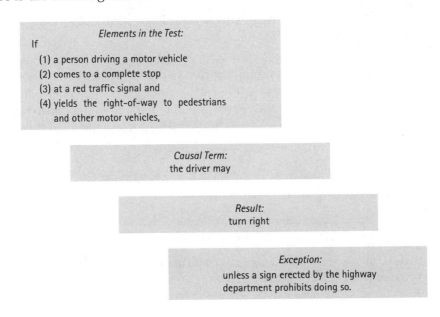

Elements in the Test:
If
(1) a person driving a motor vehicle
(2) comes to a complete stop
(3) at a red traffic signal and
(4) yields the right-of-way to pedestrians and other motor vehicles,

Causal Term:
the driver may

Result:
turn right

Exception:
unless a sign erected by the highway department prohibits doing so.

You don't need to lay out the rule exactly this way. You can use any method of diagramming that breaks up the rule so you can understand it. The point is to break up the rule visually so that it's no longer a blur of words and so that you can *see separately* the elements in the test, the causal term, the result, and any exception.

When can you combine the causal term and result? You can do it whenever that would not confuse you. If you can understand the following, you can combine, at least with this rule:

Causal Term and Result:
the driver may turn right

§2.3.2 *Step 2*: Look at Each Part Separately

Examine the details. Figure out the meaning of each element—the causal term, the result, and any exception. If you're not certain you know what a word means, look it up in a legal dictionary or read other material your teacher has assigned. Many rules seem baffling at first. Step 1 breaks the rule down into smaller parts. In Step 2, you can look at each of those parts separately to figure out what each means. Because you're looking at smaller parts now, the figuring out becomes easier.

§2.3.3 *Step 3*: Put the Rule Back Together in a Way That Helps You Use It

Sometimes that means rearranging the rule so that it's easier to understand. If when you first read the rule, an exception came at the beginning and the elements came last, rearrange the rule so the elements come first and the exception last. It will be easier to understand that way. For many rules—though not all of them—the rule's inner logic works like this:

What events or circumstances set the rule into operation?
(These are the elements in the test.)

When all the elements are present, what happens?
(The causal term and the result supply the answer.)

Even if all the elements are present, could anything else prevent the result?
(An exception, if the rule has any.)

Usually, you can put the rule back together by creating a flowchart and trying out the rule on some hypothetical facts to see how it works. A flowchart is essentially a list of questions. You will be able to make a flowchart because of the diagramming you did earlier in Step 1, which not only breaks the rule down so that it can be understood, but also permits putting it back together so that it is easier to apply. The flowchart below comes straight out of the diagram in Step 1 above.

Elements

1. Were you driving a motor vehicle?
2. Did you come to a complete stop?
3. Did you do that at a red traffic signal?
4. Did you yield the right-of-way to any pedestrians or other motor vehicles?

Exception

Did a sign erected by the highway department prohibit doing so?

Causal Term and Result
(if all the elements questions are answered "yes" and if the exception question is answered "no")

You may turn right.

Step 3 helps you add up everything to see what happens when the rule is applied to a given set of facts.

Assume that you're being tried in traffic court for making an illegal turn at a red light. The police officer testifies that you were driving a car (*element #1 satisfied*) and that this happened at a red traffic light (*element #3 satisfied*). You are representing yourself. (No lawyer represents you.) On cross-examination, you ask the police officer the following:

Q: Did I come to a complete stop before turning right?
A: Yes. *(element #2 satisfied)*
Q: Did any pedestrians have a "walk" signal?
A: No. *(starting element #4)*
Q: Did any approaching cars have a green light?
A: No. *(element #4 satisfied)*
Q: Did any signs at this intersection prohibit right-turn-on-red?
A: No. *(exception does not apply)*

A few minutes later, this happens:

You: Your Honor, the evidence satisfies all the elements in the test that gives me discretion to turn red on a red light, and the evidence does not substantiate the exception to that rule. Therefore, I was legally entitled to turn right.

Judge: Not guilty. Charge dismissed.

Voices: Hurray! Knew you could do it!

Judge: Order in the court!

Newspaper headline: Law Student Wins First Trial!
Attributes Success to Understanding Structure of Rules

§2.3.4 The Three Steps Summarized

Here are three steps (explained above) in digesting a rule to figure out what it means:

Step 1: Break the rule down into its parts *(§2.3.1).*

Step 2: Look at each of those parts separately *(§2.3.2).*

Step 3: Put the rule back together in a way that helps you use it *(§2.3.3).*

Exercise I. A Rule on Late Papers

Below is a rule that appears in a teacher's syllabus—not *your* teacher's syllabus.

If a student submits a paper after the deadline, the student's grade on that paper will be reduced five per cent for every hour the paper is late unless the student submits written proof that the student or a member of the student's family had been hospitalized or otherwise gravely at risk within 24 hours before the deadline.

Use the three-step process in §2.3 to analyze the rule. Identify any parts of it that need further definition. What questions would you ask of this teacher to make sure you understand the full meaning of parts of the rule?

Exercise II. A Rule on the Internet

Below is a rule from a course syllabus.

A student who accesses the Internet during class will be counted as absent for the entire class.

Before class, a student sets his cell phone to vibrate. During class, a friend in the parking lot sends him a text message saying the student's car is being stolen. The teacher spots the student reading the message and marks him as absent. The student protests. Under this rule as written, who is right? Who *should* be right? In light of your answers to these questions, how should the rule be rewritten?

More about Rules

I try not to break the rules but merely to test their elasticity.

—*Bill Veeck*

§3.1 Remedies, Causes of Action, and Affirmative Defenses

A very large proportion of the rules you will study in law school define causes of action or affirmative defenses, which together determine whether a party can get a remedy.

A plaintiff sues to get a *remedy*. A remedy (also called *relief*) is what the law can do to solve a problem. The most common remedy is damages—money, paid by someone responsible for causing harm, to compensate the person who suffered the loss. Sometimes a court will order a party to do something that does not involve paying money.

A harm the law will remedy is called a *cause of action* (or in federal courts and some other courts, a *claim*). If a plaintiff cannot prove a cause of action, the plaintiff cannot get a remedy. Even if a plaintiff does prove a cause of action, a court will not order a remedy if the defendant proves an *affirmative defense*.

For example, when a plaintiff proves that a defendant intentionally confined him and that the defendant was not a law enforcement officer acting within the scope of an authority to arrest, the plaintiff has proved a cause of action called *false imprisonment*. Here's the rule:

> False imprisonment consists of (1) a confinement (2) of the plaintiff (3) by the defendant (4) intentionally (5) where the defendant is not a sworn law enforcement officer acting within that authority.

But if the defendant can prove that she caught the plaintiff shoplifting in her store and restrained him only until the police arrived, she might have an affirmative defense called a *shopkeeper's privilege*. When a defendant proves a shopkeeper's privilege, a court will not award the plaintiff damages, even if he has proved false imprisonment. Here's the rule:

> A shopkeeper or a shopkeeper's employee is not liable for false imprisonment where (1) the shopkeeper or shopkeeper's employee (2) has reasonable cause to believe that (3) the plaintiff (4) has shoplifted (5) in the shopkeeper's place of business and (6) the confinement occurs in a reasonable manner, for a reasonable time, and no more than needed to detain the plaintiff for law enforcement purposes.

§3.2 Where Rules Come From (Sources of Law)

Our legal system has two primary sources of law: statutes and case law.

§3.2.1 Statutes

Legislatures create rules of law by enacting statutes such as the Freedom of Information Act, which gives you the right to read and copy certain government documents. The federal legislature—Congress—enacts federal statutes. Each state has a legislature of its own to enact state statutes.

In addition, some rules of law are found in materials that resemble statutes but were not enacted by legislatures. Statute-like provisions include constitutions, administrative regulations, and court rules. Administrative regulations are promulgated by government agencies, and court rules are promulgated usually, but not always, by courts.

§3.2.2 Case Law

Our law is derived from English law. In England, courts existed before legislatures gained the power to make law. Without legislation, those courts not only enforced law but also created the law they were enforcing. The central tool English courts used in this process was a rule called *stare decisis*, Latin for "let stand that which has been decided," or, more loosely, "follow the rules courts have followed in the past." A past court decision is a *precedent*, which later courts, within limits, are required to take into account. Courts record their decisions in judicial opinions. Lawyers use the words *cases, case law, decisions, opinions*, and *precedents* interchangeably to refer to these decisions and to the opinions that explain them.

In modern American law, the common law continues to exist to the extent it has not been superseded by legislation. Most of what you will study in the course on Torts, for example, is common law because legislatures have enacted few statutes on the subject. For a common law issue, the rules come exclusively from case law. Common law is not frozen in time. Courts, having created the common law, can change it and periodically do, in decisions that enforce the law as changed.

In addition, statutes have ambiguities, and often we do not know what a statute means until the courts interpret it—through judicial decisions enforcing the statute. If the statute is ambiguous, we have to read the case law to find out what it means. By interpreting the statute, courts essentially finish the process of law creation that the legislature started by enacting the statute in the first place.

Thus, courts make law in two ways. They created the common law centuries ago and continue to change it. And when they interpret statutes they add to what the legislature has done.

Each state has its own courts, enforcing that state's law, and in addition the federal government has courts throughout the country, enforcing federal law. Federal courts include general trial courts (the United States District Courts), intermediate appellate courts (the United States Courts of Appeals), and a final appellate court (the United States Supreme Court). The Courts of Appeals are divided geographically into thirteen Circuits.

Most large and medium-sized states have a similar structure: a general trial court, an intermediate appellate court, and a final appellate court. Smaller states might not have an intermediate appellate court. Both federal and state systems also include specialized courts, such as the United States Tax Court or a state's family court. Court names differ from state to state.

§3.3 Some Questions about Rules

1. **Must the elements always come before the rest of the rule?** No. There could be a simple causal term and result together with a long list of elements, you can list the elements last. For example:

> Common law burglary is committed by breaking and entering the dwelling of another in the nighttime with intent to commit a felony therein.[1]

If the elements were listed first, this would be a lot harder to understand.

---

[1] This was the crime at common law. Because of the way its elements are divided, it does a good job of illustrating several different things about rule structure. But the definition of burglary in a modern criminal code will differ. A statute might break up the crime into gradations (burglary in the first degree, burglary in the second degree, and so on). A typical modern statute would not require that the crime happen in the nighttime, and at least the lower gradations would not require that the building be a dwelling.

2. If there are lots of elements, or if they are complicated or ambiguous, how can you make it clear where one element ends and the next begins? You can enumerate:

Common law burglary is committed by (1) breaking and (2) entering (3) the dwelling (4) of another (5) in the nighttime (6) with intent to commit a felony therein.

3. How can you tell how many elements are in a rule? Think of each element as an integral fact, the absence of which would prevent the rule's operation. If you can think of a scenario that has a realistic chance of occurring in real life and if in that scenario part of what you believe to be one element could be true but another part not true, then you actually have two or more elements. For example, is "the dwelling of another" one element or two? A person might be guilty of some other crime, but he is not guilty of common law burglary when he breaks and enters the restaurant of another, even in the nighttime and with intent to commit a felony therein. The same is true when he breaks and enters his own dwelling. In each instance, part of "the dwelling of another" is present, and part is missing. "The dwelling of another" thus includes two elements: the nature of the building (a residence) and the identity of its resident (not the defendant).

Often you cannot know the number of elements in a rule until you have consulted the judicial decisions that interpret it. Is "breaking and entering" one element or two? The cases define "breaking" in this sense as the creation of a gap in a building's protective enclosure, such as by opening a door, even when the door was left unlocked and the building was thus not damaged. The cases further define "entering" for this purpose as placing inside the dwelling any part of oneself or any object under one's control, such as a crowbar. Can a person "break" without "entering"? Yes. If you open a window by pushing it up from outside the building, and if, before you do anything else, the police appear and arrest you, you "broke" by opening the window, but you did not enter. "Breaking" and "entering" are therefore two elements. But to know that, you would have to read the judicial decisions that define these terms.

4. Do all rules have elements? No. Instead of elements, some rules have criteria or factors that function as guidelines. These rules often authorize a court or other authority to make discretionary decisions, and the criteria define the scope of the decision-maker's discretion. For example, this Illinois statute guides a court's discretion in deciding who should receive custody of a child:

§602. Best Interest of Child.[2]

   (a) The court shall determine custody in accordance with the best interest of the child. The court shall consider all relevant factors including:
      (1) the wishes of the child's parent or parents as to his custody;

---

[2] 750 Ill. Comp. Stat. §5/602 (2007).

(2) the wishes of the child as to his custodian;

(3) the interaction and interrelationship of the child with his parent or parents, his siblings and any other person who may significantly affect the child's best interest;

(4) the child adjustment to his home, school and community;

(5) the mental and physical health of all individuals involved;

(6) the physical violence or threat of physical violence by the child's potential custodian, whether directed against the child or directed against another person;

(7) the occurrence of ongoing or repeated abuse as defined in Section 103 of the Illinois Domestic Violence Act of 1986, whether directed against the child or directed against another person;

(8) the willingness and ability of each parent to facilitate and encourage a close and continuing relationship between the other parent and the child; and

(9) whether one of the parents is a sex offender; and

(10) the terms of a parent's military family-care plan that a parent must complete before deployment if a parent is a member of the United States Armed Forces who is being deployed.

Only seldom would all of these criteria tip in the same direction. With a rule like this, a judge does something of a balancing test and would choose the option that the criteria, as a whole, tilt toward.

5. What if you read a rule that does not specify who has a legal duty, or who is prohibited from doing something, or who has discretion to act? For example:

A motion for a new trial must be filed no later than 28 days after the entry of judgment.[3]

"Shall" means "has a legal duty to." Here, it's a legal duty to file this kind of motion "no later than ten days after entry of judgment." Who has that duty? The rule doesn't say. You need to figure it out from the context. A judgment is the document that terminates a lawsuit, such as after a trial. Who would want a new trial? The party who lost at trial might want another chance to win. If that person wants a new trial, she or he has a legal duty to file a motion for one no later than ten days after entry of judgment.

6. What if all the complexity in a rule seems to be in the result? You may have to recast the rule to find out what the elements really are. For example:

A lawyer shall not make a false or misleading communication about the lawyer or the lawyer's services.[4]

---

[3] Rule 59(b) of the Federal Rules of Civil Procedure.
[4] Rule 7.1 of the ABA Model Rules of Professional Conduct.

Being a lawyer is an element because only lawyers have this duty. Other people do not. And that seems like the only element. The causal term is simple ("shall not"). But the result is complicated. You could even divide it up the way you divide a test into elements. To violate this rule, the lawyer would do three things:

1. make a communication
2. that is false or misleading
3. about the lawyer or the lawyer's services

If a lawyer lies about where tomorrow night's Beyoncé concert will be held, has the lawyer violated this rule? No. The communication is not about the lawyer or the lawyer's services. Something is missing from these facts, and that something is acting like an element. We could even recast the result as part of the test:

> If (1) a lawyer (2) makes a communication that is (3) false or misleading (4) about the lawyer or the lawyer's services . . . .

If we recast the rule this way, what is the causal term and what is the result? This rule comes from the American Bar Association Model Rules of Professional Conduct, which defines unethical conduct. From that context, we could reword the rule as follows:

> If (1) a lawyer (2) makes a communication that is (3) false or misleading (4) about the lawyer or the lawyer's services, the lawyer commits an unethical act.

The causal term becomes "the lawyer commits," and the result is "an unethical act."

Exercise. Nansen and Byrd

Part A. With the aid of §§16 and 221(a) of the Criminal Code (below), outline the rule in §220 into a list of elements and exceptions. Annotate the list by adding definitions for the elements and for any exceptions you might come across.

Criminal Code §16

When a term describing a kind of intent or knowledge appears in a statute defining a crime, that term applies to every element of the crime unless the definition of the crime clearly indicates that the term is meant to apply only to certain elements and not to others.

Criminal Code §220

A person is guilty of criminal sale of a controlled substance when he knowingly sells any quantity of a controlled substance.

Criminal Code §221(a)

As used in section 220 of this code, "sell" means to exchange for goods or money, to give, or to offer or agree to do the same, except where the seller is a licensed physician dispensing the controlled substance pursuant to a permit issued by the Drug Enforcement Commission or where the seller is a licensed pharmacist dispensing the controlled substance as directed by a prescription issued by a licensed physician pursuant to a permit issued by the Drug Enforcement Commission.

Part B. You have interviewed Nansen, who lives with Byrd. Neither is a licensed physician nor a licensed pharmacist. At about noon on July 15, both were arrested and charged with criminal sale of a controlled substance. Nansen has told you the following:

Byrd keeps a supply of cocaine in our apartment. He had been out of town for a month, and I had used up his stash while he was gone. I knew that was going to bend Byrd completely out of shape, but I thought I was going to get away with it. I had replaced it all with plaster. When you grind plaster down real fine, it looks like coke. For other reasons, I had decided to go to Alaska on an afternoon flight on July 15 and not come back. Byrd was supposed to get back into town on July 16, and by the time he figured out what had happened, I would be in the Tongass Forest.

But on the morning of the 15th, Byrd opened the door of the apartment and walked in, saying he had decided to come back a day early. I hadn't started packing, yet—I wouldn't have much to pack anyway—but I didn't know how I was going to pack with Byrd standing around because of all the explaining I'd have to do. I also didn't want Byrd hanging around the apartment and working up an urge for some cocaine that wasn't there. So I said, "Let's go hang out on the street."

We had been on the sidewalk about ten or fifteen minutes when a guy came up to us and started talking. He was dressed a little too well to be a regular street person, but he looked kind of desperate. I figured he was looking to buy some drugs. Then I realized that that was the solution to at least some of my problem. I took Byrd aside and said, "This guy looks like he's ready to buy big. What do you think he'd pay for your stash?" Byrd looked reluctant, so I turned to the guy and said, "We can sell you about three ounces of coke, but we have to have a thousand for it." When the guy said, "Yeah," Byrd said, "Wait here" and ran inside the apartment building. A thousand was far more than the stuff was worth.

Byrd walked out onto the stoop with the whole stash in his hand in the zip-lock bag he kept it in, and while he was walking down the steps, about ten feet away from me and the guy who wanted to buy, two uniforms appeared out of nowhere and arrested Byrd and me.

The "guy" turned out to be Officer D'Asconni, an undercover policeman who will testify to the conversation Nansen has described. The police laboratory reports that the bag contained 2.8 ounces of plaster and 0.007 ounces of cocaine. When you told Nansen about the laboratory report, he said the following:

> I didn't think there was any coke in that bag. What they found must have been residue. I had used up every last bit of Byrd's stuff. I clearly remember looking at that empty bag after I had used it all and wondering how much plaster to put in it so that it would at least look like the coke Byrd had left behind. I certainly didn't see any point in scrubbing the bag with cleanser before I put the plaster in it.

Part C. Will Nansen or Byrd be convicted of criminal sale of a controlled substance?

Criminal Code §221

As used in section 220, "controlled substance" includes any of the following: . . . cocaine. . . .

Criminal Code §10

No person shall be convicted of a crime except on evidence proving guilt beyond a reasonable doubt.

Using your annotated outline of elements, decide whether each element can be proved beyond a reasonable doubt, and whether any exceptions are satisfied. Then predict whether Nansen or Byrd will be convicted.

Inside a Statute and Outlining One

Elizabeth: Wait! You have to take me to shore. According to the Code of the Order of the Brethren . . . .

Captain Barbossa: First, your return to shore was not part of our negotiations nor our agreement so I "must" do nothing. And secondly, you must be a pirate for the pirate's code to apply and you're not. And thirdly, the code is more what you'd call "guidelines" than actual rules. Welcome aboard the Black Pearl, Miss Turner.

—*Pirates of the Caribbean: The Curse of the Black Pearl*

§4.1 Inside a Statute

If you open the statutory supplement in your Contracts course to §2-702 of the Uniform Commercial Code, here is what you will find:

§2-702. Seller's Remedies on Discovery of Buyer's Insolvency

(1) Where the seller discovers the buyer to be insolvent he may refuse delivery except for cash including payment for all goods theretofore delivered under the contract, and stop delivery. . . .

(2) Where the seller discovers that the buyer has received goods on credit while insolvent he may reclaim the goods upon demand made within ten days after the receipt, but if misrepresentation of solvency has been made to the particular seller in

writing within three months before delivery the ten day limitation does not apply. Except as provided in this subsection the seller may not base a right to reclaim goods on the buyer's fraudulent or innocent misrepresentation of solvency or of intent to pay.

(3) The seller's right to reclaim under subsection (2) is subject to the rights of a buyer in ordinary course or other good faith purchaser . . . . Successful reclamation of goods excludes all other remedies with respect to them.

"Are these words on steroids?" you might ask. Do they actually mean something?" The answers are no and yes. Nothing is wrong here. Statutes look pretty much like this. And they contain a great deal of meaning.

Statutes are different from everything else you've ever read before. A statute does not describe or explain anything. It has no story or characters. *Almost every word in a statute is part of a legal rule.* That's all statutes are—groups of legal rules.

A statute makes much more sense once you look for the rules and outline the statute.

§4.2 Outlining a Statute

Outlining a statute is not easy to learn. But once you learn how, you will probably do it instinctively for the rest of your career, whenever you read an unfamiliar and complicated statute.

§4.2.1 *Step 1*: Decide How Many Legal Rules Are in the Statute

Remember that legal rules are either mandatory (require something), prohibitory (forbid something), discretionary (permit something), or declaratory (state something). Look for requirements, prohibitions, permissions, and declarations. Those lead you into the individual rules within the statute.

For example, §2-702 contains five rules. The first one gives a seller permission to refuse delivery if certain elements are satisfied *(subsection (1))*. The second rule gives a seller permission to reclaim goods if other elements are satisfied *(subsection (2), first sentence)*. The third rule declares that a seller does not have any other "right to reclaim goods on the buyer's fraudulent or innocent misrepresentation of solvency or of intent to pay" *(subsection (2), second sentence)*. The fourth rule declares that a seller's right to reclaim "is subject to the rights of a buyer in ordinary course or other good faith purchaser" *(subsection (3), first sentence)*. And the fifth rule declares that "reclamation of goods excludes all other remedies with respect to them" *(subsection (3), second sentence)*.

In Step 1, we don't care what these words mean. We'll figure that out in Step 2. In Step 1, we are just trying to separate one rule from another.

§4.2.2 *Step 2*: Digest Each Rule in the Statute to Figure Out What It Means

For each rule you have identified, use the method explained in Chapter 2 to take the rule apart to figure out what it means. First, break the rule down into its parts (see §2.3.1 in Chapter 2). Second, look at each of those small parts separately (§2.3.2). And third, put the rule back together in a way that helps you use it (§2.3.3).

When you do that to the rule in UCC §2-702(1) on the first page of this chapter, here is the flowchart you end up with:

Element (only one here)

> Has the seller discovered the buyer to be insolvent?

Exception

> Has the buyer offered to pay cash including payment for all goods theretofore delivered under the contract?

Result and Causal Term
(if the elements question is answered yes and the exception question is answered no)

> The seller may refuse delivery and may stop delivery under this Article.

What are goods? When is a buyer insolvent? To find out, you would look for definitions elsewhere in the statute. "Goods" are defined in UCC §2-105(1), and "insolvent" is defined in UCC §1-201(23). If the statute does not provide definitions like these, you would consult a legal dictionary if you're preparing for your Contracts class. But if you are writing a memorandum or appellate brief, you would research how the cases interpreting the statute have defined the words.

§4.2.3 The Two Steps Summarized

Here are the two steps (explained above) in outlining a statute:

Step 1: Decide how many legal rules are in the statute *(§4.2.1).*

Step 2: Digest each rule in the statute to figure out what it means *(§4.2.2):*
  (a) Break the rule down into its parts *(§2.3.1).*
  (b) Look at each of those parts separately *(§2.3.2).*
  (c) Put the rule back together in a way that helps you *use* it *(§2.3.3).*

Exercise I. What to Do When a Judge Can't Finish the Case

Outline Rule 63 of the Federal Rules of Civil Procedure, which appears below.

If a judge conducting a hearing or trial is unable to proceed, any other judge may proceed upon certifying familiarity with the record and determining that the case may be completed without prejudice to the parties. In a hearing or trial, the successor judge must, at a party's request, recall any witness whose testimony is material and disputed and who is available to testify again without undue burden. The successor judge may also recall any other witness.

Exercise II. The Uniform Commercial Code and Unconscionability

Outline §2-302(1) of the Uniform Commercial Code, which appears below.

If the court as a matter of law finds the contract or any term of the contract to have been unconscionable at the time it was made the court may refuse to enforce the contract, or it may enforce the remainder of the contract without the unconscionable term, or it may so limit the application of any unconscionable term as to avoid any unconscionable result.

Inside a Judicial Opinion ("a Case")

§5.1 What's in a Judicial Opinion

When law teachers refer to "a case," they mean a judicial opinion through which a court makes a decision. A judicial opinion can include up to ten ingredients:

1. the case name and citation
2. the factual story (what happened *before* the lawsuit began)
3. the procedural story (what happened *during* the lawsuit)
4. the issue or issues to be decided by the court
5. the arguments made by each side
6. the court's holding on each issue
7. the rule or rules of law the court enforces through each holding
8. the court's reasoning
9. dicta
10. the remedy the court granted or denied

Most opinions don't include *all* these things, although a typical opinion probably has most of them.

When you first look at an opinion, it can seem mysterious. Reading the opinion is a lot easier if you label each passage as one or another of these ingredients. That breaks the opinion down into smaller chunks so that you can more easily understand its parts. It also helps you see how the parts are related to each other and produce the court's decision.

The *case name* is made up of the names of the plaintiff and defendant separated by "v." (That's how lawyers abbreviate "versus.") The *citation* is the volume, publication, and page where opinion can be found, together with the date.

Opinions often begin with the *factual story*. What did the parties and other people do before the lawsuit began? The court can know this story from what the parties allege in their pleadings or from what the witnesses testify to or what other evidence shows. For that reason, sometimes it's hard to separate this part of the opinion from the next part (the procedural story).

Often the court will next describe the *procedural story*, which lawyers and teachers more often call the *procedural history*. What did the lawyers and judges do? Examples are motions, trial, judgment, and appeal. Although a court might ascribe a procedural action to a party ("The defendant moved to dismiss . . ."), that's really a lawyer's work. As you will learn later in this book, and in your course in Civil Procedure, the manner in which an issue is raised determines the method a court will use to decide it.

A court might also set out—or at least imply—the *issue or issues* to be decided and *the arguments* made by each side. A court will further state, or at least imply, the *holding* on each of the issues and the *rule or rules of law* the court enforces in making each holding, together with the *reasoning*— often called the *rationale*—for its decision. The reasoning often discusses or hints at the *policy* behind the rules the court enforces. A rule's policy is its purpose, what the law tries to accomplish generally through the rule. Somewhere in the opinion, the court might place some *dicta*, which is discussion unnecessary to support a holding and therefore not part of binding precedent.

An opinion usually ends with *the relief granted or denied*. If the opinion is the decision of an appellate court, the relief may be an affirmance or a reversal of the lower court's decision. If the opinion is from a trial court, the relief is most commonly the granting or denial of a motion.

In an appellate court, several judges will decide together. An appellate court's decision is announced in *the court's opinion* or *the majority opinion*. If one of the judges does not agree with some aspect of the decision, that judge may write a *concurrence* or *dissent*. A dissenting judge thinks the court reached the wrong result. A concurring judge agrees with the result the majority reached but would have used different reasoning to get there. Concurrences and dissents are not binding precedent. Only the court's opinion has that authority.

§5.2 Why Reading in Law School Is Different— and What to Do about It

In college, most assigned reading is in textbooks. Textbook authors try to write in a way that communicates efficiently to their audience, which is primarily students.

Law school is different. Law students read mostly judicial opinions and statutes. A judge writing a judicial opinion does not wonder, "How should I write this so that any first-year law student can understand it?" A judge instead writes for an audience of lawyers and judges—who quickly understand wording and concepts that may baffle students.

Several studies have shown that an important part of success in the first year of law school is learning to read the way that experienced lawyers do.[1] Experienced lawyers don't move from sentence to sentence waiting for meaning to appear. Instead, they read *aggressively*, dissecting the opinion as they go through it.

You can start to develop this skill by carving up judicial opinions, looking for the ingredients listed at the beginning of this chapter and marking each ingredient with handwritten notes in the margin. Experienced lawyers identify the ingredients quickly and almost unconsciously. Because of their experience, they no longer need to write notes in the margin, but they instantly recognize, for example, the end of the factual story and the beginning of the procedural story. They also interpret to find meaning at every step along the way, asking themselves questions like, "Now that I know the factual story, what does that tell me about what's going on here?"

Learning how to read like a professional takes time. Most law students are challenged by this task at the beginning, but within a few months they will begin to become more efficient. You will see much more meaning in what you read and take less time to read it. But it will take time and work to get there.

Exercise. Dissecting the Text of *Conti v. ASPCA*

Read *Conti v. ASPCA* below and determine where (if anywhere) each of these ingredients occur. Mark up the text generously so you can discuss your analysis in class. Look up in a legal dictionary every unfamiliar word as well as every familiar word that is used in an unfamiliar way.

CONTI v. ASPCA
77 Misc. 2d 61, 353 N.Y.S.2d 288
(Civ. Ct., Queens Co. 1974)

Rodell, J.

Chester is a parrot. He is fourteen inches tall, with a green coat, yellow head and an orange streak on his wings. Red splashes cover his left shoulder. Chester is a

---

[1] See Ruth Ann McKinney's book, *Reading Like a Lawyer: Time-Saving Strategies for Reading Law Like an Expert* (2005), as well as the following law review articles: Leah M. Christensen, *Legal Reading and Success in Law School: An Empirical Study*, 30 Seattle U. L. Rev. 603 (2007); Laurel Currie Oates, *Beating the Odds: Reading Strategies of Law Students Admitted through Alternative Admissions Programs*, 83 Iowa L. Rev. 139 (1997).

show parrot, used by the defendant ASPCA in various educational exhibitions presented to groups of children.

On June 28, 1973, during an exhibition in Kings Point, New York, Chester flew the coop and found refuge in the tallest tree he could find. For seven hours the defendant sought to retrieve Chester. Ladders proved to be too short. Offers of food were steadfastly ignored. With the approach of darkness, search efforts were discontinued. A return to the area on the next morning revealed that Chester was gone.

On July 5, 1973 the plaintiff, who resides in Belle Harbor, Queens County, had occasion to see a green-hued parrot with a yellow head and red splashes seated in his backyard. His offer of food was eagerly accepted by the bird. This was repeated on three occasions each day for a period of two weeks. This display of human kindness was rewarded by the parrot's finally entering the plaintiff's home, where he was placed in a cage.

The next day, the plaintiff phoned the defendant ASPCA and requested advice as to the care of a parrot he had found. Thereupon the defendant sent two representatives to the plaintiff's home. Upon examination, they claimed that it was the missing parrot, Chester, and removed it from the plaintiff's home.

Upon refusal of the defendant ASPCA to return the bird, the plaintiff now brings this action in replevin.

[I]f [the parrot] is in fact Chester, who is entitled to its ownership?

The plaintiff presented witnesses who testified that a parrot similar to the one in question was seen in the neighborhood prior to July 5, 1973. He further contended that a parrot could not fly the distance between Kings Point and Belle Harbor in so short a period of time, and therefore the bird in question was not in fact Chester.

The representatives of the defendant ASPCA were categorical in their testimony that the parrot was indeed Chester, that he was unique because of his size, color and habits. They claimed that Chester said "hello" and could dangle by his legs. During the entire trial the court had the parrot under close scrutiny, but at no time did it exhibit any of these characteristics. The court called upon the parrot to indicate by name or other mannerism an affinity to either of the claimed owners. Alas, the parrot stood mute.

Upon all the credible evidence the court does find as a fact that the parrot in question is indeed Chester and is the same parrot which escaped from the possession of the ASPCA on June 28, 1973.

The court must now deal with the plaintiff's position, that the ownership of the defendant was a qualified one and upon the parrot's escape, ownership passed to the first individual who captured it and placed it under his control.

The law is well settled that the true owner of lost property is entitled to the return thereof as against any person finding same.

This general rule is not applicable when the property lost is an animal. In such cases the court must inquire as to whether the animal was domesticated or ferae naturae (wild).

Where an animal is wild, its owner can only acquire a qualified right of property which is wholly lost when it escapes from its captor with no intention of returning.

Thus in *Mullett v. Bradley* (24 Misc. 695) an untrained and undomesticated sea lion escaped after being shipped from the west to the east coast. The sea lion escaped and was again captured in a fish pond off the New Jersey coast. The original owner sued the finder for its return. The court held that the sea lion was a wild animal (ferae naturae), and when it returned to its wild state, the original owner's property rights were extinguished.

In *Amory v. Flyn* (10 Johns. 102) plaintiff sought to recover geese of the wild variety which had strayed from the owner. In granting judgment to the plaintiff, the court pointed out that the geese had been tamed by the plaintiff and therefore were unable to regain their natural liberty. . . .

The court finds that Chester was a domesticated animal, subject to training and discipline. Thus the rule of ferae naturae does not prevail and the defendant as true owner is entitled to regain possession.

The court wishes to commend the plaintiff for his acts of kindness and compassion to the parrot during the period that it was lost and was gratified to receive the defendant's assurance that the first parrot available would be offered to the plaintiff for adoption.

Judgment for defendant dismissing the complaint without costs.

Reading a Case for Issues, Rules, and Determinative Facts

§6.1 How to Identify Issues, Rules, and Determinative Facts

Many facts are mentioned in an opinion just to provide background, continuity, or what journalists call "human interest." Of the remaining facts, some are related to the court's thinking but are not crucial. Still others *caused* the court to come to its decision.

This last group could be called the *determinative facts* or the *essential facts*. They're essential to the court's decision because they determined the outcome: if they had been different, the decision would have been different. The determinative facts lead to the rule of the case—the rule of law for which the case stands as precedent—and discovering that rule is the most important goal of reading cases. Of course, when several issues are raised together in a case, the court must make several rulings and an opinion may thus stand for several different rules.

The determinative facts can be identified by asking the following question: *If a particular fact had not happened, or if it had happened differently, would the court have made a different decision?* If so, it's one of the determinative facts. This can be illustrated through an example of a decision that has nothing to do with law.

Suppose you're trying to find a place where you can live while attending school. A rental agent has just shown you an apartment. The following are also true:

A. The apartment is located half a mile from the law school.

B. It is a studio apartment (one room plus a kitchenette and bathroom).

C. The building appears to be well maintained and safe.

D. The apartment is at the corner of the building, and windows on two sides provide ample light and ventilation.

E. It is on the third floor, away from the street, and the neighbors do not appear to be disagreeable.

F. The rent is $500 per month, furnished.

G. You have a widowed aunt, with whom you get along well and who lives alone in a house 45 minutes by bus from the law school, and she has offered to let you use the second floor of her house during the school year. The house and neighborhood are safe and quiet, and the living arrangements would be satisfactory to you.

H. You have taken out substantial loans to go to law school.

I. You neither own nor have access to a car.

J. Reliable local people have told you that you're not likely to find an apartment that is better, cheaper, or more convenient than the one you have just inspected.

Which facts are *essential* to your decision? For example, if the apartment had been two miles from the law school (rather than a half-mile), would your decision have been different? If the answer is no, fact *A* could not be determinative. It might be part of the factual mosaic and might explain why you looked at the apartment in the first place, but you would not base your decision on it.

The determinative facts, the issue, the holding, and the rule all depend on each other. In the apartment hypothetical, for example, if the issue were different—say, "How should I respond to an offer to join the American Automobile Association?"—the selection of determinative facts would also change. (In fact, the only determinative one would be fact *I*: "You neither own nor have access to a car.") You will often find yourself using what the court tells you about the issue or the holding to fill in what the court has not told you about the determinative facts, and vice versa.

Often, courts do not explicitly state the issue, the holding, or the rule for which the case stands as precedent, and courts do not usually label the determinative facts as such. Whenever a court gives less than a full explanation, we have to use what's explicitly stated to pin down what's only implied.

If the court states the issue but doesn't identify the rule or specify which facts are determinative, you might discover the rule and the determinative facts by answering the following questions:

Who is suing whom over what series of events and to get what relief?

What issue does the court say it intends to decide?

How does the court decide that issue?

On what facts does the court rely in making that decision?

What rule does the court enforce?

Facts from a case can often be reformulated to be more general than the court described them. In the hypothetical above, for example, a generalized reformulation of fact *G* might be the following: "You have a rent-free alternative to the apartment, but the alternative would require 45 minutes of travel each way plus the expense of public transportation." Why would you generalize the facts in this way? The generalized version of the facts can supply a guide to deciding later cases where the factual details are not identical. For example, suppose a later case involves a person who is a member of the clergy in a religious organization that has granted a leave of absence to attend law school and who may continue to live rent-free in the satisfactory quarters the religious organization has provided, but getting to the law school would require walking for 15 minutes and then riding a subway for 30 minutes, at the same cost as a bus ride. Isn't this really the same situation, but with different details? The generalized reformulation covers both sets of facts.

§6.2 Formulating a Narrow, Middling, or Broad Rule

When a court does not state a rule of the case, you might be able to formulate the rule by converting the determinative facts into elements of a rule. Often, you can interpret the determinative facts narrowly (specifically) or broadly (generically). Notice how different formulations of a rule can be extracted from the apartment example. If the student decides to stay with the aunt, a narrow rule formulation might be the following:

> A law student who has a choice between renting an apartment and living in the second floor of an aunt's house should choose the latter when the student has had to borrow money to go to law school and when the apartment's rent is $500 per month but the aunt's second floor is free except for bus fares.

Because this formulation is limited to the specific facts given in the hypothetical, it could directly govern only a tiny number of future decision-makers. But it could be stated more broadly to govern a wider range of situations:

> A student on a tight budget should not pay rent when a nearly free alternative is available.

An even more general formulation would govern an even wider circle of applications:

> A person with limited funds should not lease property when there is a satisfactory and nearly free alternative.

The following, however, is so broad as to be meaningless:

> A person should not spend money unnecessarily.

Policy and Why Courts Care about It

In the Bookstore

(Time: August. Place: the campus bookstore. Student walks up to a counter, behind which stands a store clerk.)

Student: I'd like to return these books.

Clerk: Do you have a receipt?

Student: No.

Clerk *[points to sign]*: The rule is *[reading sign aloud]* "No returns without a receipt."

Student *[frustrated]*: But I just bought them.

Clerk *[looks at sign]*: It doesn't say, "except when you just bought them."

Student: But I just bought them.

Clerk: Maybe I should rephrase the rule: "If you have a receipt, you may return the books." You don't have a receipt, so you may not return the books. Sorry.

Student: Look, I bought them half an hour ago. When I got back to my dorm room, there was an email message from the registrar saying they switched me into a different section, where the teachers are different, and those teachers assigned different books. I don't have any choice in this. I'm a first-year law student, and all the courses are required. They assign me to a section. I need completely different books for five courses.

Clerk *[in a snide tone]*: Did your dog eat your receipt?

Student: No. I just can't find it. Don't you ever lose things?

Clerk: Not within a half hour. A rule's a rule. Sorry.

Student: But every rule has a purpose. What's the purpose of this rule?

Clerk: To protect the store from people who bring in books they found or stole or bought more cheaply elsewhere. A rule's a rule.

Student: But a rule should be applied in a way that's consistent with the rule's purpose. I can prove that I didn't find or steal them or buy them more cheaply elsewhere. I bought them half an hour ago from that clerk over there.

Second Clerk *[looks up]*: I did ring up a sale to you. I don't remember what books you bought. I just scan the bar codes. Bring them over here and let's see if my register recorded the book titles.

(The two clerks compare the books to the register's record and explain to a supervisor who has wandered over.)

Supervisor *[to student]*: We'll take all these books back and give you credit toward the books you need to buy now. The only reason we can do this is because we're confident that in these circumstances you actually did buy these books from us. Don't assume in the future that you can return things without a receipt.

§7.1 What Is Policy?

Notice the *method* through which the student wins this argument. The student showed store employees that the purpose of the rule could be accomplished without enforcing the rule in the most obvious way. Instead, the store enforced the rule in a novel way—by treating the second clerk's memory and the store's internal records together as the equivalent of a receipt. If the student had not been able to persuade store employees to interpret their rule in light of its purpose, the student would have lost the argument.

Every rule of law, whether found in a statute or a case, has a purpose—a reason for being. That purpose is called the rule's *policy* or the *policy behind the rule*. Some policies are obvious. Why is it illegal to drive while intoxicated? You probably already know the answer.

Other policies are more complicated, and understanding them requires some special knowledge. Why is your internet service provider (ISP) not liable if you send email messages to a million people accusing Britney Spears of stealing another singer's style. (She did *not* do that.) An ISP provides access to the internet. Every email message is sent through the sender's ISP and received through the recipient's ISP. And every website is accessible through the website owner's ISP. For several reasons, Congress enacted a statute exempting ISP's from liability for publishing defamatory material. If every ISP had to read and screen every email message that a website transmitted or made accessible through its equipment, the internet would suddenly become very slow and very expensive to use. And ISP's often wouldn't be able to tell what is defamatory and what is not.

Policy also exists in a wider sense—not tied to one specific rule. A broad policy might lead the law to adopt many separate rules. For example, courts everywhere like solutions that are easily enforceable, promote clarity in the law, are not needlessly complex, and do not allow true wrongdoers to profit from illegal acts. Other policy considerations may differ from state to state. In many Sunbelt states, for example, public policy favors development of land by building homes and businesses, while in states like Vermont policy prefers preservation of the environment and agriculture. Some states favor providing tort remedies even if that slows down courts because of additional lawsuits, although in others the reverse is true.

§7.2 Why Courts Care about Policy

> It is revolting to have no better reason for a rule of law than that so it was laid down in the time of Henry IV. It is still more revolting if the grounds upon which it was laid down have vanished long since, and the rule simply persists from blind imitation of the past.
>
> —*Justice Oliver Wendell Holmes*

Law is not just rules. It is rules *plus* their policies. To understand a rule, it's not enough to know its elements, results, and exceptions. You also need to know what the law is trying to accomplish through the rule.

Wherever there's doubt about what a rule means or how it should be applied, the rule's purpose provides one solution to the problem. If you're not sure what a rule means, choose the meaning that is most consistent with its purpose. If you're not sure how to apply the rule, apply it in whatever way is most consistent with its purpose. If you know the rule but not its purpose, you don't really know what to do with the rule. And if rules did not have policies, they could be arbitrary and might cause more harm than good.

Policy is also important in a different context. When the law does not yet have a rule on a given subject and courts or legislators have to decide what rule to adopt, they consider the policies the law already has for other rules and those the law should have, and they try to choose a rule that is consistent with and achieves those policies. Policy thus is valuable not only in the interpretation and enforcement of existing rules but also in the adoption of new rules.

Policy as an extra layer of analysis might seem like a burden. "Why can't we just have rules and stop there," you might ask. We can't stop there because lawyers and judges will always have questions about what a rule means and how to apply it, and we have to know a rule's policy to resolve those questions. And you can understand and write about law more easily and more effectively—in this course and on exams in other courses—if you frequently ask yourself questions like, "What is the law trying to accomplish through this rule?" and "Why does this rule exist?"

§7.3 How to Recognize Policy in a Judicial Opinion

A rule itself doesn't tell you its policy. You have to look in the judicial decisions and statutes that are the sources of most law, or in commentaries on the law, such as law review articles. Sometimes, courts openly say something like, "The policy behind this rule is. . . ." But more often a court will discuss policy without calling it policy—for example, by explaining what would happen if the rule didn't exist. The rule's purpose is to prevent that from happening. It may be confusing for courts to talk about policy without calling it policy. But with some practice, you'll be able to spot a policy discussion in a judicial decision—and write about it in this course.

In the case below, the court uses policy to decide whether to adopt a new rule.

ASH v. NEW YORK UNIVERSITY DENTAL CENTER
164 A.D.2d 366, 564 N.Y.S.2d 308 (1st Dep't 1990)

Ellerin, J.

The issue before us in this dental malpractice action is the validity of an agreement that plaintiff Arthur Ash was required to sign as a precondition to obtaining treatment at defendant New York University Dental Center which prospectively exculpated the various defendants from any liability for negligence in treating plaintiff.

Plaintiff seeks to recover for injuries suffered as a result of his aspiration, during dental treatment, of two dental crowns, which became lodged in his right lung and required surgical removal. Plaintiff [needed] substantial dental work which would cost over $6,000[, and he therefore sought treatment at the clinic associated at the defendant's dentistry school], where the work could be done [by dentistry students under supervision] for $3,000. . . .

When plaintiff arrived at the clinic . . . , he was required to sign a form containing the following provision: "In consideration of the reduced rates given to me by New York University, and in recognition of the risks inherent in a clinical program involving treatment by students, I hereby release and agree to save harmless New York University, its trustees, doctors, employees and students from any and all liability, including liability for its and their negligence, arising out of or in connection with any personal injuries (including death) or other damages of any kind which I may sustain while on its premises or as a result of any treatment at its Dental Center or infirmaries."

[P]laintiff testified that he believed the signing of this form was an insignificant registration procedure and he was never told, nor did he imagine, that he was relinquishing any of his legal rights. . . .

. . . There is no decision of the Court of Appeals [the state's highest court] that expressly deals with this precise issue. . . .

It is clear that the State's substantial interest in protecting the welfare of all of its citizens, irrespective of economic status, extends to ensuring that they be provided with health care in a safe and professional manner. Toward that end, the State carefully regulates the licensing of physicians and other health care professionals and monitors such activities to prevent untoward consequences to the public from "the ministrations of incompetent, incapable, ignorant persons". A similar concern for the enforcement of established minimum standards of professional care provides the underlying rationale for a cause of action for malpractice in favor of those who have been subjected to substandard care. Unquestionably public clinics such as defendant, which are used primarily by those who are unable to pay the rapidly escalating fees for private medical and dental care, play an important role in delivery of such care to those who may not otherwise be able to obtain it. However, important as this role is, it cannot serve as a basis for excusing such providers from complying with those minimum professional standards of care which the State has seen fit to establish. It is the very importance of such clinics to the people who use them that would create an invidious result if the exculpatory clause in issue were upheld—i.e., a de facto system in which the medical services received by the less affluent are permitted to be governed by lesser minimal standards of care and skill than that received by other segments of society.

There is, of course, no public policy against allowing patients of such clinics to agree to fewer amenities, longer waits or greater inconvenience in exchange for lower prices than they would pay elsewhere. Nor is there any public policy against such a clinic limiting itself to certain types of care or refusing to perform certain procedures. There cannot, however, be any justification for a policy which sanctions an agreement which negates the minimal standards of professional care which have been carefully forged by State regulations and imposed by law. . . .

The fact that defendant New York University Dental Center is a clinical program associated with an educational institution does not alter this conclusion. Defendant, of course, has a substantial interest in providing its students with clinical experience as part of their education. However, this interest cannot negate the State's overriding concern in seeing that defendants fulfill their equally important obligation to their patients. That obligation includes ensuring that students are sufficiently prepared and supervised so that the treatment which is provided to human patients is at least at the minimally acceptable reasonable level of skill and care. If defendants cannot fulfill this obligation, they must not hold themselves out as being providers of dental care. . . .

Other jurisdictions which have addressed attempts by health care professionals to relieve themselves of liability, particularly to those who stand in a disadvantageous bargaining position, have arrived at a conclusion similar to the one we have reached.

[For example, i]n *Emory Univ. v Porubiansky* . . . the Supreme Court of Georgia refused to enforce a very similar contract in a setting identical to the one herein, stating: "A contract between a medical practitioner and patient must be examined in light of the strong policy of the state to protect the health of its citizens and to regulate those professionals that it licenses. . . ."

This court is able to create new law only because existing law had a gap in it. How do we know there's a gap? The fifth paragraph tells us: "There is no decision of the Court of Appeals [the state's highest court] that expressly deals with this precise issue." The court uses policy as a guide in filling that gap.

Selecting the Most Appropriate Cases, Statutes, and Other Authority

This chapter explains how to select the best available authority. The next two chapters explain how to use the two most important kinds of authority: cases (Chapter 10) and statutes (Chapter 11). In reading this chapter, remember that the federal government and each state have separate bodies of law, which in most respects are independent of each other.

§8.1 The Hierarchy of Authority

Primary authority is a *source* of law. It creates or determines law, and its words are the words of the law. The most often used primary authorities are cases and statutes. Others are constitutions, court rules, and regulations promulgated by administrative agencies. Primary authority is produced by a legislature, a court, or some other governmental entity with the power to make or determine law.

   Secondary authority is *commentary about* the law. It explains the law but does not create it. Examples are treatises and law review articles written by legal scholars. Secondary authority is only a description of what a private person or a private group believes the law to be. The author of secondary authority may know a lot about the law but lacks the power to create law.

Courts use a complicated set of preferences—called the *hierarchy of authority*—to determine which authority they will follow. You can follow the hierarchy of authority more easily if you visualize it this way:

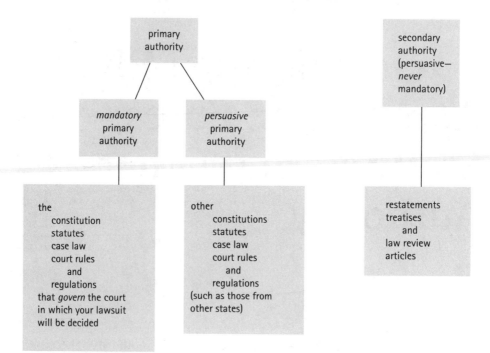

§8.1.1 Primary Authority

Primary authority is subdivided into mandatory authority and persuasive primary authority.

Mandatory authority—which *must* be followed—includes statutes and statute-like materials of the government whose law controls the question to be resolved. It also includes the decisions—the precedents—of the appellate courts to which an appeal could be taken from the trial court where the issue is being or could be litigated. The appellate courts' precedents must be followed because those courts have the power to reverse a decision of the trial court.

Within a state or the federal government, some mandatory authority outranks other mandatory authority. A constitution prevails over all other forms of authority from the same government. A constitution is the fundamental law creating a government in the first place. A legislature can enact only those kinds of statutes allowed by a constitution, and the courts' power to create and reinterpret common law is also subservient to the constitution that created the government of which the courts are a part. A statute trumps a court rule or administrative regulation because statutes gave courts and administrative agencies the power to adopt court rules and regulations. Statutes trump case law because the legislature's power to make law prevails over the courts' power to interpret or reinterpret statutes and common law. And case law made by higher courts prevails over inconsistent case law made by lower courts.

What happens if two mandatory authorities of the same rank are inconsistent with each other—for example if one statute preserves the cause of action for alienation of affection and another abolishes it? If the two cannot be reconciled, dates matter. A later statute prevails over the earlier one, and a later case prevails over the earlier one from the same court.

Persuasive primary authority can be followed, or it can be ignored. It usually comes from a jurisdiction other than the one whose law controls the matter at issue. In this context, another jurisdiction means another state or another federal circuit.

You can see a map of the federal circuits at http://www.uscourts.gov/ courtlinks/ or by looking in the front of any volume of Federal Reporter, Third Series (Fed. 3d). A federal circuit is made up of the United States Court of Appeals for that circuit and the federal district courts that are geographically within the circuit. A federal district court is a trial court, from which appeals would go to the Court of Appeals.

Suppose Wyoming law controls. And suppose that the issue is one of common law, which means that it was part of the common law developed by courts and no Wyoming statute has changed it. Decisions of the Wyoming Supreme Court are mandatory authority (they must be followed). But suppose those cases don't settle the issue, which means there's a gap in Wyoming law. Cases from other states' supreme courts are persuasive primary authority. They're primary because courts have the power to make law. But in Wyoming they're at most persuasive because Wyoming courts are not required to obey the courts of other states. A Wyoming court might follow the reasoning of a South Carolina decision if the Wyoming court is persuaded that the South Carolina case's reasoning does a good job of filling a gap in Wyoming law.

Persuasive primary authority includes (1) decisions by courts of other states (for example, the South Carolina precedent in a Wyoming court); (2) decisions by coordinate appellate courts, to which an appeal could *not* be taken from the trial court where the issue would be or is being litigated (an example is given in the next paragraph); (3) decisions made by trial courts anywhere; and (4) dicta in any decision.

To be mandatory, a decision must have been made by an appellate court to which the matter at hand could be or already has been appealed. For example, the United States Court of Appeals for the Sixth Circuit hears appeals from federal trial courts in Kentucky, Michigan, Ohio, and Tennessee, while the Court of Appeals for the Third Circuit decides appeals from federal trial courts in Delaware, New Jersey, and Pennsylvania. An opinion by the Sixth Circuit is mandatory authority to a

United States District Court in Ohio, because the Sixth Circuit can reverse, on appeal, a decision of that trial court. The same opinion is mandatory to the Sixth Circuit itself, which is bound by its own prior decisions. But that opinion is only persuasive authority to a United States District Court in Pennsylvania, because the Third Circuit—not the Sixth—hears appeals from federal trial courts in Pennsylvania. And that opinion is only persuasive authority in the Court of Appeals for the Third Circuit (a coordinate court to the Sixth Circuit) and in the Supreme Court of the United States (which is superior to all the circuits).

Decisions by the United States Supreme Court, on the other hand, are mandatory in every federal court because the Supreme Court has the power ultimately to reverse a decision by any federal court. But decisions of the United States Supreme Court are mandatory authority in a state court only on issues of federal law because the United States Supreme Court has no jurisdiction to decide matters of state law.

§8.1.2 Secondary Authority

Mandatory authority always trumps secondary authority. But in the hierarchy of authority, persuasive primary authority and secondary authority start out approximately equal. A court can either follow them or ignore them. A court's decision to follow or ignore depends on how impressed it is with the reasoning and credibility of a persuasive primary authority or a secondary authority. The most significant forms of secondary authority are (1) restatements, which are formulations of the common law drafted by scholars commissioned by the American Law Institute; (2) treatises written by scholars; and (3) articles and similar material published in law reviews.

Since 1923, the American Law Institute has commissioned restatements in contracts, property, torts, and several other fields in an attempt to express some consensus about the common law as it has developed in the 50 states. When a restatement is no longer up-to-date, it is superseded by a second or third version. Thus, the Restatement (Third) of Property replaced the Restatement (Second) of Property. A restatement consists of a series of black-letter law rules organized into sections followed by commentary.

The authoritativeness of a treatise depends on the reputation of its author and on whether the treatise has been kept up to date. Some of the outstanding treatises have been written by Wigmore (evidence), Corbin (contracts), Williston (contracts), and Prosser and Keeton (torts). Some treatises are multivolume works, and some double as hornbooks.

Law reviews print two kinds of material: articles (written by scholars, judges, and practitioners) and comments and notes (written by students). If an article is thorough, insightful, or authored by a respected scholar, it may influence a court and might therefore be worth citing. Most articles, however, do not fit that description, and the mere fact that an article has been published does not mean that it is influential. Only in the most unusual circumstances does a student comment or note influence a court. But even when law review material would not influence a court, it might nevertheless stimulate your thinking, and its footnotes can help you find cases, statutes, and other authority.

Legal encyclopedias, legal dictionaries, digests, and *American Law Reports* are not really authority. Their true function is to provide background information and to help you research the law. All except dictionaries collect cases and summarize them. The true authority is the cases they cite. Years ago, lawyers and judges cited to legal encyclopedias and dictionaries because at that time genuine authority was harder to find. You will see that done occasionally in older opinions printed in your casebooks, but the practice is no longer considered acceptable.

§8.2 How Courts Use Dicta

In a court's opinion, only the holding and the reasoning necessary to support it (including rules of law) are mandatory authority. Comments in an opinion that are not needed to state and support a holding are *obiter dicta*—words said in passing.[1]

Because *dicta* is not a holding or support for a holding, it cannot be mandatory authority. If that is so, why do courts write dicta in the first place? Often, dicta adds clarity to an opinion. Here are some examples:

- A court may want to make clear what the case is *not*: "If the plaintiff had presented evidence of injury to his reputation, he might be entitled to damages." Because that issue was not before the court, whatever the court says about it is not a holding.
- The court may want to illustrate the possible ramifications of its decision: "When a minor is at the controls of a power boat—or for that matter a car or an airplane—she is held to the standard of care expected of a reasonable adult." If the quote comes from a powerboat case, the case stands for a rule on power boats but it's only dicta on cars and airplanes.
- The court may make a suggestion to a lower court on remand: "Although the parties have not appealed on the question of appropriate damages, that issue will inevitably arise in the new trial we order, and we believe it necessary to point out . . . ." Because damages were not part of this appeal, whatever the court says about them is dicta.

Sometimes dicta is accidental: A judge might get carried away with extravagant wording or might formulate the issue or the rule or the determinative facts so that

---

[1] Although in Latin *dictum* is the singular and *dicta* is the plural, *dictum* is falling into disuse among lawyers and judges, who now often use *dicta* as both the singular and the plural.

it is not clear whether a particular comment is really within the scope of the decision. Sometimes, it's not clear what is holding and what is dicta: Even when a judge is careful in defining the issue, rule, and determinative facts, readers might reasonably disagree about whether a particular comment is necessary to the resolution of the issue.

Sometimes a court decides that it has two separate and independent grounds for a holding, either of which alone would have been sufficient. When that happens, neither ground is dicta. Both were the basis of the decision, even if only one would have been needed.

It is not wrong to rely on dicta, but it is wrong to use it inappropriately. Dicta can never take the place of a holding, and it is inappropriate to treat it as though it could. When you use dicta, identify it as such—for example, "The court said in dicta that . . . ." A holding is introduced differently: "The court held that . . . ." or "The court decided that . . . ." or other words describing something the court *did*. Dicta is talk. A holding is a decision.

§8.3 How Courts React to Precedent from Other Jurisdictions

If you cite a Missouri case to a Kansas court, how will the Kansas judge react? If you are in a federal court in the Ninth Circuit, how will the judge react if you cite precedent from the Eighth Circuit? These are the two most common situations where case law from another jurisdiction might be involved—precedent from another state (if you are or could be litigating in state court) or from another federal circuit (if you are or could be in federal court).

Courts rely on cases from other jurisdictions only for guidance and only when a gap appears in local law. A gap exists when a state's or circuit's case law does not settle an issue. Courts can fill a gap in local law in two situations. One is where the issue is one normally resolved through the common law. Because courts developed the common law, they can continue to fill gaps in it and in doing so are often guided by precedent from other states.

The other situation is where a statute is unclear and courts must decide what it means. Courts can fill that gap, although only some types of precedent from other jurisdictions will be relevant. Opinions interpreting a statute from another state might persuade, but only if the other state's statute is similar to your statute. If the two are *identical*, precedent from the other state can be particularly persuasive. Two statutes can be virtually identical even if there are minor differences in wording that do not affect the statutes' meaning. When the *substance* of the statutes is different, precedent from the other state has more limited value. If the two statutes take radically different approaches to solving the same problem, precedent from the other state is usually irrelevant.

If your state has no statute on the subject, precedent interpreting statutes from other states has no value at all. If your state treats the issue as one of common law, it will consider only precedent based on other states' common law.

What impresses a court when you cite case law from other jurisdictions? First, a court that must fill a gap will want to know what the majority rule is in other states or other circuits. Second, if a majority of states or circuits follow one rule but there is a modern trend toward a second rule (in other words, the majority is declining), a gap-filling court would want to know that. The modern-trend rule might be more appropriate to current conditions than an older, declining majority rule. Majority, by the way, means number of states or circuits, not number of cases. For this purpose, count a state or circuit only once. Third, a gap-filling court will care about how well courts elsewhere have reasoned their way to a solution. Careful and thoughtful reasoning impresses.

§8.4 How to Use Nonmandatory Authority to Fill a Gap in Local Law

How do you fill a gap in local law? First, lay a foundation by defining the gap. Second, use nonmandatory authority to fill the gap.

§8.4.1 *Step 1*: Laying the Foundation

Because nonmandatory precedent is used only to help fill gaps in local law, you can use it *only after laying a foundation* for it. A foundation is laid when you define the gap and specify how local law does not dispose of the controversy. A particularly deep gap occurs when the issue is one of "first impression" in the state or circuit where you are or could be litigating. "First impression" means that the appellate courts there have never before had occasion to resolve the issue.

Another possibility is that local cases, even from the highest court in the jurisdiction, may be questionable from age or poor reasoning. But be careful: A precedent is not infirm just because it is old or just because you don't like its reasoning. Age weakens a precedent when society has so changed that the precedent no longer represents public policy on the matter in question. And a precedent can be questionable if other courts criticize it or if it has been criticized by scholars in treatises or law review articles.

If other states have statutes on the question and your state has none, that's not necessarily a gap in the law. Your state's courts might hold that when their legislature did not enact such a statute, the legislature, in effect, rejected the statutes adopted elsewhere.

To lay the foundation, do these:

(a) state the issue precisely,
(b) explain what local law *has* decided, and
(c) identify the gap (specify what local law has *not* decided).

This example lays a foundation very concisely in the first sentence:

> No court in this state has decided whether the sale of a newly built home implies a warranty of habitability. However, a common law warranty of habitability has been recognized, as a matter of common law, in a growing number of states. . . .

Here, the gap is total: The state has no case law on the issue of whether the sale of a newly built home implies a warranty of habitability.

But things are not usually this clear cut. For example, the state might have cases that have nibbled around the edges of the issue, or cases to which analogies could be made, or cases setting out public policy, or even a case that gives the false impression of having resolved the question. If so, the foundation is not complete until you have explained—in as much detail as the reader would need in order to agree with you—why the issue is still open.

> No reported decision in this state has determined whether a violation of §432 is negligence per se. But the neighboring states of Colorado and Arizona have enacted similar statutes. *[Here, explain why they are similar.]* Courts in those states have interpreted those statutes to mean that . . . .

Here, the state has a statute, but the courts have not yet decided a certain aspect of its meaning (whether a violation is negligence per se). The foundation is the first sentence, which explains that.

Don't lecture the reader on basic principles of the hierarchy of authority ("since there are no reported decisions in this state on this issue, it is necessary to look to the law of other jurisdictions"). The reader knows that that is the standard way of filling gaps.

§8.4.2 *Step 2*: Filling the Gap

Once the foundation has been laid, summarize your nonmandatory authority ("Sixteen states have adopted this cause of action, and four have rejected it"). Then explain your nonmandatory authority in detail. Nonmandatory authority can include out-of-jurisdiction precedent, restatements, and the views of scholarly commentators in treatises and law review articles. But your focus usually should be on the case law. The views of commentators generally play a secondary role.

§8.4.3 The Two Steps Summarized

Here are the two steps (explained above) in using nonmandatory authority to fill a gap in local law:

Step 1:   Lay the foundation *(§8.4.1)*:
                (a) state the issue precisely,
                (b) explain what local law has decided, and
                (c) identify the gap (specify what local law has *not* decided).

Step 2:   Fill the gap *(§8.4.2)*.

§8.5 How to Select Nonmandatory Precedent

When selecting nonmandatory precedent to fill a gap, how do you choose the opinions to rely on? Answer the following questions, in approximately this order of priority:

1. Is the precedent on point with the issue before your court, or, if not on point, can a sound analogy make it useful anyway? If the opinion is easily distinguished, your court will not be influenced.

2. How good is the precedent's reasoning? Is the logic of the holding sound? Is it careful, thoughtful, and complete?

3. What court decided the case? Is it the highest court in its jurisdiction? Is it a court that has in the past influenced the courts of your state or circuit? Is it in a state where the relevant conditions are similar to those prevailing in your state?

4. Is the precedent's policy consistent with the policy in your state? Some states have historically been leaders in creating new tort causes of action. If your state only reluctantly does that, precedents from those states will not easily influence your courts.

5. How has the precedent (or the rule it stands for) been treated in other reported opinions? Is the precedent or rule discussed with approval or with skepticism? Is it part of a general trend or a widely accepted body of law? Or is it a lonely straggler that the rest of the law seems to be leaving behind?

6. When was the precedent decided? Judges often treat newer opinions as more authoritative than much older ones, simply because changing social conditions can make a rule no longer apt. On the other hand, a holding so new as not to have been tested through experience may be treated a little warily at first.

Exercise. The Hierarchy of Authority

You're working on a case that's now being litigated in the United States District Court for the District of Nevada. You've been asked to find out whether a defendant who made and lost a motion to dismiss for insufficient service of process can subsequently move to dismiss for failure to state a claim on which relief can be granted. You've found the following authority, all of which squarely addresses your issue. Without considering the logic and wording of each authority, rank them preliminarily solely from the information provided here. Nevada is in the Ninth Circuit. If you're not familiar with the boundaries of the federal circuits, see the map at http://www.uscourts.gov/courtlinks/ or in the front of any volume of Federal Reporter, Third Series (Fed. 3d).

Catdog v. Amundsen—4th Circuit, 2004

Great Basin Realty Co. v. Rand—Nevada Supreme Court, 1998

Matthewson's treatise on Federal Courts (published last year)

Wilkes v. Jae Sun Trading Corp.—9th Circuit, 1973

Pincus v. McGrath—United States Supreme Court, 1949

Rule 12 of the Federal Rules of Civil Procedure (revised last year)

Barking Pumpkins Records, Inc. v. Sepulveda—California Supreme Court, 2005

Garibaldi v. City of Boulder—10th Circuit, 2003

Ott v. Frazier—7th Circuit, 1931

Working with Cases

§9.1 Eight Skills for Working with Cases

If you find mandatory precedent on point—a case from the highest court in your jurisdiction deciding your issue on facts that exactly mirror yours—the issue is probably so easy that it wouldn't need to be written about. More often, you'll need to construct an answer using at least some of eight skills:

1. evaluating an opinion according to the hierarchy of authority and the principles derived from it *(Chapter 8)*
2. isolating an opinion's determinative facts and formulating rules either broadly or narrowly *(Chapter 6)*
3. analogizing *(§9.2)*
4. distinguishing, which is the opposite of analogizing *(§9.2)*
5. eliciting policy *(§9.3)*
6. synthesizing fragmented authority into a unified whole *(§9.4)*
7. reconciling conflicting or adverse authority *(§9.5)*
8. testing the results of the first eight skills for realism *(§9.6)*

The first three skills are explained earlier in this book. See the cross-references in parentheses above. The others are explained in this chapter.

§9.2 Analogizing and Distinguishing

If two situations are so parallel that the reasoning that decided the first should also govern the second, they're *analogous*. Suppose that last week on a reality TV show Martha was voted off the island because she couldn't build a functioning MP3 player out of stones and dirt. By analogy, should Sean be voted off the island this week if he can't build a cell phone from leaves and sticks? When you generalize the facts, as below, they seem to be analogous:

    A. Irrelevant raw materials (stones and dirt or leaves and sticks)
    B. Small electronic device (MP3 player or cell phone)
    C. Failure to convert *A* into *B*

Distinguishing is showing that two situations are so fundamentally dissimilar that they should be decided differently. If last week Justin was voted off the island because he sulked and refused to do his share of the work, that does not necessarily mean that this week Cynthia should be voted off the island for failing to build a seven-room house in an hour. What's the distinguishing factor? Justin decided to sulk and not work, but no matter how hard Cynthia tried, she could not have built a house in the time allowed.

Lawyers and judges are skilled at both analogizing and distinguishing. That's because the common law was developed entirely through precedent, which analogizes to and distinguishes from past decisions in resolving current issues.

Analogizing and distinguishing each happen in three steps.

Step 1:   Make sure that the issue in the precedent is the same as the issue you are trying to resolve.

Step 2:   Identify the precedent's determinative facts. Don't look for mere coincidences between the precedent and your facts. Look instead for facts that the precedent's court treated as crucial and on which it really did rely.

Step 3:   Compare the precedent's determinative facts to the facts you're trying to resolve. If they match, you have an analogy. If they don't, the precedent is distinguishable from your facts.

Here's an example.

The precedent: A landlord failed to repair a residential tenant's toilet for one week, in violation of the housing code. The court holds that the tenant can withhold rent and use the money to repair the toilet herself.

Our facts: The owner of a refrigerated warehouse fails to maintain the refrigeration device, causing the tenant's products to spoil. The lease obligates the landlord to provide refrigeration. The tenant wants to withhold rent and use the money to repair the refrigeration device.

Step 1: Is the issue the same? Yes. In both, the issue is whether the tenant may deduct the cost of repair from the rent.

Step 2: What are the determinative facts from the precedent?

A. Landlord/tenant relationship
B. Toilet problem
C. Violated housing code

Step 3: Compare the precedent's determinative facts to the facts in the current problem (below).

The Precedent	Our Facts
1. Landlord/tenant relationship	Yes
2. Toilet problem	Toilet not in dispute
3. Violated housing code	No code governs commercial leases

Does the analogy fail because a toilet is not the same as a refrigerator and because commercial leases are not governed by statute similar to the housing code? In both cases, the equipment that failed was essential to the tenant. And in both cases the landlord had an obligation to maintain the equipment that failed. The obligation to maintain the toilet came from the housing code, and the obligation to maintain the refrigeration came from the commercial lease. Once we think about it that way, Steps 2 and 3 will look like the following. Notice each way in which the steps below differ from the ones above.

Step 2: What are the determinative facts from the precedent?

A. Landlord/tenant relationship
B. Essential equipment (toilet) failed
C. Landlord violated obligation (from housing code) to repair

Step 3: Compare the precedent's determinative facts to the facts in the current problem (below).

The Precedent	Our Facts
1. Landlord/tenant	Yes—but a commercial lease, not a residential lease
2. Essential equipment failed	Yes—refrigeration essential to the tenant
3. Violated obligation to repair	Yes—obligation in the lease

In both cases, the landlord had an obligation to maintain something essential to the tenant's occupancy of the rented space. The obligation arose from different sources, but an obligation is an obligation, whether it is imposed by law generally (the housing code) or whether the parties create it through their own contract (the lease). Although it's not certain that the remedy would be the same in both cases, the analogy greatly increases the chances that if one tenant can deduct from the rent to make repairs, then the other tenant can, too.

§9.3 Eliciting Policy from Cases

Sound legal analysis answers the question, "What could a court do that would satisfy not just the elements of a rule but also the reason why the rule exists in the first place—its policy?" (Chapter 7 explains policy.)

The hypothetical in the preceding section illustrates how policy interacts with other skills discussed in this chapter. There's a good policy reason why one situation is governed by a housing code and the other isn't. Parties to a commercial lease can bargain with each other to protect themselves. If a tenant needs refrigeration, the tenant can insist that the lease be written to require the landlord to provide it. But residential tenants often lack the knowledge and market power to do that. If you've ever signed a lease, did it occur to you to negotiate for a provision requiring the landlord to fix the toilet or the stove or the heat? The legislature has therefore adopted a housing code, which is not needed in a commercial situation.

How do you find out what the law's policies are? Sometimes they're expressly stated in statutes, but more often cases are where we find policy, either stated or implied. But courts infrequently say, "We adopt this rule to achieve the following policies." More typically, a case will discuss the types of problems the court is trying to solve, the useful things the rule would accomplish, or the dangerous things that would happen if the rule didn't exist. When a court talks about any of these, the court is discussing policy even if it doesn't use the word "policy."

§9.4 Synthesis

Synthesis is the binding together of several opinions into a whole that stands for a rule or an expression of policy. By focusing on the reasoning and generalized facts that the cases have in common, synthesis finds and explains collective meaning that is not apparent from any individual case read in isolation from the others. A synthesis is plausible if it's logical, reasonable, and consistent with public policy.

A synthesis is more than a description of several cases, one after another. It's not a synthesis to describe Case A, describe Case B, describe Case C, describe Case D, and then stop. That is nothing more than a description of raw materials.

To turn a description of several cases into a unified synthesis, step back and ask yourself what the cases really have in common under the surface. Identify the threads that appear in all four cases (A, B, C, and D), tie the threads together, and organize the analysis around the threads themselves—rather than around the individual cases. The reader cares more about the threads than about the cases, and in a synthesis an individual case is important *only* to the extent that it teaches something about a thread.

It may turn out that Case B sets out the most convincing proof of whatever is at issue. Cases A and D agree and are the only out-of-state cases to have decided the issue; and Case C is a much older decision in our state, standing for the same rule but on reasoning that is less complete than that expressed in Case B, another decision from our state. An effective synthesis might explain Case B in much detail, use Cases A and D to show that other states agree, and omit Case C entirely.

If you are working out a synthesis, make that clear to the reader. First, state the synthesis in an opening sentence:

> Although the Supreme Court has not ruled on the question, the trend in the Courts of Appeals is to hold that such a prosecution is dismissable if any of three kinds of government misconduct has occurred: . . .

A synthesis like this could take many pages to prove because you would later need to show

- that the Supreme Court really has not ruled: to do that, you'd need to discuss Supreme Court cases that come close to the issue and show how they haven't resolved it
- that each of the three kinds of misconduct has been held by Courts of Appeals to be grounds for dismissal: to do so, you'd need to write a separate synthesis for each ground

When in your mind you develop or discover a synthesis, you'll usually do it from the bottom up: You'll work with the details of the cases (the bottom) until you see the threads that produce the synthesis (the top). But when you explain it in writing to your reader, you'll do the reverse. You'll start at the top by stating the synthesis and work your way down by explaining how the details support it. Your first draft might not do that very well because while writing a first draft you will often be developing your thinking as you write. (Writing is part of thinking.) But your later drafts should reflect the top-to-bottom explanations that will make sense to your reader.

§9.5 Reconciliation

Reconciliation is a hybrid of some of the other skills discussed in this chapter. If two cases on the surface seem to conflict with each other, you might be able to demonstrate that the conflict does not exist because on closer examination the two decisions actually stand for the same rule, espouse the same policy, or can be harmonized in some other way. Done that way, reconciliation has much in common with synthesis. Sometimes you might be able to reconcile by showing that one opinion is really analogous to another even if it doesn't look that way at first glance. And if you can reconcile cases, they aren't distinguishable.

§9.6 Testing for Realism

The last skill is *testing the result of your reasoning to see whether it would seem realistic to the judicial mind*. For example, would your reasoning seem reasonable and just to the typical judge? Would it produce impractical consequences?

Experience at judging creates what Roscoe Pound called "the trained intuition of the judge,"[1] an instinct for how the law ought to treat each set of facts. If the result of your reasoning would strike the judicial mind as impractical, many judges will reject what you have done, even if you've used all the other skills well. If you do everything else you are taught in law school but omit testing for realism, your analysis will be *formalistic* because it will do nothing more than comply with the forms of the law. Because the law is hardly ever certain, a judge can always fold back your reasoning and make analogies you did not make, build other syntheses, and so forth—or, worse, adopt the analogies, syntheses, and other constructs proposed by your adversary. Karl Llewellyn wrote that "rules *guide*, but they do not *control* decision. There is no precedent that the judge may not at his need either file down to razor thinness or expand into a bludgeon."[2]

To test for realism, you need to know something about how the judicial mind operates. That may take a long time to gain fully, but you are learning it now through the decisions you read in casebooks and through the writing you do in this course.

Although lawyers often write arguments based on equity, justice, and reasonability, they *never put in writing* the kind of testing described in this section.

---

[1] Roscoe Pound, *The Theory of Judicial Decision*, 36 Harv. L. Rev. 940, 951 (1923).
[2] K. N. Llewellyn, *The Bramble Bush* 180 (Oceana 1930).

How could you possibly reduce to writing a test for realism? If a lawyer concludes that the result of her or his reasoning would be inconsistent with the judge's trained intuition, the lawyer simply starts over again and builds a different analysis.

Exercise. To Surf or Not to Surf?

You're in your Contracts class, and the professor has just introduced a hypothetical problem. As you understand the hypo, one of the factors that would influence the result is the distance for delivery of a product from Cincinnati, Ohio, to either Columbus, Ohio, or Lexington, Kentucky. You think you know which is faster, but if you use your laptop to check a website like Google Maps, you will get more accurate information.

Before you go to Mapquest on your laptop while sitting in class, you recall the following:

1. The syllabus in your Contracts class allows use of a computer in class "only for purposes associated with the class."
2. Last year this same Contracts professor noticed a student bidding on Ebay during class. The professor then prohibited laptop use for the rest of the year, causing everybody else in the class to resent the student who had been caught surfing.
3. This semester, your Civil Procedure professor posted a message from a student about the Seventh Circuit's website information on standards of review. The professor's posting thanked the student for locating and sharing such useful information.

Now, use the skills of working with precedent to predict what the Contracts professor will do if you use Google Maps.

A. Try filling in the table on the next page to see if it helps you predict.
B. Synthesize. Weigh the information and determine whether, when considered together, the precedents combine to build one rule, a rule and an exception, or more than one rule.
C. Take a guess. Make a tentative prediction about the result, based on the rule or rules you just produced.
D. Assess your guess. Imagine the arguments that can be made for each side. Would a narrow or broad interpretation of the rule lead to differing results? Are there facts in this situation that seem significantly different from the rule?
E. Weigh the arguments for the competing results. Be the judge. Which side is more likely to win and why? This answer will be your final prediction.

	Is it mandatory or not?	Narrow reading of this authority	Broad reading of this authority	Policy behind this authority
Syllabus rule				
Last year's Ebay incident				
Internet value in civ pro class				

Working with Statutes

[T]he statutes of this Commonwealth . . . do not always mean what they say.
—*Henry David Thoreau*

§10.1 Eleven Tools of Statutory Interpretation

Chapter 4 explained how to outline a statute. This chapter explains how to figure out what the words and phrases in a statute mean.

If the highest court in the jurisdiction has definitively interpreted the statute, it means whatever that court said it means. Without such a definitive case, however, lawyers and judges use eleven tools to determine a statute's meaning:

1. the *words* of the statute (which create a mandatory rule, a prohibitory rule, a discretionary rule, or a declaratory rule—see Chapters 2 and 4)
2. statutorily provided *definitions* of terms used (usually found in a nearby section of the same statute)
3. any *statement of purpose* found in the statute
4. the *context* at the time of enactment: the events and conditions that might have *motivated* the legislature to act
5. announcements of *public policy* in other statutes and in case law
6. judicial interpretations of the statute—or some part of it
7. judicial interpretations of similar statutes

8. the statute's *legislative history*, which consists of the documents, like committee reports, created by various parts of the legislature during the course of enactment
9. a collection of maxims known as the *canons of statutory construction*
10. interpretations of the statute by administrative agencies charged with enforcing it
11. interpretations of the statute in treatises and law review articles by scholars who are widely recognized as experts in the field

Although legislative history (number 8 in this list) would seem to be the most direct evidence of the legislature's purpose, it's sometimes viewed with suspicion. Because of the chaotic nature of legislative work, legislative history can be incomplete and internally contradictory. But some portions of the typical legislative history are viewed by courts as particularly reliable. Those are the reports of the committees that considered the bill and the floor comments of the sponsors of the bill.

The canons of construction (number 9 in this list) are guidelines courts use in interpreting statutes. Although scholars have frequently criticized many of the canons, courts continue to use them regularly. Few scholars would reject all the canons, and some canons are never criticized. Among the never-criticized canons are the following:

A statute is to be construed in light of the harm the legislature intended to remedy.

Statutory words and phrases are to be construed in the context of the entire statute of which they are a part.

Statutes on the same subject (*in pari materia*) are to be construed together.

Statutes in derogation of the common law are to be narrowly construed.

Canons are rules of law and must be proved with authority, usually case law.

§10.2 How to Discuss Statutes in Writing

Writing about a statutory question focuses on the *words of the statute* because a legislature signals its intent primarily through the words it enacts. The crucial term or phrase should appear (inside quotation marks) when you state the issue, your conclusion, the rule on which you rely, and the most important steps of logic in the analysis. In the Exercise below, two courts do that repeatedly with variations of a single word in the statute at issue ("carry" and "carries").

Because statutes are drafted to govern wide ranges of factual possibilities, a rule expressed entirely in statutory language may need to be reformulated for practical application. (Chapters 3, 4, and 5 explain how.) Be careful when you reformulate the statutory language into a useful expression of a rule. If you oversimplify or distort, trouble awaits. Quoting the key phrases of the statute helps.

From there, use other tools of statutory interpretation to the extent they reveal what the statute means for your issue. Only rarely will all of the tools do that. If a tool doesn't help, skip it and use others. In the Exercise below, you can see examples of the tools in use.

Exercise I. The Tools in Action

Section 924(c)(1) of Title 18 of the United States Code provides that "any person who, during and in relation to any crime of violence or drug trafficking crime . . . for which the person may be prosecuted in a court of the United States, uses or *carries a firearm* . . . shall, in addition to the punishment provided for such crime of violence or drug trafficking crime . . . be sentenced to a term of imprisonment of not less than 5 years" (italics added).

Most, but not all, of the tools of statutory interpretation are illustrated in the two cases that follow, which interpret the statutory words "carries a firearm." Can you identify which tool is being used where?

UNITED STATES v. FOSTER
133 F.3d 704 (9th Cir. 1997)

Kozinski, Circuit Judge.

What does it mean to "carry a gun"? . . .

Leon Foster and Sandra Ward manufactured methamphetamine. In 1989 the police got wise to them, pulled Foster over while he was driving his pickup truck and arrested him. In his truck bed, in a zipped up bag under a snap-down tarp, they found a loaded 9 mm semiautomatic and a bucket. Inside the bucket were a scale, plastic baggies, and some hand-written notes with prices.

Foster and Ward were convicted of conspiracy to manufacture and distribute methamphetamine in violation of 21 U.S.C. §§841(a)(1) and 846. Foster was also convicted of possessing methamphetamine, in violation of 21 U.S.C. §844, and of carrying a firearm during and in relation to a drug trafficking crime, in violation of 18 U.S.C. §924(c)(1). . . .

. . . Was Leon Foster carrying a gun when he drove with it in his truck bed?

. . . "Carry" has two differing relevant uses. It may mean to transport or even to arrange for something to be transported: "I had to carry my piano all the way across the country." But it may also mean to hold an object while moving from one place to another: "I carried that ball and chain wherever I went." This narrower sense applies particularly to weapons. If I were to say "Don Corleone is carrying a gun"—or even just "Don Corleone is carrying"—you would understand that the Don has a sidearm somewhere on his person. A synonym for carry in this sense is to "pack heat." Criminals who pack heat are obviously much more dangerous than those who do not.

In our caselaw, we first adopted the broad definition of "carry" as transporting in *United States v. Barber*, 594 F.2d 1242 (9th Cir. 1979). Interpreting section 924(c)(1)'s predecessor, we said "[i]n ordinary usage, the verb 'carry' includes transportation or causing to be transported. Nothing in the legislative history indicates that Congress intended any hypertechnical or narrow reading of the word 'carries.'" *Id.* at 1244. After [the Supreme Court's decision in *Bailey v. United States,* 516 U.S. 137 (1995)], we switched to the narrower (packing heat) sense in *United States v. Hernandez*, 80 F.3d 1253 (9th Cir. 1996). We held that "in order for a defendant to be convicted of 'carrying' a gun in violation of section 924(c)(1), the defendant must have transported the firearm on or about his or her person. . . . This means the firearm must have been immediately available for use by the defendant." *Id.* at 1258 (citations omitted). A number of recent cases follow the *Hernandez* definition . . . .

We can also speculate* as to what purpose a prohibition on carrying a gun during and in relation to a violent or drug trafficking crime might serve. Using or carrying guns makes those crimes more dangerous. A drug dealer who packs heat is more likely to hurt someone or provoke someone else to violence. A gun in a bag under a tarp in a truck bed poses substantially less risk. . . .

On balance, the arguments point to the narrower definition: It fits the more specific dictionary definition, follows *Bailey* more closely, harmonizes better with the full statute, and flows from the likely purpose of section 924(c)(1). . . . A final argument for the narrower definition is the rule of lenity. Where a criminal law is ambiguous, we are wary of imposing criminal liability for conduct that the law does not clearly prohibit. See *Bifulco v. United States*, 447 U.S. 381, 387 (1980) . . . .

The rule of lenity applies only where a statute has resisted the ordinary tools of statutory interpretation. See *Hanlester Network v. Shalala*, 51 F.3d 1390, 1397 (9th Cir. 1995) ("Canons of statutory construction, such as the Rule of Lenity, are employed only where 'reasonable doubt persists about a statute's intended scope even *after* resort to the language, and structure, legislative history and motivating policies of the statute.'") (citations omitted) (emphasis in original). We think these ordinary tools of interpretation point to the narrow definition; at worst (for Mr. Foster) they leave the scope of section 924(c)(1) in doubt. If Congress wants us to put people like Leon Foster in prison for a longer time, it can re-write

---

*There is mercifully little legislative history on "carry" to burden our discussion. The original version of the section was added as a floor amendment by Representative Poff. See *United States v. Anderson*, 59 F.3d 1323, 1327 (D.C. Cir. 1995) (en banc). The general aim of the section seems to have been to ensure that violent criminals receive longer sentences, and to deter the use of guns. See 114 Cong. Rec. 22,231 (1968) (remarks of Representative Poff); see also *id.* at 22,230 (remarks of Representative Casey) and at 22,234 (remarks of Representative Harsha). The only references to "carry" concerned a proposed amendment to delete the word, apparently because it might affect people such as policemen who were authorized to carry a gun, then committed an assault without using the gun. "Carry" was deleted from Representative Casey's version of section 924(c)(1), but eventually Representative Poff's version, "carry" included, passed. See *United States v. Ramirez*, 482 F.2d 807, 814 (2d Cir. 1973).

the law to give us clearer instructions, perhaps by using the word "transport" in section 924(c)(1) as it does in various other sections of the firearm statutes.

We reaffirm our holding in *Hernandez* and its progeny that "in order for a defendant to be convicted of 'carrying' a gun in violation of section 924(c)(1), the defendant must have transported the firearm on or about his or her person. . . . This means the firearm must have been immediately available for use by the defendant." *Hernandez*, 80 F.3d at 1258. . . .

Shortly after the Ninth Circuit decided *Foster*, the U.S. Supreme Court came to the opposite conclusion in the following case.

MUSCARELLO v. UNITED STATES
524 U.S. 125 (1998)

Justice BREYER delivered the opinion of the Court.

A provision in the firearms chapter of the federal criminal code imposes a 5-year mandatory prison term upon a person who "uses or carries a firearm" "during and in relation to" a "drug trafficking crime." 18 U.S.C. §924(c)(1). The question before us is whether the phrase "carries a firearm" is limited to the carrying of firearms on the person. We hold that it is not so limited. Rather, it also applies to a person who knowingly possesses and conveys firearms in a vehicle, including in the locked glove compartment or trunk of a car, which the person accompanies. . . .

We begin with the statute's language. . . . Although the word "carry" has many different meanings, only two are relevant here. When one uses the word in the first, or primary, meaning, one can, as a matter of ordinary English, "carry firearms" in a wagon, car, truck, or other vehicle that one accompanies. When one uses the word in a different, rather special, way to mean, for example, "bearing" or (in slang) "packing" (as in "packing a gun"), the matter is less clear. But, for reasons we shall set out below, we believe Congress intended to use the word in its primary sense and not in this latter, special way. . . .

This Court has described the statute's basic purpose broadly, as an effort to combat the "dangerous combination" of "drugs and guns." *Smith v. United States*, 508 U.S. 223, 240 (1993). And the provision's chief legislative sponsor has said that the provision seeks "to persuade the man who is tempted to commit a Federal felony to leave his gun at home." 114 Cong. Rec. 22231 (1968). . . .

From the perspective of any such purpose (persuading a criminal "to leave his gun at home") what sense would it make for this statute to penalize one who walks with a gun in a bag to the site of a drug sale, but to ignore a similar individual who, like defendant Gray-Santana, travels to a similar site with a similar gun in a similar bag, but instead of walking, drives there with the gun in his car?

How persuasive is a punishment that is without effect until a drug dealer who has brought his gun to a sale (indeed has it available for use) actually takes it from the trunk (or unlocks the glove compartment) of his car? It is difficult to say that, considered as a class, those who prepare, say, to sell drugs by placing guns in their cars are less dangerous, or less deserving of punishment, than those who carry handguns on their person.

We have found no significant indication elsewhere in the legislative history of any more narrowly focused relevant purpose. . . .

We are not convinced by petitioners' remaining arguments to the contrary. First, they say that our definition of "carry" makes it the equivalent of "transport." Yet, Congress elsewhere in related statutes used the word "transport" deliberately to signify a different, and broader, statutory coverage. The immediately preceding statutory subsection, for example, imposes a different set of penalties on one who, with an intent to commit a crime, "ships, transports, or receives a firearm" in interstate commerce. 18 U.S.C. §924(b). Moreover, §926A specifically "entitles" a person "not otherwise prohibited . . . from transporting, shipping, or receiving a firearm" to "transport a firearm . . . from any place where he may lawfully possess and carry" it to "any other place" where he may do so. . . .

[P]etitioners say that our reading of the statute would extend its coverage to passengers on buses, trains, or ships, who have placed a firearm, say, in checked luggage. To extend this statute so far, they argue, is unfair, going well beyond what Congress likely would have thought possible. They add that some lower courts, thinking approximately the same, have limited the scope of "carries" to instances where a gun in a car is immediately accessible, thereby most likely excluding from coverage a gun carried in a car's trunk or locked glove compartment. See, e.g., [*United States v. Foster*, 133 F.3d 704, 708 (9th Cir. 1998)] (concluding that person "carries" a firearm in a car only if the firearm is immediately accessible). . . .

In our view, this argument does not take adequate account of other limiting words in the statute—words that make the statute applicable only where a defendant "carries" a gun both "during *and* in relation to" a drug crime. §924(c)(1) (emphasis added). Congress added these words in part to prevent prosecution where guns "played" no part in the crime. See S. Rep. No. 98-225, at 314, n. 10. . . .

[P]etitioners argue that we should construe the word "carry" to mean "immediately accessible." And, as we have said, they point out that several Courts of Appeals have limited the statute's scope in this way. See, e.g., *Foster*, supra, at 708. . . . That interpretation, however, is difficult to square with the statute's language, for one "carries" a gun in the glove compartment whether or not that glove compartment is locked. Nothing in the statute's history suggests that Congress intended that limitation. And, for reasons pointed out above, . . . we believe that the words "during" and "in relation to" will limit the statute's application to the harms that Congress foresaw.

Finally, petitioners and the dissent invoke the "rule of lenity." The simple existence of some statutory ambiguity, however, is not sufficient to warrant application of that rule, for most statutes are ambiguous to some degree. Cf. *Smith*, 508 U.S. at 239 ("The mere possibility of articulating a narrower construction . . . does not by itself make the rule of lenity applicable"). "The rule of lenity applies only if, 'after seizing everything from which aid can be derived,' . . . we can make 'no more than a guess as to what Congress intended.' " *United States v. Wells*, 519 U.S. 482 (1997). . . . To invoke the rule, we must conclude that there is a "'grievous ambiguity or uncertainty' in the statute." *Staples v. United States*, 511 U.S. 600, 619, n. 17 (1994) . . . . Certainly, our decision today is based on much more than a "guess as to what Congress intended," and there is no "grievous ambiguity" here. The problem of statutory interpretation in this case is indeed no different from that in many of the criminal cases that confront us. Yet, this Court has never held that the rule of lenity automatically permits a defendant to win. . . .

For these reasons, we conclude that the petitioners' conduct falls within the scope of the phrase "carries a firearm." The decisions of the Courts of Appeals are affirmed . . . .

Justice GINSBURG, with whom the CHIEF JUSTICE, Justice SCALIA, and Justice SOUTER join, dissenting.

. . . I would read the words to indicate not merely keeping arms on one's premises or in one's vehicle, but bearing them in such manner as to be ready for use as a weapon. . . .

For indicators from Congress itself, it is appropriate to consider word usage in other provisions of Title 18's chapter on "Firearms." . . .

Section 925(a)(2)(B), for example, provides that no criminal sanction shall attend "the transportation of [a] firearm or ammunition carried out to enable a person, who lawfully received such firearm or ammunition from the Secretary of the Army, to engage in military training or in competitions." . . .

. . . "Courts normally try to read language in different, but related, statutes, so as best to reconcile those statutes, in light of their purposes and of common sense." *McFadden*, 13 F.3d at 467 (Breyer, C. J., dissenting). So reading the "Firearms" statutes, I would not extend the word "carries" in §924(c)(1) to mean transports out of hand's reach in a vehicle.

Section 924(c)(1), as the foregoing discussion details, is not decisively clear one way or another. The sharp division in the Court on the proper reading of the measure confirms, "[a]t the very least, . . . that the issue is subject to some doubt. Under these circumstances, we adhere to the familiar rule that, 'where there is ambiguity in a criminal statute, doubts are resolved in favor of the defendant.' " *Adamo Wrecking Co. v. United States*, 434 U.S. 275, 284-285 (1978) . . . ; see *United States v. Granderson*, 511 U.S. 39, 54 (1994) ("[W]here text, structure, and history fail to establish that the Government's position is unambiguously correct—we apply the rule of lenity and resolve the ambiguity in [the defendant's] favor."). "Carry" bears many meanings, as the Court and the "Firearms" statutes demonstrate. The narrower "on or about [one's] person" interpretation is hardly implausible nor at odds with an accepted meaning of "carries a firearm." . . .

The narrower "on or about [one's] person" construction of "carries a firearm" . . . fits plausibly with other provisions of the "Firearms" chapter, and it adheres to the principle that, given two readings of a penal provision, both consistent with the statutory text, we do not choose the harsher construction. . . .

Exercise II. Plagiarism and the Board of Bar Examiners

Hardy and Tisdale were enrolled in a law school legal writing course. On the first assignment of the semester, Tisdale wrote a draft of the first half of his paper before Hardy did, and Hardy asked to see it. That was forbidden by the course rules because the assignment's due date had not yet arrived. Tisdale showed Hardy what he had written anyway and let Hardy borrow the computer disk on which Tisdale's work was stored.

Hardy copied Tisdale's work onto a disk of his own. He then changed as many of the words as he could. When he was finished, the first half of the two papers had approximately the same organization, although about 80% of the words were different—similar, but different.

Tisdale and Hardy then had a falling out. Each of them said unkind things about the other's choice of ringtone, clothing, sports loyalties, and career goals. They stopped speaking to each other. On the due date, they submitted their papers.

The teacher instantly recognized the similarity between the first half of Hardy's paper and the first half of Tisdale's. In the second half of Hardy's paper, the teacher noticed phrases that did not "sound like" him. The teacher had a vague memory of having seen those phrases previously somewhere else. The teacher logged onto Lexis and then onto Westlaw, typing in the suspect phrases from Hardy's paper and looking for sources in which they might appear. (This is one way a teacher can easily check a student's paper for plagiarism.) The teacher found a number of instances where Hardy had copied passages word for word from sources he did not cite and without quote marks around the copied words.

When confronted with all this, Hardy claimed that by changing most of the words in Tisdale's draft he had not misrepresented someone else's work as his own, and that the plagiarism in the second half of his paper was not deliberate. He said that while researching he must have written down the phrases in question, then misplaced the cites, and later assumed that the words in his notes were his own. The teacher properly rejected that explanation and gave Hardy a failing grade for the course. The law school suspended him for a year. (Tisdale was also punished, but Hardy poses the issue here.)

After a year, Hardy returned to the law school that had suspended him. Last spring, he graduated. He has applied for admission to the Wisconsin bar.

In every state, an applicant for admission to the bar must prove to the bar examiners that she or he has the type of character needed to practice law. After passing the bar examination, the applicant must fill out a detailed character questionnaire and submit supporting documents, including an affidavit from the applicant's law school. A false, misleading, or incomplete answer on the questionnaire is itself grounds for denying the application for admission. Every state's questionnaire asks, among other things, whether the applicant has ever been accused of academic dishonesty, and the law school's affidavit must answer the same question.

On his questionnaire, Hardy described what he had done and what the school had done. And in its affidavit, the law school reported—as it must—the same thing.

After admission to the bar, a lawyer can be professionally disciplined if the lawyer commits professional misconduct in violation of the state's code governing lawyers' ethics. One agency reviews the character of bar applicants, and a different agency investigates complaints of unethical conduct by lawyers. Admission to the bar and discipline of already-admitted attorneys are two separate processes, although the two share some underlying purposes.

The statute-like provisions governing admission to the bar are usually found in a state's court rules as well as in the bar examiners' own rules. A state's ethics code, too, is often found in the state's court rules. The primary difference between a court rule and a statute is that court rules are adopted by courts and statutes are enacted by legislatures. Otherwise, court rules and statutes are drafted and interpreted using the same skills (which are explained in this chapter).

Your research has found the following:

1. SCR 20:8.4(c), a Wisconsin Supreme Court Rule setting out one of the grounds for disbarring or otherwise disciplining an attorney (a person already admitted to the bar);
2. SCR 40.06, a Wisconsin Supreme Court Rule, and BA 6.01 and 6.02, Wisconsin Board of Bar Examiner Rules, all of which govern applications for admission to the bar;
3. *In re Scruggs*, a Wisconsin case interpreting SCR 20:8.4(c); and
4. four out-of-state cases, each interpreting a statute or court rule quoted within the case.

What will happen when Hardy applies for admission to the Wisconsin bar?

Wisconsin Supreme Court Rules

SCR 20:8.4(c) Misconduct

It is professional misconduct for a lawyer to . . . engage in conduct involving dishonesty, fraud, deceit or misrepresentation . . . .

SCR 40.06 Requirement as to character and fitness to practice law

(1) An applicant for bar admission shall establish good moral character and fitness to practice law. The purpose of this requirement is to limit admission to those applicants found to have the qualities of character and fitness needed to assure to a reasonable degree of certainty the integrity and the competence of services performed for clients and the maintenance of high standards in the administration of justice.

. . .

(3) An applicant shall establish to the satisfaction of the board that the applicant satisfies the requirement set forth in sub. (1). . . .

. . .

(5) The dean of a law school in this state shall have a continuing duty to report to the board any information reflecting adversely upon the character and fitness to practice law of an applicant for bar admission. . . .

Rules of the Wisconsin Board of Bar Examiners

BA 6.01 Standard of character and fitness.

A lawyer should be one whose record of conduct justifies the trust of clients, adversaries, courts and others with respect to the professional duties owed to them. A record manifesting a deficiency in the honesty, diligence or reliability of an applicant may constitute a basis for denial of admission. The Supreme Court Rules place on the applicant the burden of producing information sufficient to affirmatively demonstrate the character and fitness appropriate for bar admission.

BA 6.02 Relevant conduct.

The revelation or discovery of any of the following should be treated as cause for further inquiry before the Board decides whether the applicant possesses the character and fitness to practice law.

. . .

(b) academic misconduct

. . .

(d) acts involving dishonesty or misrepresentation

. . .

In re Scruggs
475 N.W.2d 160 (Wis. 1991)

[Respondent is a lawyer admitted to the bar of this state.]

[Before he was admitted, and as a third-year law student applying to a law firm for a job, respondent] provided the firm with what purported to be a copy of his law school transcript, showing a grade point average of 3.2. In fact, the transcript was not that of [respondent.] . . . It appears from the record that [respondent] submitted the transcript of a fellow student on which he had substituted his own name and biographical information.

. . .

After his employment with that firm was terminated[, he made similar misrepresentations when applying for another job.] . . .

[At least some of this conduct occurred after respondent was admitted to the bar.]

The referee [who heard the evidence] concluded that [respondent] engaged in conduct involving dishonesty, fraud, deceit and misrepresentation in violation of SCR 20:8.4(c). . . .

. . . [We suspend respondent's] license to practice law for two years.

In re Zbiegien
433 N.W.2d 871 (Minn. 1988)

[The petitioner has graduated from law school and has applied for admission to the bar of this state.]

[In a law school seminar in products liability, the petitioner submitted a draft paper that] was plagiarized in large part from the works of other authors. Nearly all of the first 12 pages were taken verbatim or nearly verbatim from a number of law review articles without proper citation in the endnotes. In addition, some endnotes were taken from other sources in such a way as to give the appearance that they were petitioner's own work. Several other portions of the paper were paraphrased or had words or phrases omitted or substituted for the originals as they appeared in various published sources. Again, no proper citation was given. . . . [The petitioner received] a course grade of "F". . . .

[The petitioner] admitted the extensive plagiarism . . . both in the form of direct quotes not properly indented and footnoted and paraphrased passages not appropriately credited to the original sources. [He said that his computer printer had not been printing properly, and he did not proofread the paper as it came out of the printer because at the time his wife was disabled from an auto accident, and his teenage son had run away from home.] . . .

The [State Board of Law Examiners, however,] found that not only had petitioner plagiarized a substantial amount of text and footnotes taken verbatim, or nearly verbatim, from various published sources without proper identification [and] that the alleged computer problems did not explain away the plagiarism. . . .

Petitioner appeals from that determination. . . .

Rule II.A of the Minnesota Rules of the Supreme Court for Admission to the Bar provides that an applicant must establish good character and fitness to the satisfaction of the Board.

"Good character" is defined as "traits that are relevant to and have a rational connection with the present fitness or capacity of an applicant to practice law." Definition 4, Minn. R. Admis. Bar (1986). . . .

Plagiarism, the adoption of the work of others as one's own, does involve an element of deceit, which reflects on an individual's honesty. . . . The petitioner clearly plagiarized large sections of his paper. . . .

It is the view of this court that [this] petitioner's conduct, wrongful though it was, does not demonstrate such lack of character that he must be barred from the practice of law. He has been punished [already in practical terms because the Board's investigation has delayed his admission to the bar] for over a year. [In dealing with law school officials and when testifying before the Board, the petitioner was filled with genuine remorse and shame.] We . . . believe that this conduct will not be repeated. We hold that, under the facts and circumstances of this case petitioner will not be barred from the practice of law. . . .

KELLEY, J. (dissenting):

. . . When this court admits an applicant to the practice of law, it certifies to the public that . . . it knows of no reason why the applicant-admittee does not possess the character which the profession demands of all admitted attorneys in this state. We judge an applicant's character by the standard that it must reflect those traits of integrity, honesty and trustworthiness necessary for a lawyer to possess when he or she represents clients, when dealing with professional peers, and when appearing before the courts. Yet, in this case, notwithstanding that we know that this petitioner has . . . recently engaged in outright dishonesty by plagiarizing and claiming as his own the intellectual works of others with no attempt at appropriate attribution of source, the majority would conclude, even as it condemns the petitioner's conduct, that he has been "punished" enough by the delay in his admission. . . .

[D]enial of admission . . . has not as its purpose punishment but rather protection of the public and the integrity of the legal system. . . .

Even though I would deny the petition, I would not foreclose forever, petitioner's admission to the Bar. I would, however, require that he prove that after a reasonable period of time had elapsed he then . . . demonstrates that from the experience he has learned to conduct his affairs in a manner that this court can, with confidence, certify to the public that his character does reflect traits of integrity and trustworthiness.

In re Lamberis
443 N.E.2d 549 (Ill. 1982)

[The respondent is a lawyer admitted to the bar of this state.]

In writing a thesis which he submitted to [a law school] in satisfaction of a requirement for a [post-J.D.] master's degree in law, the respondent [while a member of the bar] "knowingly plagiarized" . . . [i]n preparing pages 13 through 59 of his 93-page thesis [by using two books' words] substantially verbatim and without crediting the source. . . .

The purpose for which respondent used the appropriated material . . . displays a lack of honesty which cannot go undisciplined, especially because honesty is so fundamental to the functioning of the legal profession. . . .

[Under] DR 1-102(A)(4) of the [Illinois Code of Professional Responsibility] "[a] lawyer shall not . . . engage in conduct involving dishonesty, fraud, deceit, or misrepresentation." . . .

Having decided that the respondent's conduct warrants some discipline, we must decide whether to impose disbarment, suspension or censure. The Hearing Board recommended censure; the Review Board recommended suspension for six months; and the Administator argues here for disbarment. . . .

[I]n the 10 years since respondent entered private practice, no client has ever complained about his conduct, professional or otherwise. . . .

[Although] the respondent's conduct undermined the honor system that is maintained in all institutions of learning[, the law school involved] has already . . . expelled [him], an act which will also undoubtedly ensure that the respondent will be hereafter excluded from the academic world.

In view of the respondent's apparently unblemished record in the practice of law and the disciplinary sanctions which have already been imposed by [the law school], we choose censure as the most appropriate discipline for the respondent.

Iowa Sup. Ct. Bd. of Professional Ethics & Conduct v. Lane
642 N.W.2d 296 (Iowa 2002)

An Iowa attorney passed [off] someone else's writing as his own and claimed he spent almost two weeks writing that which he used. . . . We . . . suspend Lane's license for six months.

After the conclusion of a trial in federal court . . . attorney Lane submitted a post-trial brief to the court. The legal portion of the brief was in great part plagiarized from a treatise written by Barbara Lindemann and Paul Grossman. See Lindemann & Grossman, Employment Discrimination Law (3d ed. 1996). Lane later applied to the court for attorney fees. Among other charges, Lane requested compensation for eighty hours of work spent to prepare the questioned brief. Charging $200 per hour, Lane asked for $16,000 to write the brief that was largely copied from an uncredited source. . . .

The Ethics Board alleges violations of DR 1-102(A) . . . [which provides that a lawyer shall not]

(1) Violate a disciplinary rule; . . .

(3) Engage in illegal conduct involving moral turpitude;

(4) Engage in conduct involving dishonesty, fraud, deceit or misrepresentation;

(5) Engage in conduct that is prejudicial to the administration of justice; and

(6) Engage in any other conduct that adversely reflects on the fitness to practice law.

. . .

Lane plagiarized from a treatise and submitted his plagiarized work to the court as his own. This plagiarism constituted, among other things, a misrepresentation to the court. . . .

Plagiarism itself is unethical. "Plagiarism, the adoption of the work of others as one's own, does involve an element of deceit, which reflects on an individual's honesty." *In re Zbiegien*, 433 N.W.2d 871, 875 (Minn. 1988). . . .

Equally troubling is Lane's application for attorney fees. Lane copied the entire portion of his legal argument out of a book and then claimed it took him eighty hours to write the brief containing the copied material. He requested attorney fees for this work at the rate of $200 per hour. . . . Because he plagiarized the entire legal argument, the chances are remote that it took Lane eighty hours to write the argument. . . . These circumstances only support the conclusion Lane endeavored to deceive the court.

In re Widdison
539 N.W.2d 671 (S.D. 1995)

[The applicant has graduated from law school and applied for admission to the bar of this state.]

[During his] second year of law school, he wrote and submitted a casenote for law review publication [which] included . . . material from secondary sources which he had failed to cite. . . . The faculty advisor . . . assigned [the applicant] a failing grade in the law review course. . . .

[After the applicant took the final exam in the course on Worker's Compensation, the professor discovered two students' examination answers] were strikingly similar. . . . [T]he professor assigned a failing grade to each examination[, one of which was the applicant's].

[The applicant] has the burden of proving by clear and convincing evidence his qualifications for admission to practice law in this state. . . . One of those qualifications is that he "be a person of good moral character." SDCL 6-16-2. SDCL 16-16-2.1 defines "good moral character" as including, but not limited to, "qualities of honesty, candor, trustworthiness, diligence, reliability, observance of fiduciary and financial responsibility, and respect for the rights of others and for the judicial process." That statute also provides that "[a]ny fact reflecting a deficiency of good moral character may constitute a basis for denial of admission." SDCL 16-16-2.1 (emphasis added). Good moral character is a prerequisite to practice law in every state. . . .

"The state bears a special responsibility for maintaining standards among members of the licensed professions" such as attorneys at law. [Citations omitted.] . . . The same zeal to protect the public from the unfit within the bar must also be applied to the unfit who would seek to enter the bar. . . .

[The applicant] has not met his burden of proving good moral character. [We affirm the order denying his application for admission to the bar], with leave to reapply at a future date provided [the applicant] is able to rectify his character deficits and show he has gained an understanding of, and the ability to put into practice, the qualities of honesty, candor, and responsibility required [of lawyers].

The Process
of Writing

Getting to Know Yourself as a Writer

§11.1 Product and Process

A writing course focuses on improving both the *product* created through writing and the *process* of creating it. An office memo is an example of product. What should it look like? What should it accomplish? The process of writing is what you do at the keyboard while creating the memo, including what you're thinking while you type.

Process is much harder to teach than product. Product is tangible. It can be held in the hand, and a sample office memo, like the one in Appendix A, can be discussed in class to learn what makes it effective or ineffective. Process is much harder to observe because it's a series of events that happen mostly in your mind. Imagine a teacher sitting next to you as you write. The teacher would have a difficult time figuring out what you're doing—and you might want the teacher to leave.

There are many different *effective* processes of writing. If you put the 50 best-selling book authors in America into one room and asked them how they write, they would probably give you 50 different answers. But most effective processes of writing share a few basic traits, which we discuss in this and later chapters of this book.

Beyond that, finding the process that works best for you will happen through experimentation in which you simultaneously do *and* think about what you are doing. Notice how you write and reflect on it, by yourself or with your teacher or another student. Reflecting on what you do and how you do it is the most effective way of improving your process of writing.

§11.2 What Do You Do When You Write?

How do you go about writing? What have you done in the past, and how are you doing it in law school? Be completely accurate. If you're asked how you write, it might be tempting to say that you used exactly the process someone recommends—simply because it's human nature to confuse what you set out to do with what you actually did do. (For most people, it takes reflection to separate the two.) If you're open and self-critical about your process, you'll be able to improve it more quickly.

What do you *like* about the way you write? What *frustrates* you? What seems to cause the frustrations? How would you like to be able to write? (What would you like your process to be?) What might it take for you to be able to accomplish that? What methods have you tried out to get there?

When teachers ask individual students questions like these, often the students themselves do most of the brainstorming—because they know themselves better than anybody else can know them and because they really want to find a process that works well for them. That means that you don't need to wait until your next conversation with your teacher to work on your writing process. You can brainstorm with another thoughtful student. Or, while writing, you can have an internal dialog with yourself about what in your process is working and why.

§11.3 Voice

Voice is a personal quality in a person's writing, something that speaks from the page in that writer's own way. Most people have only a slight voice in their writing—and prefer not to write in a way that's unique. There's nothing wrong with that.

Some students enter law school with distinctive written voices of their own. In legal writing courses, they learn that their writing must conform to a number of professional standards. Does that mean that you can no longer write in a voice that is yours? No, but you might need to adapt it to a professional situation. Your voice in professional documents will grow into something different from what it was before law school, but it will still be yours and distinctive—although recognizably professional. Most people who enter law school with distinctive written voices say later, after they have developed a professional voice, that they like the professional version.

§11.4 Confidence

Learning a skill at a higher level of proficiency, with new requirements, can make you feel as though the competency you thought you had before has been taken away from you. Most students feel at least some of that while learning to write at the professional level. The feeling of doubt is sharpest near the beginning. But gradually—very gradually—it is replaced with a feeling of *strength*. By the end of the legal writing course, many students feel much stronger as writers than ever before because they have *become* stronger. For now, please remember this: If in the weeks ahead you fall into doubt about your writing abilities, it will be because you're quickly learning a lot. *It does not necessarily mean you're a bad writer. You might be a good one. Once you absorb what you are learning and start producing professional writing—and that will happen—your prior confidence will return and be stronger than before because you'll now be reaching for mastery.*

Many law students and young lawyers report that while learning legal writing they felt discouraged, but that later they experienced a first moment of validation. That moment might have come late in a semester, when a legal writing professor told them that they had done something really well. Or it might have come in a summer or part-time job, when a supervising lawyer complimented them on a well-written memo. Or it might have come in court when a judge leaned over the bench and said, "It was a pleasure to read your brief, counselor." That first moment of validation was the beginning of the recognition of *mastery*. Mastery was not yet complete; it would take much longer for that to happen. But it had begun.

Many students and young lawyers also say that they wished someone had told them while they were working so hard in legal writing that a moment marking the beginning of mastery would eventually come. That's why we're telling you now that if you're like most students—and even if you feel deeply discouraged along the way—that moment *will* eventually come.

§11.5 Learning Styles and Writing

This section explains three of the most often discussed learning styles. Most people have some of the characteristics of two or all three styles.

Rather than classify yourself in one style or another, you might figure out which style or styles provide your strengths and whether other styles illustrate strengths you want to try to develop. To become effective at learning writing or any other skill, it helps to identify your strengths so you can capitalize on them and identify areas where you need to grow so you can consciously work at causing that growth.

Auditory/sequential learners, or ASLs, absorb information most efficiently by listening. They would rather hear driving directions than look at a map. They tend to think in words rather than pictures. "Sequential" in "auditory/sequential" refers to thinking in a series of ideas that add up in a progression to larger conclusions, like this:

| if police violate the Constitution during search or interrogation | → | evidence inadmissible at trial |

if police seize stolen property and get a confession	→ both need justification
probable cause for police to stop a car in traffic	→ police had legal authority to do so
no probable cause to search trunk	→ evidence found there should be inadmissible
but driver consented to search	→ evidence found is admissible even though no probable cause
driver in custody after stolen property found in trunk	→ *Miranda* warnings required
driver knowingly and voluntarily waived *Miranda* rights	→ confession admissible
evidence and confession admissible	→ *driver will be convicted of possessing stolen property*

Visual/spatial learners, or VSLs, absorb information most efficiently through seeing—either reading words or looking at pictures, diagrams, or demonstrations. They would rather look at a map than listen to someone give driving directions. More than other people, they think in images, although they also think in words. When reading a story, they often "see" the action in their minds, as though watching a movie, or they create a mental diagram of the relationships among the people involved. "Spatial" in "visual/spatial" refers to several aspects of thinking, among them a tendency to start from an idea and branch out in several directions, sometimes simultaneously, like this:

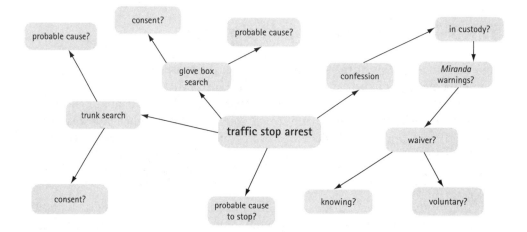

Tactile/kinesthetic learners, or TKLs, absorb information most efficiently through action. They learn best by doing something rather than by reading or hearing about it or looking at it, especially when doing so involves use of the sense of touch. They also learn well from experience. They would rather explore than look at a map or hear directions. They often think through doing because activity creates insights. While studying, TKLs often feel a desire to move about or do something with their hands because motion is thought.

Imagine that you buy something complicated, perhaps a PC with monitor, keyboard, printer, and speakers. Connecting everything and learning how to use it will be difficult. Inside the boxes are owner's manuals. If you have auditory/sequential strengths, your first instinct might be to read carefully the text in the manuals. If you have visual/spatial strengths, you might look first at the diagrams in a manual and consult the text only if the diagrams don't tell you what you need to know. If you have tactile/kinesthetic strengths, you might toss the manuals aside and start fiddling with the equipment until you've figured out how to install it and how to use it.

This example is somewhat of an oversimplification, but researchers sometimes use it to illustrate differences among the three styles. Manufacturers know about learning styles. They put lots of diagrams in manuals for VSLs, and for TKLs they sometimes include a separate one- or two-page insert with essential information, titled something like "If You Hate Manuals, Use This."

When it comes to writing, people with auditory/sequential strengths tend to focus on the details, and in legal writing, they might intuitively understand how to show the steps of their reasoning in a logical sequence. Regardless of learning style, most students need to improve at explaining their reasoning steps *in depth*. But ASLs and VSLs can be strong at *sequencing* the steps.

People with visual/spatial strengths might more quickly understand an entire situation. They might see the big picture at once. They can seem to sculpt a document rather than writing it from beginning to end. According to a leading researcher in this field,

> For visual-spatials, writing is a lot like painting a picture. They may paint with broad strokes at first, filling in the details as they refine their pictures. In a painting, there's no particular order. You can start in the middle and work toward either end, or you can start at the end and work toward the beginning. I know a VSL who's a superb writer . . . . She cannot show anyone her rough drafts because they are full of holes. These are real gaps in the flow of writing where the picture hasn't formed yet. Being nonsequential in her thinking, she skips around the text, filling in the parts that are clear in her mind, and leaving large, gaping holes. Sometimes these holes are filled in her dreams, as her unconscious supplies the missing words or missing pieces of the picture.[1]

Less is known about TKLs and writing, except that some people with tactile/kinesthetic strengths say that writing helps them think because of the physical activity involved, especially when typing. Some describe this as thinking through their fingers.

---

[1] Linda Kreger Silverman, *Upside-Down Brilliance: The Visual-Spatial Learner* 300 (2002).

In legal writing, *all* of these strengths can be valuable. You can continue to build your skills around the ones you already have. It's *not* necessary to build up the others equally. No one is perfect or equally rounded, and all of us have uneven strengths. Many of the most famous writers can describe in abundant detail where they are weak in the writing process. And everyone can become more effective by identifying areas where they're not strong and by trying to improve there.

Much of education is based on the erroneous assumption that all learners are auditory/sequential. A teacher stands at the front of the room and talks. Students are supposed to sit still for long periods of time. Textbooks are masses of words, and in higher education they have few or no diagrams. In law school, an exception to all this is in skills courses, where students learn to do things, like write memos or cross-examine witnesses.

Some researchers include learning style categories other than those discussed here, for example *verbal* (learning through reading and writing) and *oral* (learning through talking). These overlap with some of the categories explained earlier in this section. Researchers are still discovering new aspects about learning styles, and much remains to be discovered.

If you want to know more about your learning style or styles, you might look at the books and articles listed in the footnote.[2] And you might do a Web search for the phrase "learning style." The books, articles, and websites explain how people with various learning styles can study more effectively and create more effective learning environments for themselves.

---

[2] Books: Ann L. Iijima, *The Law Student's Pocket Mentor: From Surviving to Thriving* 59-76, 103-106 (2007) and Michael Hunter Schwartz, *Expert Learning for Law Students* (2d ed. 2008). Articles: Robin A. Boyle & Rita Dunn, *Teaching Law Students Through Individual Learning Styles,* 62 Alb. L. Rev. 213 (1998); M.H. Sam Jacobson, *Learning Styles and Lawyering: Using Learning Theory to Organize Thinking and Writing,* 2 J. ALWD 27 (2004); M.H. Sam Jacobson, *How Law Students Absorb Information,* 8 J. of Leg. Writing 175 (2002); and M.H. Sam Jacobson, *A Primer on Learning Styles: Reaching Every Student,* 25 Seattle L. Rev. 139 (2001).

Inside the Process of Writing

Learning how to write like a lawyer is the beginning of learning how to make professional decisions. Partly those are analytical decisions, such as determining how a statute affects the client. And partly they're practical decisions, such as how to communicate most effectively to the reader.

§12.1 Five Phases of Writing

Writing happens in five phases:

1. researching authorities and analyzing what you find *(see §12.3)*
2. organizing your raw materials into an outline *(§12.4)*
3. producing a first draft *(§§12.5-12.6)*
4. rewriting it through several more drafts *(§12.7)*
5. polishing it *(§12.9)*

Writing teachers say that writing is recursive and not linear. That means that writers rarely, if ever, start at the beginning, write until they get to the end, and then stop (which would be in a line, or linear). And they do not go through the five phases of writing in strict order, finishing one phase before starting the next one (which also would be linear).

Instead, writers often circle back (recursively) to reopen something already done and redo some aspect of it. You will, for example, continue to analyze while organizing, writing the first draft, and rewriting, although much of the analytical work comes at the beginning. While writing the first draft, you might decide to go back and rewrite something you wrote a few pages ago. While rewriting, you might reorganize.

Still, it helps to think about writing in the five phases listed above. Each phase is a different *kind* of work, requiring somewhat different skills.

§12.2 Managing Time

Suppose your teacher distributes an assignment and sets a deadline three weeks later for submitting your work. On the day you receive the assignment, you have two options.

The first is to toss it aside when you get home so you can try not to think about it for at least two weeks, leaving only the last few days before the deadline to do the entire job. Many students did this in college and turned in their first draft as their final product. When they try it again in law school, the result is usually disappointing because law school writing requires much more preparation and many more drafts. When you're learning professional skills, each new task will usually take longer to accomplish than you might think because the complexities of the task are not immediately apparent. (Later, with experience, you will get much better at predicting how long it will take to get things done.)

The other option is to use the full three weeks to get the job done. Some students have very good internal clocks that pace them through the work without having to set a schedule for themselves. But for most students, time will get out of control unless they schedule. In this sense, planning the work is

1. estimating how long it will take you to do the research, analyze the results, organize your raw materials, produce a first draft, rewrite it through several more drafts, and polish it, and
2. budgeting your time so that you can do each one of these tasks well.

When you first get the assignment, it can seem huge and intimidating. But once you break it down into a group of smaller tasks, it's not as big any more and it seems much more doable. Here is what Amy Stein, a legal writing professor, tells her students:

> When I ask students if they have made a schedule for completing their work, they often look at me as if I have asked them to split the atom. Taking a series of complicated tasks and breaking them into manageable pieces is the best way that I know of to deal with the panic that comes from feeling that I have too much to do in too little time. Preparing a calendar will provide a master plan for all tasks, both work and play.

Students can use a paper calendar or find one on a PDA, calendaring program, or the web. . . .

Building a schedule requires a certain amount of honesty. Students must know their own strengths and weaknesses and be able to answer several questions. . . . Do you work best in short, intense bursts or longer sessions? Where do you work the best? Are you a procrastinator? Are you a morning person or a night person? A morning person should schedule research in the morning and thirty minutes on the elliptical bike at night. . . .

. . . It is marvelously satisfying to cross off what you have accomplished. . . .[1]

§12.3 Researching and Analyzing

Researching is finding relevant authority, such as statutes and cases. Your teacher has probably assigned a research textbook that explains how to research.

Analysis is deciding which authorities to rely on (Chapter 8), figuring out what they mean (Chapters 9 and 10), and how they govern the client's facts (Chapter 15). Students and lawyers usually print out or photocopy the authorities that research suggests might be relevant and mark them up while reading and rereading them, identifying the most significant passages. It helps to outline the statutes (Chapter 4).

§12.4 Organizing Your Raw Materials into an Outline

For two reasons, good organization is crucial in legal writing. First, legal writing is a highly structured form of expression because rules of law are by nature structured ideas. The structure of a rule controls the organization of its application to facts—and thus the organization of a written discussion of the rule and its application. Second, legal writing is judged entirely by how well it educates and convinces the reader that your reasoning is correct. Good organization makes your analysis more easily understandable to the reader by leading the reader through the steps of your reasoning.

Many students find that organizing in legal writing is especially challenging. That is why it takes several chapters in this book to explain how to outline and how to organize (see Chapters 13 and 16 through 19).

---

[1] Amy R. Stein, *Helping Students Understand that Effective Organization Is a Prerequisite to Effective Legal Writing,* 15 Perspectives 36, 37 (2006).

§12.5 Producing a First Draft

Many students treat the first draft as the most important phase of writing. But that is wrong: the first draft is often the *least* important phase. Most of the rest of writing does much more to cause an effective final product. And if you write on a computer, first-draft writing might not be separate from rewriting. That's because of the ease with which you can interrupt your first draft and go back to rewrite something you initially wrote only a few minutes ago.

The only purpose of a first draft is to get things down on the page so that you can start rewriting. The first draft *has no other value*. Despite its many faults, a first draft accomplishes its entire purpose merely by existing.

> All good writers write [awful first drafts]. This is how they end up with good second drafts and terrific third drafts. . . . I know some very great writers, . . . who write beautifully . . . , and not one of them . . . writes elegant first drafts. All right, one of them does, but we do not like her very much. . . .
>
> A friend of mine says that the first draft is the down draft—you just get it down. The second draft is the up draft—you fix it up. . . . And the third draft is the dental draft, where you check every tooth. . . . [2]

Do your first draft as early as you possibly can. You can't start rewriting (§12.7) until you have a first draft.

You don't have to write the first draft from beginning to end. You can start with any part of the document that you feel ready to write, no matter where in the document it will be. You can write the middle before you write the beginning, for example. If your mind is mulling over a certain part of the document, start writing that part. You can write the rest later.

§12.6 Overcoming Writer's Block

Suppose you sit down to write your first draft, but nothing happens. You stare at the computer screen, and it seems to stare right back at you. This does *not* mean you're an inadequate writer. Writer's block happens to everybody from time to time, even to the very best writers. What can you do to overcome it? Here are some strategies:

1. Do something unrelated for a while. Prepare for class, do the dishes, or jog. While you're doing something else, your unconscious mind will continue to work on the first draft. After a while, ideas will pop into your conscious mind unexpectedly, and you will need to sit down and start writing again. But be careful: In law, you're usually writing against a deadline, and doing something else cannot go on for too long.

---

[2] Anne Lamott, *Bird by Bird*, 21-22, 25-26 (1994).

2. If the beginning is blocking you, start somewhere else. The reader starts at the beginning, but you don't have to. A common cause of writer's block is starting to write at the beginning. The beginning of a document is often the hardest part to write. And in each part of the document, the first paragraph is often the hardest to write. One of the reasons is that if you're not sure exactly what you're going to say, you won't know how to introduce it at the beginning.

3. Use writing to reduce your fear. The most effective way to reduce anxiety is to start writing early—long before your deadline—and to keep on working steadily until you're finished. If you start early, you'll lose less sleep and be a happier writer. Many students procrastinate because they worry about writing. But procrastination *increases* anxiety and puts you further and further behind. The only way to break this cycle is to get started on writing so you can bring the task under control.

4. Don't expect perfection in first drafts. If you're chronically blocked when you try to do first drafts, it might be because you expect yourself to produce, in your first draft, a polished final version. That's expecting too much. Even well-known novelists cannot do it. Really bad first drafts are just fine. Keep reminding yourself that the first draft is the *least* important phase of writing. You can afford to write horribly in the first draft because you can fix everything during rewriting.

5. Start writing while researching and analyzing. While you're reading a case, some words of what you would like to say might flash through your mind. Type them or write them down. As you do, sentences might start coming to you. You sat down to research and analyze, but now you're writing. When you run out of steam while writing, go back to researching and analyzing. Experienced writers keep their computer on or a notepad handy while reading statutes, cases, and other authority because reading, thinking, and writing are all part of a single process. To read is to trigger thinking, which can trigger writing. It doesn't matter that you're writing without consulting your outline. You can figure out later where in the document what you are writing goes, or whether it goes in at all.

6. Separate yourself from distractions. If you're distracted by roommates or by the temptation to watch television or play computer games, leave the distractions in one place while you work in another.

§12.7 Rewriting

> There is no such thing as good writing. There is only good rewriting.
> *—Justice Louis Brandeis*

A first draft is for the writer. You write to put your thoughts on the page. But in subsequent drafts, the focus shifts to the reader. How much will *this* reader need to be told? Will she or he understand what you say without having to read twice? Will this reader become convinced that you're right?

To answer these questions while you read your work, pretend to be the reader for whom you're writing. Will this skeptical person see issues that you have not addressed? Will this busy person become impatient at having to wade through material of marginal value that somehow got into your first draft? Will this careful person be satisfied that you have written accurately and precisely?

You'll do a better job of impersonating the reader if, between drafts, you stop writing for a day or two, clear your mind by working on something else, and come back to do the next draft both "cold" and "fresh." Obviously, that cannot happen if you put off starting the project and later have to do the whole thing frantically at the last minute. To make sure that you have time to rewrite, start on an assignment as soon as you get it, and then pace yourself, working at regular intervals within the time allotted.

Actually, with computers, there might not be a clear dividing line between writing a first draft and rewriting it. A writer working on the sixth page of a first draft can interrupt that to rewrite part of page three; return to page six to continue first-draft writing; interrupt that again to make changes in the introduction on page one; then return to page six for more first-drafting; and so on. The writer keeps moving back and forth because while one part of the brain is working on page six, another part is thinking about other pages. This is called *recursive* rather than *linear* writing. You've finished a draft when you feel it's more or less complete, even if you know you'll need to return to it for more rewriting.

Most of the writing you'll do in the practice of law can be made effective in three to five drafts. The paragraphs you're reading now are a fifth draft. (Some parts of this book required 10 or 12 drafts however.)

To experience what the reader will experience, some writers read their drafts out loud, which can alert you to wording problems. Bad phrasing often sounds terrible when you say it. Other writers can get the same effect without speaking because they've developed the ability to "hear" in their minds a voice saying the words they read.

While rewriting, you can test your writing for effectiveness by using the checklists in many chapters of this book. Look for section titles that include the words "Ways to Test."

Don't be afraid to cut out material from your first draft. The fact that you've written something does not mean that you have to keep it.

Eventually, you'll notice, after putting the writing through several drafts, that the problems you find are mostly typographical errors and small matters of grammar, style, and citation. When that happens, you've moved from rewriting into polishing (§12.9), and the project is nearly finished.

For many people, rewriting "is the hardest task of all."[3] Set aside a lot of time for it. Sometimes during rewriting, things will seem discouraging because you will discover

---

[3] Peter Elbow, *Writing with Power: Techniques for Mastering the Writing Process* 121 (1981).

that problems you thought you had solved earlier really haven't been. At other times, when you piece things together well, you might experience relief, even exhilaration.

Rewriting may be the hardest phase of writing, but parts of it can be turned into a game. Read the preceding sentence again. During rewriting, the second part of that sentence ("parts of it can be turned into a game") went through the following evolution:

1st draft: ... there are ways of causing parts of rewriting to include the kinds of fun many people enjoy while playing games.

2d draft: ... parts of rewriting can be turned into something that includes the fun of a game.

3d draft: ... parts of it can be turned into a game.

How did this keep getting shorter and more clearer? Convoluted language was made simpler. Things that didn't add understanding were taken out. If games are usually fun, what meaning does the word *fun* add to the word *games*? Rewriting tightened the draft by finding ways to say the same thing more vividly in fewer words.

Look again at the first-draft version above. During rewriting, you would notice its weakness in either of two ways. You might reread it and ask, "What's that supposed to mean? What was I trying to say?" Or a game resembling a treasure hunt might have flagged it.

Question 7 in §21.1 includes a list of forms of the verb *to be*, which usually weakens writing. Your writing will become stronger and livelier if you try to replace *is, are, was*, and other forms of *to be* with action verbs. That doesn't always work, but if you look for opportunities to do it, you'll find some ways to make your writing stronger. (The weakness in the first draft example above begins with "there are," which is a variant of the verb *to be*.)

How can you find all the places where you've used variations of the verb *to be*? Use the "find" feature in your wordprocessor to search for *is, are*, and *was*. At every instance, think about replacing the word with an action verb. Sometimes that will strengthen your writing, and sometimes it won't. Decide one way or the other. This might not compare with a top-notch video game, but it does lend itself to thoughts like "Ha! Zapped another one!" You can make a list of words that cause you trouble and do this for each of them.

Although rewriting focuses on the sentence level, it should also consider the big picture. Is your organization natural and effective? As you reread and rewrite, do you have doubts about your analysis? Don't limit yourself to "surface-level changes," but instead use rewriting as "an opportunity to re-see [your] work" as a whole.[4]

Don't confuse rewriting with polishing (§12.9). If all you do is fix typographical errors, awkward wording, grammatical errors, and errors in citation form,

---

[4] Patricia Grande Montana, *Better Revision: Encouraging Students to See Through the Eyes of the Legal Reader*, 14 J. Legal Writing 291, 292 (2008).

you're only polishing, and you've skipped rewriting completely. Rewriting is hard because much of it involves reimagining your first draft and reexamining the decisions you made there. Experienced writers report that they can really enjoy rewriting because of what they can achieve there. "The pleasure of revision [another name for rewriting] often arises when you refine what you intend to say and *even* discover that you have more to say, a new solution, a different path, a better presentation."[5] Research on the writing process has shown that experienced writers use rewriting for deep rethinking, and usually they reorganize the earlier draft.[6]

§12.8 Using Writing to Help You Think

[T]here is no better way to master an idea than to write about it.

—Robert H. Frank

I write to discover what I think.

—Daniel Boorstin

Writing is thinking.

—Deirdre McCloskey

[L]earning to write as a lawyer is another way to learn to think as a lawyer.

—Terrill Pollman

Writing and rewriting will help you expand and refine your analysis. The writing process and the thinking process are inseparable. You can't write without rethinking what you're trying to say.

Wherever you are in writing—in the first draft, in rewriting, or even in polishing—don't be afraid to change your mind about your analysis of the law and the facts. Most writers have abandoned ideas that felt valuable when thought about, sounded valuable when spoken, but nevertheless proved faulty when—in the end—they "wouldn't write."

Most writers have experienced the reverse as well: sitting down to write with a single idea and finding that the act of writing draws the idea out, fertilizes it, causes it to sprout limbs and roots, and to spread into a forest of ideas. The amount of thought reflected in a good final draft is many times the amount that was in the first draft because the writing process and the thinking process are inseparable, each stimulating and advancing the other.

---

[5] Christopher M. Anzidei, *The Revision Process in Legal Writing: Seeing Better to Write Better,* 8 Leg. Wtg. 23, 44 (2002) (italics added).
[6] *Id.* at 40.

§12.9 Polishing

This is the last phase. Allow a day or more to pass before coming back to the writing to polish it. If you're away from it for at least a day, you'll come back fresh and be able to see things you would otherwise miss.

Print the document so you can see it exactly the way the reader will see it. Readers often see problems on the printed page that aren't so obvious on a computer screen. Before returning to the computer to fix problems, you can mark up the printed copy. This is sometimes called "a red-pen proofread," although you could use another color.

Take one last look for wording that does not say clearly and unambiguously what you mean. This is the biggest reason for waiting at least a day. When you wrote the words, they seemed clear because at that moment you knew what you were trying to say. But after some time has passed, you're no longer in that frame of mind. If you're not sure what the words mean or what you intended them to mean, fix them.

And take one last look for wording that can be tightened up. Can you say it equally well in fewer words? If you can, do so.

Look for typographical errors, awkward wording, grammatical errors, and errors in citation form. Does the formatting make the document attractive to read? If not, choose a different font (but one that looks professional), add white space so the document doesn't seem crowded, or find other ways to make it look attractive.[7] Use your word processor's spellcheck function. Make sure the pages are numbered.

Now, you're finished.

§12.10 Plagiarism

Plagiarism is using other people's words or ideas as though they were your own. You commit plagiarism if you lift words or an idea from *anywhere* else and put them into your own work without quotation marks (for words) and a citation (for words or ideas).

You already know the ethical and moral reasons not to plagiarize. You heard them in college and high school. Here are three more reasons:

First, you'll feel better about yourself if you don't steal words or ideas from someone else. You can have professional self-respect and pride in your own work only if you did the work yourself. And pride in your own work is one of life's pleasures.

Second, it's so easy to catch plagiarism that you should assume you'll be caught. A teacher can take some of your words and search for them in any of the legal research databases to find the case or article from which they were taken.

---

[7] See Ruth Anne Robbins, *Painting with Print: Incorporating Concepts of Typographic and Layout Design into the Text of Legal Writing Documents*, 2 J. ALWD 108 (2004).

Many teachers routinely do that. Teachers can also electronically search other students' papers for words like yours. A teacher who designed your assignment and grades the other students' papers knows where all the ideas came from. Even if you copy the detailed structure of your paper from another student, that can be plagiarism, and a teacher who grades both papers will notice it.

Third, your writing actually gains value from appropriate citation to the sources of words and ideas. Much of what you write will have credibility *only* if you show exactly where words and ideas come from. Proper attribution of ideas will allow your reader to rely on your work and to give you credit for ideas that are truly yours.

How Professional Writers Plan Their Writing

In college, students are sometimes told that they should do *all* the organizational work in an outline before starting the first draft. Professional writers rarely do that. Before starting the first draft, you need an organization to work from, but it can be flexible. During the first draft and during rewriting, experienced writers typically *re*organize as they write. A fluid outlining method that helps you write is explained in Chapter 19.

§13.1 Myths about Outlines

If you dislike outlining, it may be that you were taught an outlining method that seemed unnecessarily rigid. In college and high school, you might have been told that before you can start writing, you must make an outline with roman numerals, capital letters, and arabic numerals, like this (from a paper on the effectiveness of professional schools):

    I. Legal Education
       A. The First Year
          1. Large Classes
          2. The Casebook Method of Teaching
            [and so on]

B. The Second and Third Years
   [and so on]
II. Medical Education

This is a linear outline. It starts in one place and goes straight from I to II and later from III to IV to the end, with lower-level layers for detail along the way. It outlines the kind of paper you might have written in college and might write for a second- or third-year seminar in law school.

Here, the student has chosen and researched an important topic. But the linear outline might not help the student write. For some students, the linear outline might even make writing more difficult. Many professional writers do *not* plan their work by doing a linear outline in advance. Here's why:

Suppose you're sitting at the keyboard thinking about the project you are working on. Valuable thoughts are running through your mind. At that moment, you are in the groove. Ideas are flowing. This mental state—which some social scientists call "flow"—doesn't happen every day, but you're lucky enough to be in it at this moment. You look at your linear outline (like the one above) and try to find a place to put one of the ideas on your mind. While you're trying to find a place for that idea, all the other ideas in your mind recede. They seem to fly away. And it's hard to find a place in the outline for the one idea that's left because when you made the outline that idea had not yet occurred to you. Trying to deal with your outline has obstructed the flow of ideas.

Or the situation is different: You're not in flow. You haven't written anything yet. But you've made a linear outline. You stare at it and ask yourself, "What should I write under roman numeral I and before letter A?" Five minutes later, you haven't been able to answer that question. You're focused on writing what the outline tells you should be first, but your imagination is dry. The outline hurts you. If you weren't trying to satisfy it, your mind might start thinking about some other part of the project, and ideas would start coming. But as long as you're staring at the outline, your mind shuts down. In fact, "one of the only virtues of linear outlining is that it looks neat, and that very virtue is its downfall. By working to make sure the outline is neat, we effectively cut off any additions or inserts, and new ideas. After all, we do not want to mess up our neat outline."[1]

The principal myth about outlining is that a linear outline helps *everyone* write better. Linear outlining helps some writers, but it hurts others. It might help those who naturally think in a linear fashion. If you don't naturally think that way, a linear outline made before writing might inhibit you from starting to write and might obstruct the flow of ideas while you write. (By the way, if the idea of flow interests you, you might look at some of the books in the footnote.[2] Your university or public library probably has some of them.)

---

[1] Henriette Anne Klauser, *Writing on Both Sides of the Brain* 48 (1987).
[2] See Susan K. Perry, *Writing in Flow* (2001), as well as the following books by Mihaly Csikszentmihalyi: *Finding Flow* (1998), *Flow: The Psychology of Optimal Experience* (1990); *Beyond Boredom and Anxiety* (1975); *Optimal Experience* (edited with Isabella Selega Csikszentmihalyi, 1988); and *Flow in Sports* (with Susan A. Jackson, 1999).

Linear outlining can also interfere with what writing teachers call the recursive nature of writing. Writing as a process does not go neatly from one step to the next. It goes back and forth from one aspect of writing to another and in several directions at once (see Chapter 12). The process through which writers create can be messy. A messy process is fine as long as it leads to a neat and orderly final product.

This is why many students resist outlining in college. Outlining can seem like an arbitrary and useless requirement. But you still need to organize what you will say, and you will need to create an outline—but maybe not the way you were taught to do it in college.

§13.2 A Method Used by Many Professional Writers to Plan Their Writing

Organizing really means two things: For the writer, organizing is structuring the document. This is part of the *process* of writing explained in Chapters 11 and 12. For the reader, however, organization should be *visible in the product* so the reader doesn't get lost. Thus, you'll organize before the first draft, just to get the writing started in a coherent way. You'll also reorganize during the first draft and later during rewriting—so the reader can understand.

Sometimes the original organization works well and doesn't need much reworking. But often you'll need to do a lot of reorganizing while rewriting until you find a structure that works. When you reorganize a lot, that does not necessarily mean you have been making mistakes and are now fixing them. Most of the time, reorganizing happens because the act of writing teaches you the analysis you are trying to write. *Writing is thinking.* You can't rewrite without rethinking what you're trying to say. Reorganizing is a natural part of rewriting.

This makes outlining easier because it doesn't have to be perfect the first time. Before a first draft, you can do a quick-and-dirty *fluid outline.* Then in later drafts, you can reorganize, if necessary, to meet the reader's expectations. With experience, you'll gain foresight. Your first drafts will become more organized, and you'll need to do less and less reorganizing in later drafts. But even the most experienced writers reorganize a lot of what they write.

Before a first draft: Make a fluid outline, which is just a flexible collection of lists on scratch paper or on your computer. Your raw materials (cases, facts, hypotheses, and so on) flow through it and into your first draft. Begin by identifying the issues. For each issue, identify the rule of law that controls the answer. Then make a list (either on paper or on your computer screen) of everything you found through research that proves the rule is accurate and another list of everything that supports your application of the rule to the facts. With practice, you might not even make lists; you might just make piles of your photocopies or print-outs. As you write about an issue during your first draft, cross off things on your list (or move things out of your pile). When you've crossed off everything on your list, go on to the next issue. When you've done all the issues, you have completed a first draft of the Discussion if you are writing an office memo, or of the Argument if you are writing a motion memo or appellate brief. Chapter 19 explains how to do all this effectively.

Many professional writers organize this way: making lists or piles, knowing that they'll be finished when everything is crossed out or a pile is empty. This method is only a suggestion. If you develop a different procedure that works better for you, use yours instead.

In later drafts: Linear outlines are *not* inherently bad. Although linear outlines might obstruct producing a first draft, they can help to improve later drafts during rewriting. To do that, you would create *a post-draft linear outline*—a linear outline of what you've *already* written. That might seem strange, but for many writers it works. *A finished product should be organized the way a linear outline is—even if you used a fluid outline to produce your first draft.*

To find out whether this method would work for you, print out a copy of your draft and read it, asking yourself whether you've incorporated a linear outline into your writing without realizing you were doing so. If the answer is yes, that increases the odds that you have organized effectively.

At each point in your draft where you state an important conclusion or start a new topic, write a heading that reflects that. You can handwrite the headings in the margins of your printed draft. The headings will resemble the items that would be listed in a linear outline. For example, if you were writing a seminar paper on the topic partially outlined at the beginning of this chapter, you would write in the margin "The Casebook Method of Teaching" at the point where you finish talking about whether large classes work well and where you are about to start talking about casebooks.

After you've done this to your entire draft, step back and look at your headings. For the moment, look at the headings alone and ignore the rest of your draft. You're trying to see the big picture. Are the headings in a logical order? Do they cover everything? Do they lay out the analysis in a way that would be clear to the reader? If you answer yes to these questions, you might have a good organization—and you've now produced good headings, which you can insert into your draft if they would help guide the reader.

But if any of the answers is no, use the cut-and-paste feature of your word processor to rearrange portions of your draft. Then reread everything to make sure that individual sentences and paragraphs still work well in their new locations. You might need to reword some things.

§13.3 Some Other Methods Used by Professional Writers to Plan Their Writing

Some writers outline by writing on sticky notes and putting them on a wall. The outline can be reshuffled by moving the notes around.

Some outline by making flowcharts in which the things to be written about appear in boxes or ovals with arrows showing their relationship to each other and the order in which they'll be discussed. For some very visual writers, this accurately reflects how they think about what they are writing.

A few outline with mind-mapping software like Inspiration.

And some outline the linear way, with roman numerals, as illustrated at the beginning of this chapter. It has worked well for them, and they're happy with it.

III

Office Memoranda

Office Memorandum Format

§14.1 Structure of an Office Memorandum

Form follows function.

— Louis Sullivan (architect)

A lawyer writes an office memorandum to determine how the law will treat a client's situation. Often a junior lawyer will write a memo to answer a question asked by a supervisor. The supervisor might know the law generally, but not necessarily how the law treats the issues for which a memo is needed. The supervisor might use the memo to advise the client or to plan a lawsuit or other action on the client's behalf. The office memo presents the research and analysis in a format that allows the supervisor to use her or his time most efficiently.

When writing a memo, who should you imagine your reader to be? When you start working at a job, there will be nothing to imagine because you will know your supervisor. But in law school, your assignments and your readers are hypothetical. Imagine that you are writing to the typical supervising attorney described in §1.5. This person will be busy and by nature skeptical and careful. Your supervisor will read your memo for the purpose of making a decision and will probably be under some kind of pressure (especially time pressure) while reading.

Office memo format varies from law office to law office and can vary further from case to case. A typical office memorandum includes some combination of the following, often, though not always in this order:

1. a memorandum heading
2. the Issue or Issues
3. a Brief Answer
4. the Facts
5. a Discussion
6. a Conclusion or Recommendations

See the sample office memo in Appendix A.

The **memorandum heading** simply identifies the writer (you), the reader, the date on which the memorandum is submitted, and the subject matter.

The **Issue** or Issues states the question or questions that the memorandum resolves. The **Brief Answer** states your conclusion together with a short summary of your reasons. Your detailed analysis will appear in the Discussion.

Issue

Will trademark law allow Donald Trump to prevent others from using, in commerce, the phrase "You're fired!", which he says for dramatic effect on his television show?

Brief Answer

No. The words "You're fired!" are generic or descriptive. They lack the secondary meaning required for trademark protection. And many other people have used them as business names or slogans before Trump starting doing so. Trump can trademark a picture of himself pointing with his index finger and saying the words "You're fired!" But he cannot trademark the words alone.

The Issue itemizes the inner core of facts that you think crucial to the answer: Trump, his television show, and the words "You're Fired!". The Brief Answer states legal conclusions based on those facts. The Discussion explains in detail why the Brief Answer is right.

The **Facts** set out the events and circumstances relevant to the Issue. Sometimes the Facts are stated chronologically, but sometimes organizing them by topic is more clear to the reader. Emphasize dates only if they are determinative or needed to avoid confusion. A date could be determinative if the issue is based on time (such as a statute of limitations).

Include all facts you consider determinative, together with any explanatory facts needed to help the story make sense. If your supervisor is thoroughly familiar with the factual background, this part of the memo might be short because you are trying to remind the supervisor about the essential facts, rather than to make a detailed record of them.

The **Discussion** is the largest and most complex part of the memorandum. It proves the conclusion set out in the Brief Answer. Chapter 15 explains how to write predictively in a Discussion, and Chapters 16 through 19 explain how to organize it. If the Discussion is detailed or analyzes several issues, it should be broken up with subheadings to help the reader locate the portions the reader might need at any given time.

Different lawyers follow different practices concerning the **Conclusion**. Some lawyers include it only if the issue is so complicated that a reader would need a summary of the reasoning at the end of the memo. Other lawyers always include it in the belief that a reader will always need a summary. Sometimes this is a good place to explain what lawyering tasks you think need to be done next or to suggest methods of solving the client's problem. If so, this part of the memo can more accurately be called **Recommendations**. A short memo might have no Conclusion or Recommendations.

§14.2 Which Part of the Memo to Write First

One lawyer might write the Discussion before writing anything else, on the theory that the other components of the memorandum will be shaped by the insights gained while putting the Discussion together. For example, writing the Discussion might show which facts are important enough to be recited in the Facts. Another lawyer might start by writing the Facts because they seem easier to describe. And a third lawyer might be flexible, starting with whatever component first begins to take shape in the lawyer's mind and often drafting two or more components simultaneously.

Flexibility works well. One way of overcoming inertia and plunging into writing is to start with whatever part of the memo you are thinking about. *Writing is thinking*, and if you're already thinking about a part of the memo, your mind is beginning to write even if your fingers have not yet touched the keyboard.

§14.3 The Audience for an Office Memo

Your audience will usually be one person: the supervising lawyer who asked you to research and write the memo. Although the memo might eventually be read by others, you're primarily writing to your supervisor.

If you were sitting with your supervisor, looking her or him in the eye, and explaining your research and analysis, you would choose your words and tone to communicate with that one person. In an office memo, you're doing the same thing, but in writing. In a first-year writing course, how can you write to a supervisor when you don't have one?

To imagine a professional supervisor, think of someone you know whose intelligence, wisdom, and judgment you respect deeply. In your first draft, write as though you are explaining your research and analysis to this person, who in your mind is playing the role of your supervisor. Assume that she or he is educated in the law, even if that's not true. The point is to write to a real human being whose mind would be engaged if reading your document. Then, in subsequent drafts, continue writing to this person while improving your writing to satisfy the professional standards your teacher expects. In later drafts, you're really writing to two people: your imagined supervisor and your teacher.

Professional writers often do something like this. They write imagining one specific person as the reader, and they find the words that would make everything clear to that person. They do this to help connect with the people who actually will read their writing. (It works only if the imagined reader is similar to the real readers.)

Predictive Writing in an Office Memorandum

§15.1 Predicting in Writing

When a client hires a lawyer, the client often asks the lawyer to start making predictions pretty quickly: "Will I win?" "Is it worth fighting for this?" "Can the other side get away with that?" The process of making predictions might seem magical and mysterious. This chapter explains how to do it. (You might reread §1.2 on the difference between predictive writing and persuasive writing. It's short and will help you here.)

A lawyer predicts for either of two reasons. One is to help *the client* make a decision knowing how the law will respond ("if the client constructs her estate in this way, it will not be taxed"). The other is to help *the lawyer* make a tactical or strategic decision ("we can plead this complaint because it will survive a motion to dismiss").

Predictive writing is sometimes called *objective writing,* but objectivity only partly defines it. Any writing that makes a disinterested report of what the law is can be called objective. Predictive writing does more than that. It foretells how the law will resolve a particular controversy. Sometimes an office memo predicts explicitly, and sometimes it predicts implicitly:

explicitly:	Ms. Rhee will probably be awarded damages for trademark infringement.
implicitly:	Ms. Rhee probably has a cause of action for trademark infringement.

Both statements mean the same thing. You can say it either way, unless you work in an office that prefers one or the other.

The first step in predicting is to develop arguments for each side on every issue. Think of the reasons why your client should win. And think of the reasons why the opposing party should win. To predict which arguments will persuade a court, you need to know the arguments the court will hear from each side. Then, evaluate each argument by asking yourself whether it will probably persuade a judge. Bearing those evaluations in mind, how would a court rule on each issue? Then step back and consider the matter as a whole. In light of your predictions on each individual issue, how will the court decide the entire controversy?

§15.2 An Example of the Predictive Process: Taylor and Garrett

Assume that in our jurisdiction the crime of common law burglary has been codified in the following form and renamed burglary in the first degree:

> *Criminal Code §102:* A person commits burglary in the first degree by breaking and entering the dwelling of another in the nighttime with intent to commit a felony therein.

This part of the statute is preceded by a definitions section:

Criminal Code §101: Definitions:

(a) A "breaking" is the making of an opening, or the enlarging of an opening, so as to permit entry into a building, or a closed off portion thereof, if neither the owner nor the occupant has consented thereto.

(b) A "closed off portion" of a building is one divided from the remainder of the building by walls, partitions, or the like so that it can be secured against entry.

(c) A "dwelling" is any building, or any closed off portion thereof, in which one or more persons habitually sleep.

(d) An "entering" or an "entry" is the placing, by the defendant, of any part of his body or anything under his control within a building, or a closed off portion thereof, if neither the owner nor the occupant has consented thereto.

(e) "Intent to commit a felony therein" is the design or purpose of committing, within a building or closed off portion thereof, a crime classified in this Code as a felony, if the defendant had that design or purpose both at the time of a breaking and at the time of an entering.

(f) "Nighttime" is the period between sunset and sunrise.

(g) A dwelling is "of another" if the defendant does not by right habitually sleep there.

The legislature has also enacted the following:

Criminal Code §10: No person shall be convicted of a crime except on evidence proving guilt beyond a reasonable doubt.

Criminal Code §403: A battery causing substantial injury is a felony.

Assume—just to make things simpler—that none of these sections has yet been interpreted by the courts, and that you're therefore limited to the statute itself. That's a very unusual situation. You'll typically be working with judicial decisions that have interpreted the statute.

Taylor and Garrett are students who have rented apartments on the same floor of the same building. At midnight, Taylor was studying, while Garrett was listening to a Radiohead album with his new four-foot speakers. Taylor had put up with this for two or three hours, and finally she pounded on Garrett's door. Garrett opened the door about six inches, and, when he realized that he could not hear what Taylor was saying, he stepped back into the room a few feet to turn the volume down, without opening the door further. Continuing to express outrage, Taylor pushed the door fully open and strode into the room. Garrett turned on Taylor and ordered her to leave. According to Taylor, she felt this to be "too much" and punched Garrett so hard that he suffered substantial injury.

The punch was a felonious battery under Criminal Code §403. Is Taylor also guilty of burglary in the first degree under Criminal Code §102? Your first reaction might be "no," and your reasoning might go something like this: "That's not burglary. Burglary happens when somebody gets into the house when you're not around and steals all the valuables. Maybe this will turn out to be some kind of trespass." But in law a satisfactory answer is never just "yes" or "no." An answer includes a sound *reason*, and, regardless of whether Taylor is guilty of burglary, this answer is wrong because the reasoning is inadequate. The answer can be determined only by applying all the relevant rules to the facts. Anything else is a guess.

A lawyer might start *thinking* predictively in the following way:

First-degree burglary (from §102) has six elements and no exceptions. In §101, the legislature defined each of the elements as well as some terms used in the definitions.

Taylor is guilty only if each element is proved beyond a reasonable doubt (§10). So I'll make a list of the elements and annotate it with the facts:

1. *a breaking*: When she pushed the door back, she enlarged an opening into Garrett's apartment, which is a closed off portion of a building, and neither Garrett nor the landlord consented to that.
2. *and an entry*: Taylor "entered" by walking into the apartment, which neither Garrett nor the landlord consented to.
3. *of the dwelling*: Nothing suggests that Garrett does not habitually sleep in his own apartment. He was there at midnight, although he obviously wasn't sleeping at the time. It's a dwelling.
4. *of another*: And it is not Taylor's dwelling. She lives down the hall.
5. *in the nighttime*: Midnight is in the nighttime.
6. *with intent to commit a felony therein*: Taylor committed a felony under §403 when she hit Garrett. The issue is when she formed the intent to do that. Because of the way §101(e) defines this element, it's not satisfied unless she had the intent to hit him both when she broke *and* when she entered. If she formed the intent to hit him *after* she entered, the element is not satisfied. Here are the arguments:

> *guilty:*   She was already furious, and she walked right over and punched him, without hesitation.
>
> *not guilty:*   After the breaking and entering and before the punch, Garrett turned on her and ordered her to leave, and she will testify that she had a reaction to what he did. She felt it to be "too much." She may have been angry when she pushed the door open and walked in, but anger does not necessarily include an intent to hit somebody. She is not guilty unless the evidence proves beyond a reasonable doubt that she formed that intent before or during the breaking and entering—not afterward.

The not guilty argument looks better. It creates reasonable doubt that undermines the guilty argument (unless the jury decides she's not telling the truth).

So stepping back and looking at the big picture, the prosecution can prove every element except the last one. And since they'll be missing an element, she'll be acquitted.

That is how the lawyer might *think* through the process of prediction. But if the lawyer were asked to record that prediction in the Discussion portion of an office memorandum, the lawyer might *write* something like the following. (This is a simple Discussion because it does not evaluate any judicial opinions.)

Discussion

Taylor will probably be acquitted of first-degree burglary because the evidence does not show beyond a reasonable doubt that she had formed the intent to commit a felony when she broke and entered Garrett's apartment. The evidence does prove, however, that she committed the other five elements of first-degree burglary. Under §102 of the Criminal Code, a person is guilty of burglary if he or she (1) breaks and (2) enters (3) the dwelling (4) of another (5) in the nighttime (6) "with intent to commit a felony therein." Under §11, a defendant can be convicted only "on evidence proving guilt beyond a reasonable doubt."

The prosecution will easily be able to prove the third, fourth, and fifth elements. Section 101(f) defines a dwelling as "any building, or closed off portion thereof, in which one or more-persons habitually sleep." Nothing suggests that Garrett does not habitually sleep in his own apartment. Additionally, that apartment is, to Taylor, the dwelling of another. Section 101(g) would define it as her dwelling only if she habitually slept there and had a legal right ("by right") to do so. She has rented an apartment elsewhere on the same floor, and nothing suggests she has also signed the lease to Garrett's apartment. All these events transpired between sunset and sunrise, which satisfies §101(f)'s definition of nighttime.

Taylor's pushing open Garrett's apartment door was a breaking. A breaking includes, among other things, "the enlarging of an opening, so as to permit entry into . . . a closed off portion" of a building "if neither the owner nor the occupant has consented thereto." Crim. Code §101(a). Garrett's apartment is a "closed off portion" of a building, which is defined by §101(b) as "one divided from the remainder of the building by walls, partitions, or the like so that it can be secured against entry." Although Garrett's apartment is not described, it would be difficult to imagine an apartment that is not thus divided from the building in which it is located. During the incident in question, Garrett opened his front door about six inches after Taylor knocked on it to complain of noise, and, when she walked into his apartment moments later, he immediately ordered her out. The initial opening of six inches would not have been enough to admit Taylor, and Garrett's prompt order to leave shows beyond a reasonable doubt that he had not consented to her opening the door farther. And nothing suggests that Taylor had consent from an owner of the apartment, who might have been someone other than Garrett.

Taylor's walking into Garrett's apartment was an entry, which §101(d) defines as "the placing, by the defendant, of any part of his body or anything under his control within a building, or a closed off portion thereof, if neither the owner nor the occupant has consented thereto." Taylor walked into Garrett's apartment, and the circumstances do not show consent to an entry for the same reasons that they do not show consent to a breaking.

But the prosecution will not be able to prove beyond a reasonable doubt that Taylor had formed the intent to assault Garrett when she broke and entered. Section 101(e) defines "intent to commit a felony therein" as "the design or purpose of committing, within a building or closed off portion thereof, a . . . felony, if the defendant had such design or purpose both at the time of a breaking and at the time of an entering." She will testify that when Garrett turned around and ordered her to leave while she was protesting his noise, she found this to be "too much" and punched him. A reasonable explanation for her intent is that it was formed after she was already in the room. No words or action on her part show that she had the intent to punch Garrett before she actually did so. Although, in her anger, she might have contemplated an assault before or when she broke and entered, there is a difference between considering an act and having the "design or purpose of committing" it, and her actions before she struck Garrett show no more than an intent to complain.

Thus, unless the jury decides that Taylor is not telling the truth, she will be acquitted of first-degree burglary because the evidence does not show beyond a reasonable doubt that she had the intent to commit a felony when she pushed open Garrett's door and walked into his apartment.

This material could be organized effectively in other ways, too. When you write, *please resist the temptation to copy uncritically the style of this example*. It might not be appropriate to your assignment or to your own approach to the analysis. The issues here are not difficult, and the facts given were few. Even the earliest writing you do in law school will require both more extensive discussion and deeper analysis than in this example.

§15.3 How to Test Your Writing for Predictiveness

While rewriting, ask yourself the following questions. They also appear on this book's website as a checklist, which you can print out.

1. Have you refused to hide from bad news? If the client's case is weak, it's better to know that now. Predictive writing is frank diagnosis. Advocacy has another time and place.

2. Have you edited out waffling? Your readers will expect you to take a position and prove it. Mushy waffling with words like "seems," "appears," and their synonyms makes your advice less useful to clients and supervising attorneys. Supervisors and judges are grateful for concreteness, whether or not they agree with you. If somebody disagrees with you, lightning will *not* strike you down on the spot. (It is not waffling to say that "the plaintiff probably will win an appeal" or "is likely to win an appeal." No prediction can be a certainty.)

3. Have you told the reader whether your prediction is qualified in any way? For precision, a prediction should at least imply how confident you are of it. Is the underlying rule a matter of "settled law" and are the facts clear-cut? If your prediction is qualified, you can state precisely the variables on which the prediction is based, such as "The defendant will probably prevail unless . . . ."

4. Have you concentrated on solving a problem, rather than on writing a college essay? A college essay is a vehicle for academic analysis—analysis to satisfy curiosity—rather than practical problem-solving for clients. Legal writing is practical. Solve the problem you were asked to solve. Solve it completely. But don't insert into your writing essays not essential to solving the problem. For example:

> Common law courts developed the crime of burglary because in the middle ages, with no police and no electric lights, life was much more dangerous at night. People bolted their doors and windows when the sun went down, but they still felt vulnerable because of the advantage darkness gave to criminals. The courts classified burglary as a felony with the same punishment as murder (execution by hanging) so that people

could sleep at night with some sense of security. Modern statutes have reduced the punishment to imprisonment. They often retain something like the common law formulation of burglary as the most serious form of the crime. Lesser statutory forms might omit some of the elements of common law burglary and might be called second- or third-degree burglary or breaking and entering.

This is interesting. It even explains why Goldilocks would not be charged with common law burglary. She got into the bears' house during the daytime, and she didn't have a felonious intent, even if she later ate their porridge and slept in their beds. But it doesn't help predict whether Taylor will be convicted and therefore wouldn't belong in Taylor's memo.

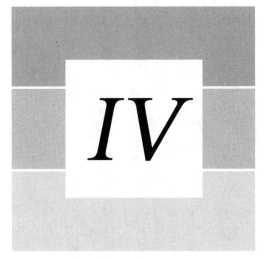

Organizing
Analysis

CREAC: A Formula for Structuring Proof of a Conclusion of Law

This and the following chapters explain how to structure the Discussion section of an office memo as well as the Argument section of a motion memo or appellate brief.

§16.1 The Need to Organize with Care (Kendrick and Jordan)

After a long day in the library studying for exams, Jordan and her friends walked to the student lounge, bought cans of apple juice from vending machines, poured the juice into clear plastic cups, sat, and chatted. One of the group suggested that before they go back to the library and study for a few more hours, they have a contest to see which of them could do the most convincing job of pretending to be drunk. Kendrick, who was eating pizza nearby, took out his cell phone and, without her knowledge, filmed Jordan, who was clearly winning the contest.

Kendrick put the film on YouTube under the title "Jordan Drunk in the Student Lounge." Nothing on the YouTube page suggested that she was not actually drunk. The day after Kendrick did this, Jordan received a very attractive job offer from a law firm. Like many job offers, this one was conditioned on a background check. Among other things, the firm searched the internet for websites on which Jordan's name appeared. When the firm came across the YouTube film clip, it rescinded the offer. Jordan tried to persuade the firm that she had not actually been drunk and that she had had nothing to do with putting the film on YouTube, but by then the firm had filled the position with another applicant. Other firms with which Jordan had interviewed are not returning her phone calls, and she thinks that is because they have done background checks of their own.

Jordan has hired your law firm, which is not the one that rescinded the job offer. Your supervisor has decided that a lawsuit would make sense only if YouTube would be liable. You and your supervisor have already determined that Jordan would win a lawsuit against Kendrick for defamation and invasion of privacy. But suing Kendrick alone would not help because it would be years before he would have earned enough money to compensate Jordan.

A television station would have been liable under your state's common law of defamation and invasion of privacy if it had broadcast Kendrick's film with the title that appeared on YouTube, and a newspaper or magazine would have been similarly liable if it had published still frames from Kendrick's film with the same words in the form of a caption. Your supervisor asked you to research whether the federal Communications Decency Act of 1996 would prevent recovery against YouTube, which is not a television station, newspaper, or magazine. After reading the statute and the case law interpreting it, you believe that Jordan cannot recover against YouTube.

When you write the Discussion section of an office memo or the Argument in a motion memo or appellate brief, *what will you say first? What will you say after that? How will you organize the many things you have to say? And in how much detail will you say them?* Those questions are answered in this and the following chapters.

§16.2 A Formula for Organizing Analysis

A supervising lawyer who reads a predictive Discussion in an office memo does so in preparation for making a decision. So does a judge who reads persuasive writing in a motion memo or appellate brief. They will make different kinds of decisions. The lawyer will decide what to advise the client or how to handle the client's case. The judge will decide how to rule on a motion or appeal. But both look for a tightly structured analysis that makes your conclusion seem inevitable.

To the reader who must make a decision, analysis is most easily understood if it is organized into the following formula—or into some variation of it.

> To prove a conclusion of law:
>
> **C:**   State your **conclusion**.
>
> **R:**   State the primary **rule** that supports the conclusion.
>
> **E:**   **Explain** and prove the rule by analyzing authority.
>
> **A:**   **Apply** the rule's elements to the facts.
>
> **C:**   *(optional)* If explaining or applying the rule is complicated, sum up by restating your **conclusion.**

What do the ingredients in the CREAC[1] formula mean?

The **conclusion** of law is your determination of how the law treats certain facts. It is what you are trying to prove. In predictive writing, it can be expressed as a determination ("The Communications Decency Act prevents recovery against YouTube") or as a prediction ("Jordan will not be able to recover against YouTube for defamation or invasion of privacy").

The **rule** is the primary rule on which you rely in reaching your conclusion. Other rules might also be involved, but this is the main one on which your analysis rests.

Rule **explanation** is proof—using authority such as statutes and cases—that the main rule on which you rely really is the law in the jurisdiction involved. The reader needs to know for certain that the rule exists in the jurisdiction, and that you have expressed it accurately. Explain how the authority supports the rule, analyze the policy behind the rule, and counteranalyze reasonable arguments that could be made against your interpretation of the rule. A subsidiary rule might help explain the main rule. A subsidiary rule is one that guides application of the main rule or works together with it in some way necessary to your analysis. An example would be the rule that evidence showing guilt beyond a reasonable doubt is required for conviction in a criminal case. In the Discussion on pages 110–111, notice how it interacts with a main rule, the definition of first-degree burglary.

Rule **application** is a demonstration that the rule + the facts = your conclusion. Explain why your result is what the law has in mind, using authority, policy considerations, counteranalyses, and any subsidiary rules needed.

Sometimes authority that you use in rule explanation might reappear in rule application, but for a different purpose. For example, suppose that *Alger v. Rittenhouse* held that a boat crew that caught a shark became its owner, to

---

[1] The CREAC formula is identical to the paradigm for structuring proof of a conclusion of law—often called just *the paradigm*—which first appeared in Richard K. Neumann, Jr., *Legal Reasoning and Legal Writing: Structure, Strategy, and Style* 111-125 (1990), and which has continued to be called *the paradigm* in subsequent editions of that book.

the exclusion of the fisherman who hooked but lost the shark an hour earlier. In your case, ranchers trapped in their corral a wild mustang that immediately jumped over the fence and ran onto your client's land, where it was captured by your client. In rule explanation, you can use *Alger* to prove that your jurisdiction has adopted the rule that wild animals become the property of the first person to reduce them to possession. And in rule application, you can use *Alger* again—this time to show that your client satisfies that rule because her facts are analogous to those of the boat crew, and that she thus owns the mustang.

A rule's *policy* is the rule's reason for being (see Chapter 7 and §9.3). Each rule of law is designed to accomplish a purpose, such as preventing a particular type of harm. When courts are unsure of what a rule means or how to apply it, they interpret the rule in the way that would be most consistent with the policy behind it. Thus, policy can be used to show what the rule is (in rule explanation) and how to apply it (in rule application).

Counteranalysis is a term used by law teachers, but not by many practicing lawyers. A *counteranalysis* evaluates the arguments that could *reasonably* be made against your conclusion. Don't waste time and space by evaluating marginal or far-fetched arguments. In predictive writing, the counteranalysis is an objective evaluation of each reasonable contrary argument, with an honest report of its strengths and weaknesses. You must say whether your conclusion can withstand attack. And you must consider the possibility that other analyses might be better than the one you've selected. In persuasive writing in a motion memo or appellate brief, a counteranalysis is called a *counterargument.* It does not objectively consider contrary points of view. It argues against them, stressing their weaknesses and showing their strengths to be unconvincing. Counteranalyses can appear in rule explanation or in rule application.

The formula explained here is designed for practical writing in office and motion memos and appellate briefs. Do not use it in this form when you take law school examinations. For exams, use the IRAC organization, which is explained in the article on Writing Exam Answers on this book's website.

Although the CREAC formula *helps* you organize, it will take some effort to learn how to use it. But once you've learned that, writing will become easier because you won't have to struggle to figure out how to organize a mass of information. The CREAC formula will organize it for you.

§16.3 Why Readers Prefer This Type of Organization

Your readers will be practical and busy people who read your memo or brief to help them make a decision. Because skepticism results in better decisions, readers will be skeptical about what you say. That means you must put all the reasons why you are right on the page for the reader to consider.

State your **conclusion** first because a practical and busy reader needs to know what you are trying to support before you start supporting it. If you state your conclusion only after the analysis that supports it (or in the middle of that analysis), some or all of your reasoning will seem pointless to the reader who does not yet know what you are trying to prove. Effective writers usually state their conclusions boldly at the beginning of a Discussion or Argument. This may take some getting used to. It's contrary to the way writing is often done in college. And many people have been socialized to state a conclusion only after a proof—even in informal conversations—to avoid appearing opinionated or arrogant.

Far from being offended, however, the reader who has to make a decision is grateful not to be kept in suspense. That kind of reader becomes frustrated and annoyed while struggling through sentences the relevance of which cannot be understood because the writer has not yet stated the proposition the sentences are intended to prove.

Next, state the **rule** because, after reading a conclusion of law, a skeptical lawyer or judge instinctively wants to know what principles of law require that conclusion. After all, a core idea of law is that things are to be done according to the rules.

Then **explain** and prove the rule because the reader will refuse to follow you further until you have established that the rule really is controlling law and until you have educated the reader on how the rule works. The skeptical lawyer or judge will not accept a rule statement as genuine unless it has been proved with authority. You need to do all this *before* you apply the rule to your facts because the reader will not accept the rule until after you've shown that it is law and how it is supposed to operate.

Then **apply** the rule. When you have done that, you have completed proof of a conclusion of law.

If what you have said is complicated, restate your **conclusion** to wrap things up.

§16.4 Ingredients of Rule Explanation

To explain a rule, do the following:

1. Prove that the rule is law in the jurisdiction where the dispute would be or is being litigated. If the jurisdiction adopted the rule by statute, quote the key words of the statute, and show how the courts' interpretation of the statute is consistent with your understanding of it. If the rule is part of the jurisdiction's common law, prove that with cases. If the jurisdiction has a gap in its law on this subject show how cases from other jurisdictions would persuade local courts to adopt the rule you are using.

2. Prove that you have stated the rule accurately. Sometimes whatever you say to prove that the rule is law also shows that you have stated it accurately.

Sometimes you will need to add some extra discussion to give the reader confidence that you have not misstated the rule.

3. Explain how the rule operates. Don't include information irrelevant to your issue. But some information about how courts have interpreted the rule will give the reader an overview before you start rule application.

4. Explain the policy behind the rule—if that would help the reader understand the rule. What is the law trying to accomplish through the rule? You don't need to explain the policy behind the cause of action for negligence. Every lawyer learned in the first year of law school that the policies behind negligence are to deter people from behaving in ways that are unreasonably dangerous to others and to compensate those who are injured through unreasonably dangerous behavior. But what about the policy behind the rule that a judge may not ask jurors to explain how they reached their verdict? That might need to be explained so that the reader can see how your analysis of the rule is consistent with its policy.

5. If any arguments could reasonably challenge your explanation of the rule, show in the counteranalysis why they are not persuasive. If you can't do that, consider changing your mind.

6. If any subsidiary rules are essential to the analysis, prove and explain them as well. A subsidiary rule is one that operates with the primary rule to resolve the issue. Usually, less explanation is needed for subsidiary rules because they are less important. Not all subsidiary rules need to be explained in rule explanation.

§16.5 Ingredients of Rule Application

To apply a rule to your facts, do the following:

1. State, in summary, what happens when you compare the facts to the rule. Here are some examples:

"All of these elements are present in the facts."

"Ms. McGillicuddy did everything the law of adverse possession requires of her."

"Cobb did not proximately cause Crawford's injury, although the other elements of negligence are present."

"None of these elements are present in the facts."

2. Show, in detail, why that result occurs. Go through the rule's elements—all of them. But concentrate on the elements that are difficult to analyze, and allocate less space to others. Use authorities to support your analysis. Show how the facts are equivalent or analogous to those in cases.

3. If it's not obvious, show how the result is consistent with the rule's policy. See paragraph 4 in §16.4.

4. If any arguments could reasonably challenge your application of the rule, show in a counteranalysis why they are not persuasive. If you can't do that, consider changing your mind.

§16.6 Separating Rule Explanation from Rule Application

Judicial opinions usually start with a statement of the facts of the case. After that, a court will typically begin discussing the law. In the law discussion, you can often see exactly where the court stops explaining the law generally and starts applying the law to the facts of the dispute. If you were to draw a line across the page at that point, above the line would be rule explanation and below the line would be rule application. If the opinion decides several issues, you might find a dividing point for each issue. If you want to get some practice in recognizing the difference between rule explanation and rule application, you might try looking for this dividing point when you read cases for other courses. The more recent the case, the more apparent the dividing point will be. Opinions written before about 1950 tend to be somewhat less well organized.

Exercise. Changing Planes in Little Rock

Wong has sued Keating in an Arkansas state court. Wong has never lived in Arkansas, and none of the events that led to *Wong v. Keating* happened in that state. But Wong sued in Arkansas because his lawyer has confidence in the juries there. The only time Keating has ever set foot on the ground in Arkansas was for

45 minutes while changing planes at the Little Rock airport. The only way for Keating to get to Shreveport, Louisiana, where she had a job interview, was to fly into Little Rock on one flight and then fly from Little Rock to Shreveport on another. During those 45 minutes, while Keating was walking in the airport from her incoming gate to her outgoing gate, a process server, acting on Wong's behalf, served Keating with a summons and complaint in *Wong v. Keating*. Keating has moved to dismiss on the ground that Arkansas has no personal jurisdiction over her. Wong claims that service in Arkansas gives Arkansas personal jurisdiction over Keating.

Below is an analysis of this issue. Find the components of the CREAC formula set out in the box in §16.2.

Arkansas has personal jurisdiction over Keating. Under the Due Process Clause of the Fourteenth Amendment, a state is authorized to exercise personal jurisdiction over a defendant who is served with a summons while the defendant is voluntarily inside the state. *Burnham v. Superior Court*, 495 U.S. 604 (1990). That is true even if service of the summons is the only connection between the state and the plaintiff, the defendant, or the plaintiff's claim. It is true when a defendant does not reside in the state, is only traveling through the state, and has no connection to the state except for the trip during which the defendant was served. *Id.* at 617-619, 635-639. And it is true even when none of the events or circumstances alleged in the plaintiff's complaint happened in the state. *Id.* at 620-621.

The defendant in *Burnham* was a New Jersey resident who had traveled on business to southern California and then to northern California to visit his children. The plaintiff was the defendant's wife, who had him served in a divorce action while he was in northern California. Four justices of the Supreme Court joined in an opinion by Justice Scalia and held that, under precedent going back two centuries, a state has "the power to hale before its courts any individual who could be found within its borders." *Id.* at 610. Another four justices joined in an opinion by Justice Brennan and held that the defendant's presence in the state at the time of service was a purposeful availment that satisfies the minimum contacts requirements of *International Shoe v. Washington*, 326 U.S. 310 (1945). The ninth justice (Stevens) concurred separately on the ground that both rationales are correct. Because there was no majority opinion, it is not settled which rationale supports the rule, although the rule had the unanimous support of all nine justices.

Regardless of the rationale, service on Keating in the Little Rock airport created personal jurisdiction in Arkansas. Keating was present in Arkansas at the moment of service. The process server's affidavit is evidence of that, and Keating concedes it. Moreover, she does not claim that she did not know she was in Arkansas or that she was in the state under duress. She bought her airline ticket knowing she would have to change planes in Little Rock, and her presence was therefore voluntary.

Keating argues, however, that she was not in Arkansas long enough to be subject to the state's jurisdiction, even if she was served in Arkansas. She points out that the *Burnham* defendant had traveled to California to conduct business there and visit his children, spending nights in hotels and purposely availing himself of the benefits of the state. Keating contends that this case is distinguishable from *Burnham* because her destination was Louisiana rather than Arkansas, and because she was on the ground in Arkansas for less than an hour and only for the purpose of getting to Louisiana.

This case cannot be distinguished from *Burnham*. The Scalia opinion stressed that the state's jurisdiction extends to any visitor, "no matter how fleeting his visit." *Id.* at 610. And the Brennan rationale would treat using the Little Rock airport for a connecting flight as purposeful availment supporting minimum contacts because Keating gained a benefit from her presence in Arkansas. Any other result would be unsupportable policy in an era of modern travel. There is no practical way to craft a rule that would clearly distinguish between a presence in the state that is too short for jurisdiction and a presence that is long enough, which is why the Supreme Court held in *Burnham* that any presence is enough if the defendant is served while present.

Moreover, Keating's presence in Arkansas was not limited to her 45 minutes inside the airport. She might have been validly served while either of the airplanes on which she flew was on the tarmac or even in the air over Arkansas. Service of process on a passenger in an airplane that flew over Arkansas but never landed in the state has been sustained because at the moment of service the passenger was inside Arkansas, even though the passenger was not on the ground. *Grace v. MacArthur,* 170 F. Supp. 442 (E.D. Ark. 1959). The *Grace* court reasoned that there is no real difference between a passenger on an airplane that passes through Arkansas airspace and a passenger who travels through the state by train or bus without disembarking. *Id.* at 447.

Thus, Arkansas has jurisdiction over Keating, and her motion to dismiss should be denied.

Varying the Sequence and Depth of Rule Explanation and Rule Application

§17.1 Varying the CREAC Formula to Suit Your Needs

The CREAC formula set out in §16.2 can be varied in two ways.

First, you can vary the **sequence** in which the components appear. The next section in this chapter explains how.

Second, in rule explanation and in rule application, you can vary the **depth** of your explanation to suit the amount of skepticism you expect from the reader. Later sections in this chapter explain how.

(In addition, you can **combine** separate CREAC analyses into a unified explanation of several issues and sub-issues. Chapter 18 explains how.)

§17.2 Varying the Sequence

In some situations, you might vary the sequence of the CREAC formula's components—for example, by stating the rule first and the conclusion second—

although the order should not be illogical or confusing. Think long and hard before deciding to vary the sequence in the box in §16.2, and, if you do vary it, you should be able, if asked, to give a good reason for doing so. Because of the reader's needs described in §16.3, *rule explanation should be completed before rule application begins.* Variations in sequence usually do not work well in an office memo. They are more useful in persuasive writing in motion memo and appellate briefs, where varying the sequence might fit into a strategy of persuasion.

§17.3 When to Vary the Depth of Rule Explanation or Rule Application

Depending on the situation, rule explanation and rule application can be very short, very long, or somewhere in between. In one instance, rule explanation might need to be only a sentence, while rule application might require three pages. In another instance, the reverse might be true. Or each of them might be four or five pages long—or four or five sentences long. How can you tell how much depth is needed? Ask yourself three questions:

First, *how much depth will convince the reader that your conclusion is correct?* That depends on the reader's level of skepticism, which in turn depends on how complicated the issue is and how important it is to the decision the reader must make.

Second, *how much depth will make it unnecessary for the reader to follow up by going to Lexis, Westlaw, or a library shelf to read the authorities you rely on?* This second question poses what might be called the need-to-read test: You have not gone into enough depth if your reader would find it hard to agree with you without actually reading the authorities you have cited. A reader's need to go to the statutes and cases depends on the context. A reader is more likely to feel that need with a crucial and difficult issue than with a simple, peripheral, or routine one.

Third, *how much depth would tell the reader what the reader needs to know to make an informed decision?* If the reader were to go to the statutes and cases, would the reader be startled to find the things you've left out? Part of your job is to leave things out. The reader is counting on you to cut out the things that do not matter. But do not leave out so much that the reader is deprived of some of the information needed to make the decision.

Don't explore an issue in more depth than a reader would need. The reader is a busy person, almost as intolerant of too much explanation as of too little. If you include a great deal of detail about peripheral issues or about routine propositions with which the reader will easily agree, the reader can feel stuck in quicksand.

Students often underestimate the skepticism of readers. If you have no idea how much analysis to include, err on the side of making a more complete analysis until you have gained a better sense of what must be fully proved.

Rule explanation and rule application can each be explored in a way that is *comprehensive, substantiating,* or *conclusory.* The rest of this chapter explains how, using the facts from §16.1.

§17.4 Comprehensive Analysis

A comprehensive explanation includes whatever analyses are needed to satisfy an aggressive skepticism. This is the full treatment. In the example below, notes in the margin show where each component of the CREAC formula begins. Can you locate policy discussions and counteranalyses?

C—*the conclusion*

YouTube has been immunized by federal law from liability for the film and words posted by Kendrick on YouTube's website.

R—*the rule*

Under the Communications Decency Act of 1996, a defendant is immune from liability if (1) the defendant is a "provider or user of an interactive computer service," which the statute defines to include a website; (2) the plaintiff has pleaded a state law claim; (3) the claim requires the plaintiff to prove that the defendant is a "publisher or speaker of any information"; and (4) the information at issue in the plaintiff's claim was "provided by another information content provider," which the statute defines to include a person other than the defendant who puts information on the defendant's website. 47

E—*rule explanation begins*

U.S.C. §230(c)(1), (e)(3), (f)(2), (f)(3) (2000). The immunity test is in §230(c)(1), (e)(3). The other subsections are definitional.

In the leading case interpreting these subsections of §230, a plaintiff sued America Online, alleging that AOL allowed anonymous messages to be posted on and to remain on its website that defamed him and put his life in jeopardy. *Zeran v. America Online, Inc.,* 129 F.3d 327 (4th Cir. 1997). According to the complaint, the messages purported to be advertisements for "Naughty Oklahoma T-Shirts" with what the court described as "offensive and tasteless slogans related to the April 19, 1995, bombing of the Alfred P. Murrah Federal Building in Oklahoma

City." *Id.* at 329. The messages said that the
t-shirts could be purchased by calling the plaintiff's home telephone number. Although the
plaintiff knew nothing about this and was not
selling t-shirts of any kind, so many outraged
people called him at home that at times he
"was receiving an abusive phone call approximately every two minutes." *Id.* The plaintiff
alleged that AOL was slow to remove these
messages from its site, and that every time one
was removed, another was posted, which AOL
failed to prevent. *Id.* Several calls included
threats to kill him, and he had to seek police
protection. *Id.*

The Fourth Circuit held that the Communications Decency Act barred the plaintiff's claims
against AOL. *Id.* at 339. Even though the messages defamed him, AOL was immunized
because, in §230(c)(1)'s words, (1) AOL is a "provider . . . of an interactive computer service"; (2)
the plaintiff's defamation and negligence claims
grew out of state law; (3) publication is an element of defamation, requiring the plaintiff to
prove that AOL is a "publisher or speaker
of . . . information"; and (4) the information at
issue in the plaintiff's claim was "provided by
another information content provider," the
anonymous poster. *Zeran,* 129 F.3d at 332.
Section 230 even immunized AOL from liability
for delays in removing the messages after the
plaintiff informed the company of their defamatory character and their effect on him. *Zeran,*
129 F.3d at 339.

The plaintiff in *Zeran* argued that a website
is no different from the publisher or distributor
of a newspaper, book, or magazine, who would
be liable for defamatory words it publishes. But
the court held that even though a website is
easily analogous to a print publisher, Congress
had immunized websites anyway. "By its plain
language, §230 creates a federal immunity to
any cause of action that would make service providers liable for information originating with a
third-party user of the service," such as the

unknown person who posted the false messages about the plaintiff. *Id.* at 330.

Other Circuits have interpreted §230 in the same way. *Doe v. GTE Corp.*, 347 F.3d 655 (7th Cir. 2003) (Internet service provider immune from liability for a user's invasion of plaintiff's privacy); *Batzel v. Smith*, 333 F.3d 1018 (9th Cir. 2003) (website operator immune for defamatory email message posted on its website); *Ben Ezra, Weinstein, & Co. v. America Online, Inc.*, 206 F.3d 980 (10th Cir. 2000) (AOL immune for inaccurate information posted bulletin boards about stocks).

According to the statute's legislative history, Congress added subsections 230(c)(1) and (e)(3) to overrule a case that held that Prodigy could be held liable for defamatory statements posted on one of its bulletin boards. S. Rep. No. 104-230, at 194 (1996); H.R. Conf. Rep. No. 104-458, at 194 (1996); 141 Cong. Rec. at H84691-70. The case was *Stratton Oakmont, Inc. v. Prodigy Services Co.*, 23 Media L. Rep. 1794 (N.Y. Sup. Ct., Nassau County 1995).

In the statute itself, Congress enunciated the reasons for this immunity: "to promote the continued development of the Internet" and "to preserve the vibrant and competitive free market that presently exists for the Internet and other interactive computer services, unfettered by Federal or State regulation." 47 U.S.C. §230(b)(1) & (2) (2000). "Congress recognized the threat that tort-based lawsuits pose to freedom of speech in the new and burgeoning Internet medium. . . . Section 230 was enacted, in part, to maintain the robust nature of Internet communication and, accordingly, to keep government interference in the medium to a minimum." *Zeran*, 129 F.3d at 330. People like the plaintiff in *Zeran* would be left without a remedy, but Congress considered the vitality of the Internet to be a greater value than insuring that every plaintiff aggrieved by information distributed over the Internet could recover. *Id.*

A—*rule application begins*

YouTube can satisfy the immunity test in subsections 230(c)(1) and (e)(3). First, YouTube operates a website. It is therefore, in the statute's words, "a provider or user of an interactive computer service."

Second, defamation and invasion of privacy are state law claims. The immunity provisions of §230 were enacted to prevent defamation claims against websites when the defamatory words were not generated by the website operator. That is why defamation claims failed in *Zeran* and *Batzel*. *Doe* treated invasion of privacy claims the same way.

Third, publication by the defendant is an element of both defamation and invasion of privacy. Thus, both claims would require Jordan to prove that YouTube was, in the statute's words, the "publisher or speaker of [the] information" that defamed her and invaded her privacy.

Finally, that information was not provided by YouTube. Instead, it was, in the statute's words, "provided by another information content provider." That was Kendrick.

This result is consistent with the reasons why Congress enacted the immunity provisions in §230. As a practical matter, YouTube cannot review every film clip posted on its website without incurring business expenses so great that they could easily make the website unprofitable and cause weeks or months of delay in the posting of the film clips that are the site's reason for existing. If the law imposed liability on YouTube for failing to conduct these investigations, the site could be forced to shut down. Congress did not immunize interactive computer service providers like websites from all information liability. They are immunized only for information provided by others, like Kendrick. They remain liable for information that they generate themselves.

Even though a television station, newspaper, or magazine would have been liable under state law for defamation and invasion of privacy for publishing images of Kendrick's film with the words that he posted on YouTube, the website has been immunized from these state law claims by §230. The courts have uniformly enforced that distinction.

C—*the conclusion, again*   Thus, Jordan will not be able to recover from YouTube.

§17.5 Substantiating Analysis

A substantiating analysis goes less deeply into the writer's reasoning. It supports the conclusion but without comprehensive detail. A substantiating analysis works when the reader has a skepticism that is less than aggressive because the issue is not central to the problem addressed by the document you've writing. A substantiating analysis is not appropriate when the issue is crucial or difficult. A substantiating analysis might look like this:

C—*the conclusion*

R—*the rule*

E—*rule explanation begins*

YouTube is immunized from liability for the film and words posted by Kendrick on YouTube's website. A defendant is immune if (1) the defendant is a "provider or user of an interactive computer service," which the statute defines to include a website; (2) the plaintiff has pleaded a state law claim; (3) the claim requires the plaintiff to prove that the defendant is a "publisher or speaker of any information"; and (4) the information at issue in the plaintiff's claim was "provided by another information content provider," which the statute defines to include a person other than the defendant who puts information on the defendant's website. 47 U.S.C. §230(c)(1), (e)(3), (f)(2), (f)(3) (2000).

In the leading case interpreting these subsections of §230, a plaintiff sued America Online, alleging that AOL allowed anonymous messages to be posted on and to remain on its website that defamed him and put his life in jeopardy. *Zeran v. America Online, Inc.*, 129 F.3d 327, 339 (4th Cir. 1997). The Fourth Circuit held that AOL is immune because, in §230(c)(1)'s words, (1) AOL is a "provider . . . of an interactive computer service"; (2) the plaintiff's defamation and negligence claims grew out of state law; (3) publication is an element of defamation, requiring the plaintiff to prove that AOL is a "publisher or speaker of . . . information"; and (4) the information at issue was "provided by another information content provider," the anonymous poster. Section 230(f)(3) defines "another information content provider" to include a person other than the defendant who puts information on the defendant's website.

Other Circuits have interpreted §230 in the same way. *Doe v. GTE Corp.*, 347 F.3d 655 (7th Cir. 2003); *Batzel v. Smith*, 333 F.3d 1018 (9th Cir. 2003); *Ben Ezra, Weinstein, & Co. v. America Online, Inc.*, 206 F.3d 980 (10th Cir. 2000). In the statute itself, Congress enunciated the reasons for this immunity: "to promote the continued development of the Internet" and "to preserve the vibrant and competitive free market that presently exists for the Internet and other interactive computer services, unfettered by Federal or State regulation." 47 U.S.C. §230(b)(1) & (2) (2000). In some circumstances, plaintiffs would be left without a remedy, but Congress considered the vitality of the Internet to be a greater value than insuring that every plaintiff aggrieved by information distributed over the Internet could recover.

A—*rule application begins*

YouTube can satisfy the immunity test in §230(c)(1) and (e)(3). First, YouTube operates a website and is therefore "a provider or user of an interactive computer service." Second, defamation and invasion of privacy are state law claims. Third, both claims would require Jordan to prove that YouTube was the "publisher or speaker of [the] information" that defamed her and invaded her privacy. Finally, that information was "provided by another information content provider" (Kendrick).

This result is consistent with the reasons why Congress enacted the immunity provisions in §230. YouTube cannot practically review every film clip posted on its website, and if the law imposed liability on YouTube for failing to conduct these investigations, the site could encounter expenses and delays that would force it to shut down.

What in the comprehensive explanation in §17.4 is missing here? If you and your supervisor were trying to figure out whether to sue YouTube, would the substantiating analysis be sufficient?

§17.6 Conclusory Analysis

A conclusory analysis does no more than allude to some of the more important reasons supporting your conclusion. The components of the CREAC formula are in the example below, but, except for the rule, they are in abbreviated form.

C—*the conclusion*	YouTube is immunized from liability for the film and words posted by Kendrick on YouTube's website. A defendant is immune if (1) the
R—*the rule*	defendant is a "provider or user of an interactive computer service," which the statute defines to include a website; (2) the plaintiff has pleaded a state law claim; (3) the claim requires the plaintiff to prove that the defendant is a "publisher or speaker of any information"; and (4) the information at issue in the plaintiff's claim was "provided by another information content provider," which the statute defines to include a person other than the defendant who puts infor-
E—*rule explanation*	mation on the defendant's website. 47 U.S.C. §230(c)(1), (e)(3), (f)(2), (f)(3) (2000).
A—*rule application begins*	YouTube can satisfy this test. First, YouTube operates a website and is therefore "a provider or user of an interactive computer service." Second, defamation and invasion of privacy are state law claims. Third, both claims would require Jordan to prove that YouTube was the "publisher or speaker of [the] information" that defamed her and invaded her privacy. Finally, that information was "provided by another information content provider," Kendrick.

A conclusory analysis is appropriate *only* when the reader will easily agree with you or when the point is not important to your analysis. In those situations, a reader would find a more detailed analysis to be tedious.

§17.7 Cryptic Analysis

Beginning students sometimes write treatments so cryptic as to be less than conclusory.

> Jordan will not be able to recover from You-Tube. YouTube meets all four of the requirements for protection from liability under the Communications Decency Act of 1996 and is therefore immune from Jordan's claim. 47 U.S.C. §230(c)(1), (e)(3), (f)(2), (f)(3) (2000).

This example omits the rule on which the conclusion is based, and it does not show in any way how the rule governs the facts. It would never satisfy a skeptical reader.

Advanced CREAC: Organizing More Than One Issue

§18.1 Introduction

If you have more than one issue, the reader will need a separately structured proof for each one. That could happen

1. where more than one element of a rule is at issue *(see §18.2)*
2. where more than one claim or defense is at issue *(see §18.3)*
3. where a dispute involves separate but related issues *(see §18.4)*

Each issue would have its own conclusion. When you add all those issue conclusions together, you get an ultimate conclusion. When you organize your writing, you would state the ultimate conclusion first, and it would cover all the issues—like a big umbrella:

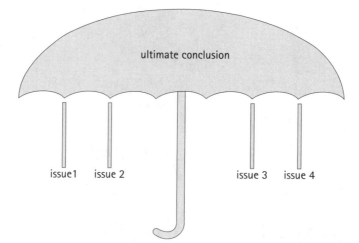

§18.2 How to Organize When More Than One *Element* Is at Issue

If you need to resolve more than one element of a test, you will have an ultimate conclusion for the rule as a whole, together with a conclusion for each element:

Ultimate Conclusion	Ferguson will probably be able to gain title through adverse possession to the land known as Ironwood Tract.
Conclusions on Issues	*Element 1:* Ferguson has been in actual possession of the Ironwood Tract.
	Element 2: Ferguson's possession has been continuous for at least ten years.
	Element 3: Ferguson's possession has been open and notorious for the entire ten years.
	Element 4: Ferguson's possession has been hostile to the rights of the client.
	Element 5: Ferguson's possession has been under a claim of right or title.

When this analysis is written out, the opening, or *umbrella* passage, would state the ultimate conclusion ("Ferguson will probably be able to gain title to the client's Ironwood Tract") and the essence of the reason ("because she has satisfied all the elements of adverse possession"). The umbrella passage would also recite the *rule* on which it is based (the test for adverse possession). The umbrella passage would at first seem to be an incomplete CREAC structure because it would *not include rule application and definitions of the elements*. But the discussion of the elements will provide that. The umbrella passage covers and organizes the subordinate proofs of the elements.

The umbrella passage also sets out a roadmap for what follows. It tells the reader what issues you will consider, their relative importance or unimportance, and sometimes the order in which you will consider them.

After the umbrella passage would be CREAC-structured discussions for the elements—a separate CREAC for each element. Each element is an issue for which you would have a *conclusion*. Each element would have to be defined through a definitional or other declaratory *rule* ("Actual possession means exclusive occupation of the land"). The definition would have to be proved through authority in *rule explanation*. And you would apply the definition to the facts in *rule application*.

§18.3 How to Organize When More Than One *Claim or Defense* Is at Issue

Suppose your supervising attorney wants to know whether the client will be awarded damages in a tort case. You need to figure out whether the client has a cause of action (one issue or a cluster of issues). And you anticipate that the defendant will raise the affirmative defense of sovereign immunity. Although this situation is more complex than the one where several elements of a single rule are in dispute, you would handle it in the same way (see §18.2).

You can build an umbrella CREAC structure, and underneath it you can prove the conclusions through separate CREAC-structured analyses. The ultimate conclusion might, for example, be that the client will be awarded damages because she has a cause of action (first conclusion) and the defendant has waived sovereign immunity (second conclusion). Thus:

Ultimate Conclusion   The client will be awarded damages.

Conclusions on Issues *Issue 1:*
                          The client has a cause of action for negligence.

> *Subissue 1:*   The defendant owed the client a duty.
> *Subissue 2:*   The defendant breached it.
> *Subissue 3:*   The client suffered injury.
> *Subissue 4:*   The breach proximately caused the injury.

> *Issue 2:*
> The defendant has waived sovereign immunity.

Because negligence has four elements, the first issue would be divided further into the four subissues shown above. That means that at the beginning of your analysis of Issue 1, you would include an umbrella passage limited to whether the client has a cause of action for negligence.

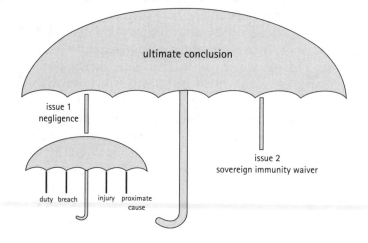

§18.4 How to Organize *Other Types of Separate but Related Issues*

Suppose someone sues your client, and your supervising attorney wants to know whether this lawsuit can be dismissed on forum selection grounds (that it was brought in the wrong court). You will have to resolve some or all of the following issues: Does this court have subject matter jurisdiction over this kind of case? Does this court have personal jurisdiction over your client? Is this court the right venue for this lawsuit? To resolve these issues, you would use the same umbrella CREAC structure explained in §18.2:

Ultimate Conclusion　　This lawsuit is not dismissible on forum selection grounds.

Conclusions on Issues　　*Issue 1:*
This court has subject matter jurisdiction.

Issue 2:
This court has personal jurisdiction over our client.

Issue 3:
Venue is proper in this court.

Here, too, if an issue involves a test with more than one element, you would include an umbrella passage limited to that issue.

§18.5 How to Work with Multi-Issue Situations

Many students feel confused when faced with multi-issue situations, but within a few weeks, you might begin to gain confidence in organizing this way. Within a year or two, most students instinctively think in structured proofs—it has become second nature. This section provides some suggestions for getting to that point.

Step 1: While researching and planning your writing, ask yourself how many issues you have. If you have a hard time identifying issues, ask yourself how many conclusions of law a court would need to make to resolve the dispute.

Step 2: Now, figure out what kind of issues you have. For each issue, is it part of the cause of action, part of a defense, part of a procedural requirement, or something else? This will help you choose one of the structures described in this chapter.

Step 3: Select one of the multi-issue structures explained in this chapter, and adapt it to your case. Make a list of every conclusion of law you will write in your memo or brief (like the lists of issues earlier in this chapter). Organize the conclusions logically—for example, elements of a cause of action first, then defenses. Treat this as the beginning of an outline. Chapter 19 explains how to complete this outline and turn it into a memo or brief.

Step 4: At the beginning of an umbrella passage, use a roadmap paragraph to explain your umbrella CREAC to the reader. A roadmap paragraph maps out your discussion so the reader knows what to expect. It states your ultimate conclusion ("The client should be awarded damages," for example) and then states the conclusions that support that ultimate conclusion. If some elements of a test are at issue and others are not, the roadmap paragraph is the place to make that clear. Most judges say that a well-written roadmap paragraph is very important or essential in helping them understand what you are trying to say.[1] Here is a typical roadmap paragraph, which you might use to introduce the discussion outlined in §18.3:

> The plaintiff will be awarded damages. The evidence supports all four of the elements of negligence. The defendant owed a duty to the plaintiff to keep the loading

---

[1] Kristen K. Robbins, *The Inside Scoop: What Federal Judges Really Think about the Way Lawyers Write*, 8 J. Leg. Writing Inst. 257, 273 (2002).

dock clear and breached that duty by leaving explosive materials on the loading dock overnight. The plaintiff's injury, destruction of the warehouse, is uncontested. It was proximately caused by the breach when the materials exploded. In addition, sovereign immunity has been waived by § 419 of the Highways Code.

After reading this, a reader would know that you will discuss each of these issues in detail.

Step 5: Use headings to show your reader where your analysis of each issue begins. Lawyers and judges will not read your work from beginning to end. They will read parts of it at a time, and headings help them find the parts they need. If you are writing an office memo, look at the way headings are used in Appendix A. If you are writing a persuasive memo or an appellate brief, you will write point headings, which are explained in Chapter 31.

Working with CREAC in First Drafts and in Later Drafts

§19.1 Using CREAC to Outline and to Begin Your First Draft

The CREAC formula explained in the preceding chapters can help you organize. It will also help keep your material from getting out of control. Getting used to writing with the CREAC formula takes some effort, but once you are used to it, organizing your writing becomes much easier *because the formula shows you where to put things.*

This section describes one method of starting to work with the formula. It is only a suggestion for the first time you write. If you develop a different procedure that works better for you, use that instead.

In the method described here, you will label everything so that you know where it goes and then just plug it into whatever variant of the formula best fits your situation. The first time you try this, it might seem a little awkward. But by the second or third time, it will begin to feel more natural because it fits the way people instinctively work and takes less effort than other methods of organizing.

Step 1: Figure out how many issues you have. Each one will be analyzed through a separate CREAC structure. Chapter 18 explains how to do this.

Step 2: For each issue, identify the rule that is central to and governs the answer. You might also use other rules but, for the moment, focus on the rule that—more than any other—compels your answer.

Step 3: Inventory your raw materials. For each issue or subissue, sort everything you have into two categories: rule explanation and rule application. Some methods of sorting may work better for you than for others, and over several writing assignments you might experiment to find the method that fits best into the way you write.

One method is to go through your notes and write "RE" in the margin next to everything that you might use in rule explanation and "RA" next to everything that might help the reader understand how to apply the rule. Some ideas or authorities might be useful in both rule explanation and rule application and might get a notation of "RE/RA." If you have several issues, you can work out a shorthand for marking them separately, such as "#3RE" for "rule explanation on issue 3" or "#1RA" for "rule application on issue 1." If you've printed out cases, write these notations next to each part of the case that you will use. Go through your facts, too, marking the ones that are important enough to talk about during rule application.

Step 4: Think about how all these things add up. If you have not yet drawn a conclusion, do it now. If you decided previously on a conclusion, check it against your raw materials to see whether it still seems like the best conclusion.

Step 5: Make a fluid outline. Your notes are now complete enough to be organized into some variation of the CREAC formula. You can do that by making the fluid outline described in §13.2.

For each issue, take a piece of paper and write four headings on it, using abbreviations for the CREAC components (for example: "concl," "rule," "RE," and "RA"). You can do this on a computer instead if you feel more comfortable typing than writing. Under "concl," write your conclusion for that issue in whatever shorthand will remind you later of what your thinking is (for example: "no diversity—Wharton citizen of Maine"). Under "rule," do something similar. Under "RE," list your raw materials for rule explanation. For each item listed, do not write a lot—just enough to remind you at a glance of everything you have. If you're listing something found in a case you've printed out, a catch-phrase and a reference to a page in the case might be enough (for example: "intent to return— *Wiggins* p.352"). Under "RA," do the same for rule application. Make sure that everything you have on that issue is on that page.

Suppose that for rule explanation on a certain issue you have listed six resources (cases, facts, and so on). You have not yet decided the order in which you will discuss them when you explain the rule. In most situations, the decision will be easier and better if you do *not* make it while outlining. The best time to decide is just before you write that issue's rule explanation in your first draft. *You do not need to know exactly where everything will go before you start the first draft.* When you decide, just write a number next to each item ("1" next to the first one you will discuss, "2" next to the second, and so on).

Step 6: Start writing. Choose the issue with which you feel most comfortable. Put that issue's outline page (see Step 5) where you can see it while you work. Using what you have on the outline page, write a complete sentence stating your conclusion for that issue. Then write the other CREAC components.

As you cover each thing you have listed on the issue's outline page, cross it off. When everything has been crossed off, go on to another issue and use the same process to write it.

Your first draft probably will not use everything that you've listed on your outline pages. Some material will not seem as useful while you are writing as it did when you were sorting. But don't throw anything away yet. During rewriting, you might change your mind and want to use it after all.

§19.2 How to Test Your Writing for Effective Organization

While rewriting, ask yourself the following questions. They also appear on this book's website as a checklist, which you can print out.

1. Have you organized around tests and elements, rather than around cases? Readers don't like it if you dump before them the cases you found in the library. A mere list of relevant cases, with discussion of each, does not help a decision-maker, who needs to understand how the *rules* affect the facts. The law is the rules themselves, and a case merely proves a rule's existence and accuracy. Teachers sometimes call this fault *case-by-case-itis.* It's easy to spot in a student's paper: The reader sees a series of paragraphs, each of which is devoted to discussion of a single case.

2. Have you collected closely related ideas, rather than scattering them? If you have three reasons why the defendant will not be convicted, list them all in one place and then explain each separately. The reader looking for the big picture can't follow you if you introduce the first reason on page one; mention the second for the first time on page four; and surprise the reader with the third on page six. If you have more than one item or idea, listing them at the beginning helps the reader keep things in perspective. It also forces you to organize and evaluate your thoughts. Roadmap paragraphs help tell the reader where you are going.

3. Have you accounted for all of the issues and discussed them in a logical order? If you have several issues, have you organized them so the reader understands how everything fits together?

4. For each issue, have you stated your conclusion? If so, where? State it precisely so the reader knows from the very beginning what you intend to demonstrate. In an office memo, your conclusions will be predictions, either expressed ("Kolchak will probably be acquitted of robbery") or implied ("The evidence does not establish beyond a reasonable doubt that Kolchak is guilty of robbery").

5. For each issue, have you stated the rule or rules on which your conclusion is based? If so, where? Don't merely describe the cases and let the reader decide what rule they stand for. Formulate a credible rule, and prove it by analyzing the authority.

6. For each issue, have you explained the rule? If so, where? See §16.4 for how to evaluate your rule explanation.

7. For each issue, have you applied the rule to the facts? If so, where? See §16.5 for how to evaluate your rule application.

8. Have you completed rule explanation before starting rule application? Before you start rule application, the reader needs to know that you have accurately stated it and that it really is law. If you don't do those things first during rule explanation, many readers will find it harder to agree with your rule application. You might use some authorities in rule explanation and again in rule application. But that doesn't mean rule application and rule explanation can be mixed.

9. In both rule explanation and rule application, have you explained your reasoning fully? Explain each step in your reasoning. Don't leave anything out. One way to discipline yourself to do this is to ask yourself about each statement you make, "Why is that true?" Then make sure that your writing completely answers that question.

10. Have you created a post–draft linear outline? A post-draft linear outline is explained in §13.2. Other methods can accomplish essentially the same thing. Here is what one writing professor suggests to her students:

> . . . I encourage a color-coding system. . . . I tell the students that once they have completed a given section or subsection, they must proofread specifically for the [CREAC formula]. They can either change the color of the font, or use highlighters or colored pencils, but they must identify each element of the [CREAC formula] to be certain that they have prepared their paper properly. I want to see the conclusion, the rule, the rule [explanation] and rule application clearly delineated.
>
> I encourage students that I know are having trouble to bring a marked up copy to my office so we can look it over together. . . . I recently had a transfer student who was

quite concerned about the [CREAC formula]. To solve his problem, he wrote the paper as he saw fit, changed the font color for conclusion, rule, rule [explanation], rule application, and then literally cut up his draft and rearranged it. I thought his method was a great idea, and he ended up getting an A.[1]

---

[1] Amy R. Stein, *Helping Students Understand that Effective Organization Is a Prerequisite to Effective Legal Writing,* 15 Perspectives 36, 39 (2006).

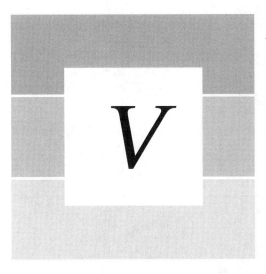

Working Effectively with Details

20

Paragraphing

This chapter explains how to structure paragraphs to help the reader see your reasoning.

§20.1 How Paragraphs Reveal the Details of Your Organization

Most readers unconsciously use paragraph divisions to learn how a writer's thoughts fit together. They assume that each paragraph substantiates or explores a separate and distinct idea or subject. They also assume that the first or second sentence in each paragraph states or implies that idea or subject and, if necessary, shows how it is related to matters already discussed. To the extent that you frustrate these assumptions, your writing will be less helpful to the reader and therefore less influential.

An effective paragraph has five characteristics. First, it has *unity*: It proves one proposition or covers one subject. Material more relevant to other propositions or subjects has been removed and placed elsewhere. Second, an effective paragraph has *completeness*: It includes whatever is needed to prove the proposition or cover the subject. Third, an effective paragraph has *internal coherence*: Ideas are expressed in a logical sequence that the reader can follow without having to edit the paragraph mentally while reading. Fourth, an effective paragraph is of *readable length*: It's neither so long that the reader gets lost nor so short that valuable material is underdeveloped or trivialized. Fifth, an effective paragraph announces or implies its purpose at the outset: Its *first or second sentence states or implies its thesis or topic* and, if necessary, makes a transition from the preceding material.

§20.2 Descriptive Paragraphs and Probative Paragraphs

The way you write a paragraph depends on whether you are describing something or proving something. Compare these paragraphs:

Descriptive	*Probative*
In January in Death Valley, the average high temperature is about 65°, and the average low is about 37°. Spring and fall temperatures approximate summer temperatures elsewhere. In April and in October, for example, the average high is about 90°, and the average low about 60°. July is the hottest month, with an average high of about 116° and an average low of about 87°. The highest temperature ever recorded in Death Valley was 134° on July 10, 1913. Average annual rainfall is about 1½ inches.	The climate in Death Valley is brutal. At Furnace Creek Ranch, the highest summer temperature each year reaches at least 120° and in many years at least 125°. The highest temperature recorded in Death Valley—134°—is also the highest recorded in the Western Hemisphere and the second highest recorded anywhere on earth. (The highest is 136°—in the Sahara.) In the summer sun, a person can lose four gallons of perspiration a day and—in 3% humidity—die of dehydration.

A topic is a category of information, such as "weather in Death Valley." After reading the descriptive paragraph, you know some weather details about Death Valley. Descriptive paragraphs are *about* things.

A proposition, on the other hand, can be proved or disproved—such "the climate of Death Valley is brutal." After reading the probative paragraph, you have a reaction to that proposition. You might agree with it or disagree. A probative paragraph should try to *prove* something.

If a descriptive paragraph confuses a reader, the reader might ask, "What is this paragraph about?" But if a probative paragraph confuses, the reader might instead ask, "What is this paragraph supposed to prove?"

Probative and descriptive writing can occur in the same document. In an office memo, for example, the fact statement is mostly descriptive, and the Discussion is mostly probative.

Even in probative writing, some paragraphs are descriptive. If it takes three pages to prove a particular proposition, at least a few paragraphs in those three pages will have to describe the raw materials involved—statutes, cases, or facts, for example. Proof is explaining *how* the raw materials support the proposition being proved. Sometimes we have to describe the raw materials before we can explain how they prove something.

§20.3 Proposition Sentences, Topic Sentences, and Transition Sentences

A probative paragraph begins by stating a proposition. The first or second sentence in the paragraph states the proposition and is the *proposition sentence*. The rest of the paragraph should prove the proposition.

A descriptive paragraph provides details about a topic. The first or second sentence in the paragraph, the *topic sentence*, can expressly state the topic or imply it. Sometimes the topic sentence can be omitted if the context implies the topic.

Although in descriptive writing a topic can often be implied, in probative writing the proposition should be expressly stated. A practical reader needs to know what you are trying to prove before you start proving it.

With either type of paragraph, a *transition phrase or sentence* can show the reader how the paragraph is connected to the material before it or the material after it. Although a transition is not required, it often helps the reader understand what you are doing. A transition most often appears at the beginning of a paragraph and less often at the end, as a bridge into the next paragraph. Often the first sentence of a paragraph can both state a proposition or topic and make a transition.

§20.4 How to Test Your Paragraphs for Effectiveness

In first drafts, paragraphs are seldom put together well. To identify the paragraphs in need of rehabilitation, ask yourself the following questions. They also appear on this book's website as a checklist, which you can print out.

1. Does each paragraph have one purpose? Prove one proposition or describe one subject. Remove and place elsewhere material that is more relevant to other propositions or subjects.

2. Have you told the reader, near the beginning of each paragraph, the paragraph's proposition (for a probative paragraph) or its topic (for a descriptive paragraph)? If the reader does not learn the paragraph proposition or topic at the beginning, the reader often must read the paragraph two or three times to figure out its purpose. A topic sentence is unnecessary when the topic is clearly implied by the context.

3. Have you broken up paragraphs that were so large that a reader would get lost in them? Paragraphs that wander aimlessly or endlessly confuse a reader. When that happens, you have probably tried to develop two or more complex and separable themes in a single paragraph, perhaps without realizing it. Identify the individual themes and then break up the material accordingly into digestible chunks—which become separate paragraphs.

4. Within each paragraph, have you expressed your ideas in a logical and effective sequence? When a paragraph confuses but nothing is wrong with its size or with the wording of individual sentences, the paragraph usually lacks internal coherence. That happens when ideas within the paragraph are presented in a sequence that makes it hard for the reader to understand them or how they fit together to prove the proposition or illuminate the topic.

Exercise. The First Month or Two of Law School (Probative and Descriptive Paragraphs)

Write two paragraphs—one descriptive and the other probative—about the first month or two of law school.

Descriptive paragraph: Summarize what happened during your first month or two in law school. Describe some of the things you saw, heard, read, and wrote. Do *not* try to prove any belief you might have about the first month or two of law school.

Probative paragraph: The opening sentence of this paragraph should be "The first month or two of law school is hard"—or "puzzling" or "exciting" or "cruel" or "challenging" or any other characterization you choose—"because"—and here you complete the sentence by stating whatever you believe to be the cause of your characterization. The rest of the paragraph should prove the proposition expressed by that sentence.

Writing an Effective Sentence

§21.1 How to Test Your Sentences for Effectiveness

Sentences usually don't become effective until later drafts. While rewriting, ask yourself the following questions. They also appear on this book's website as a checklist, which you can print out.

1. Have you gotten the reader to the verb as fast as possible? The verb holds a sentence together. In fact, a sentence is usually incomprehensible until the reader has identified both a subject and a verb. For example:

> The defendant's use of email spam to solicit contributions to a fake charitable organization purportedly engaged in disaster relief and his use of the contributions to buy a vacation home for himself constitutes fraud.

This sentence cannot be understood in a single reading because it's "front-loaded." You don't reach the verb and object ("constitutes fraud") until after you have plowed through a subject 32 words long. Then, you have to read the sentence again because everything you read before finding the verb made no sense the first time you read it.

During first drafts, writers often ask themselves, "What shall I talk about next?" and then write down the answer. That becomes the subject of a sentence, no matter how unreadable the result. We all do this in first drafts, but in rewriting you can recognize the problem and fix it.

You can fix a front-loaded sentence by reshuffling it to bring the reader to the verb quickly:

> The defendant committed fraud by using email spam to solicit contributions for a fake charitable organization purportedly engaged in disaster relief and by using the contributions to buy a vacation home for himself.

Or you can break up the sentence into two or more shorter sentences:

> The defendant committed fraud. He used email spam to solicit contributions for a fake charitable organization purportedly engaged in disaster relief, and he used the contributions to buy a vacation home for himself.

2. Have you put the verb near the subject and the object near the verb? Many readers get lost in a sentence where something has been inserted between a subject and a verb or between a verb and an object:

> The Wabash Garage Orchestra, even though it includes 32 musicians, some with cellos or other large instruments, played the Philip Glass Violin Concerto while sitting in trees in Fabian Smedley's back yard.

Move the problem words to the end or to the beginning of the sentence, leaving the subject and verb (or a verb and an object) relatively close together.

move phrase or clause to the end of the sentence:	The Wabash Garage Orchestra played the Philip Glass Violin Concerto while sitting in trees in Fabian Smedley's back yard, even though the orchestra includes 32 musicians, some with cellos or other large instruments.
move phrase or clause to the beginning of the sentence:	Even though it includes 32 musicians, some with cellos or other large instruments, the Wabash Garage Orchestra played the Philip Glass Violin Concerto while sitting in trees in Fabian Smedley's back yard.

3. Have you put the most complicated part of the sentence at the end? To understand a sentence, a reader has to figure out its structure. Readers do this quickly and unconsciously while they read. When they can't figure out the structure easily, they have to read the sentence again—or they ignore the sentence and keep reading without ever learning what the sentence meant. Compare these:

complicated part at the beginning:	Because the defendant's website is interactive and allows a person in any state to order a

catalogue, send a message to the defendant, and purchase beer or wine by typing in credit card and other information, the court held that it has jurisdiction over the defendant.

**complicated part
in the middle:**

The court held that, because the defendant's website is interactive and allows a person in any state to order a catalogue, send a message to the defendant, and purchase beer or wine by typing in credit card and other information, the court has jurisdiction over the defendant.

**complicated part
at the end:**

The court held that it has jurisdiction over the defendant because the defendant's website is interactive and allows a person in any state to order a catalogue, send a message to the defendant, and purchase beer or wine by typing in credit card and other information.

Most readers find the third example the easiest to read because the first thing they see is simple ("The court held that it had jurisdiction over the defendant"). Once they understand that, the complicated part makes sense.

4. Have you put what you want to emphasize at the beginning or at the end of the sentence? The beginning or end of a sentence is more obvious than the middle. Sometimes, the end is more obvious just because that is the last thing the reader reads before going on to something else. And sometimes the beginning is more obvious—for example, if the sentence is the first one in a paragraph.

5. If you need to contrast one thing from another, have you used the most effective sentence structure and wording? Some sentence structures and words show contrast better than others do. For example:

> The Supreme Court has held that a defendant waives the objection by not making it at trial, but the Court has also held that, even without an objection, a conviction should be reversed where a prosecutor's conduct was as inflammatory as it was here.

The word *but*, buried in the middle of a long sentence, only weakly alerts the reader that one idea (the rule about waiver) is being knocked down by another (the exception for inflammatory prosecutorial conduct). Everybody writes this kind of thing in rough drafts, but it should be recognized and cured during rewriting:

> Although the Supreme Court has held that a defendant waives the objection by not making it at trial, the Court has also held that, even without an objection, a conviction should be reversed where a prosecutor's conduct was as inflammatory as it was here.

Although tells the reader right away that the sentence's first clause will turn out not to matter. When *but* appears at the beginning of a sentence, it, too, can show contrast well:

> The Supreme Court has held that a defendant waives the objection by not making it at trial. But the Court has also held that, even without an objection, a conviction should be reversed where a prosecutor's conduct was as inflammatory as it was here.

No rule of grammar forbids starting a sentence with *but* or *and*. Doing it constantly, though, can make your writing tedious.

6. Have you made the subject of a sentence or clause someone or something who is, was, or will be doing something? And have you used a verb in the active voice? If the answer to these questions is no, do you have a good reason for using the passive voice? First, figure out who or what is, was, or will be doing something. Make them or it the subject of the sentence or clause. Then choose a verb in the active voice that expresses what they are doing, have done, or will do. But don't do any of this if you have a good reason to use the passive voice.

In the active voice, the subject of the sentence acts ("Maguire sued Schultz"), but in the passive voice the subject of the sentence is acted upon ("Schultz was sued by Maguire"). Here are two more examples:

passive:	The deadline was missed by the student.
active:	The student missed the deadline.

The passive voice can be vague, weak, and boring. Although most sentences should be in the active voice, sometimes the passive voice works better. The passive may be more effective when you do not know who acted, when the identity of the actor is unimportant, when you want to deemphasize the identity of the actor, or when you want to emphasize something other than the actor. For example, compare these:

passive:	Ms. Blitzstein's assistance-to-needy-family benefits have been wrongfully terminated fourteen times in the last six years.
active:	The Department of Public Welfare has wrongfully terminated Ms. Blitzstein's assistance-to-needy-family benefits fourteen times in the last six years.

Depending on the context, the passive sentence might not be vague. Here, the reader might know that the Department is the only agency capable of terminating aid-to-dependent-family benefits, or at least that the Department is being accused of doing so in this instance. And, again depending on the context, the passive sentence may be the stronger and more interesting of the two. If the reader is a judge who is being asked to order the Department to stop this nonsense, the passive is the stronger sentence because it emphasizes the more appealing idea. Generally, a judge is more likely to sympathize with a victim of bureaucratic snafus than to condemn a government agency for viciousness or incompetence.

Sometimes, the passive voice is a good way of avoiding sexist pronouns. See §22.4, question 11.

7. Have you found ways to avoid the verb "to be" ("is," "was," etc.)? In law, people do things to other people and to ideas and objects, which you can describe with verbs that let the reader *see* the action. For example:

weak:	The ginger in the soup was the source of the wonderful smell that was in our house.
much better:	The ginger in the soup made our house smell wonderful.
weak:	There is a possibility of action in the near future by the EPA to remove these pesticides from the market.
much better:	The EPA might soon prohibit sale of these pesticides.

In the "weak" examples, you can barely tell who has done what to whom because the lofty tone obscures the action, and because the nouns and verbs do not stand out, take charge, and create action. In the "much better" examples, the reader immediately knows what's happening and does not have to read the same words twice.

The verb *to be* creates problems. *To be* includes *is, are, was, were,* and some other forms that occur less often. They do a good job of describing condition or status ("the defendant is guilty"). But they obscure action. Legal writing creates temptations to use *there is* and its variations (*there are, there were*). Often—though not always—editing them out creates stronger and tighter wording:

weak:	There are four reasons why the plaintiff will not recover. . . .
much better:	For four reasons, the plaintiff will not recover . . . .

Early drafts often include sentences like the "weak" examples above, but rewriting can produce final drafts that more closely resemble the "much better" ones. While rewriting, look for sentences like the "weak" ones, where the verb obscures action. Figure out what's *really* going on (who is doing what?). You can even use your word processor's "find" function to locate instances where you have used one of the four most common forms of the verb *to be—is, are, was*, and *were*. You'd have to search separately for each form. When you find one, ask yourself whether it obscures what's really going on. If the answer is yes, redo the sentence with an action verb. If the answer is no, leave the sentence as it is.

8. If a sentence is too long or too complicated to be understood easily the first time it is read, have you either streamlined it or broken it up into two or more sentences? You can express the sentence's ideas in fewer words. Or you can split the sentence into two or more shorter sentences. Or you can do both.

9. Have you violated any of these guidelines *only* when you have a good reason for doing so. Writing is creative work, and guidelines are meant to be violated—when you have a good reason. To test whether your reason is a good one, try to articulate for yourself exactly what it is. Your teacher might ask, too.

Exercise

See the Exercise at the end of Chapter 22.

Effective Style: Clarity, Vividness, and Conciseness

In first drafts, style is usually pretty awful. Most writers achieve effective style only through rewriting, as they look for opportunities to make the earlier drafts clearer and more vivid and concise.

§22.1 Clarity and Vividness

> If the reader thinks something you wrote is unclear, then it is, by definition.
> —*Deirdre N. McCloskey*

Unclear writing can make it hard or impossible for your reader to agree with you. Even if a reader could—with effort—figure out what you mean, readers in the legal profession usually cannot give you that effort. They don't have the time. A disappointed senior lawyer may return your memo to you and ask you to rewrite it, which may damage your credibility. A judge may rule against you because the judge could not understand your arguments.

Vividness goes a step further. Clear writing communicates a message. Adding a vivid image can make the message memorable and convincing. Vividness isn't always necessary. It's usually enough to concentrate on clarity and to add vividness only when you see an opportunity to do so in a professional way.

Unfortunately, many students arrive in law school without a solid instinct for effective style because much of the assigned reading in college lacks clarity and vividness.

Important-sounding words can be less clear and vivid than simple and straightforward ones. You might be able to sound like a lawyer but fail to *communicate* like one—for example by writing *ingested* (an impressive but vague word) instead of something that would tell exactly what happened, such as *ate* or *drank* or *swallowed.* Judges and senior lawyers want to read straightforward English. In one experiment, some appellate judges and their law clerks were asked to appraise contorted writing in "legalese," while others were asked to evaluate the same material rewritten into "plain English." They thought the original legalese "substantively weaker and less persuasive than the plain English versions."[1] And the judges and law clerks assumed that the lawyers who wrote in plain English worked in higher prestige jobs.[2]

§22.2 Conciseness

The present letter is a very long one simply because I had no time to make it shorter.

—Pascal

First drafts are usually too wordy. In later drafts, you can tighten up the writing by finding ways to say the same things in fewer words so your work can more easily be read and understood. Later drafts might grow in length, however, when you add *ideas* that weren't in the first draft because the process of rewriting helps you see what's missing intellectually. Rewriting for conciseness can help make room for these new ideas.

---

[1] Robert W. Benson & Joan B. Kessler, *Legalese v. Plain English: An Empirical Study of Persuasion and Credibility in Appellate Brief Writing,* 20 Loyola L.A. L. Rev. 301, 301 (1987).
[2] *Id.* at 301-02.

Compare two versions of the same sentence. The facts—though not the words—come from *Sherwood v. Walker*,[3] a classic mutual-mistake-of-fact case discussed in many Contracts casebooks.

verbose: It is important to note that, at the time when the parties entered into the agreement of purchase and sale, neither of them had knowledge of the cow's pregnant condition.

concise: When the parties agreed to the sale, neither knew the cow was pregnant.

How did the verbose first draft become the tight rewrite?

It is important to note that	*was deleted*	
at the time when	*became*	when
entered into the agreement of purchase and sale	*became*	agreed to the sale
neither of them	*became*	neither
had knowledge of	*became*	knew
had knowledge of the cow's pregnant condition	*became*	knew the cow was pregnant

Be careful, though, not to edit out needed meaning. It would be a mistake to eliminate so much that a reader would not know that the cow was pregnant when sold or that the parties did not know of the pregnancy at the time.

As you write and rewrite, avoid the temptation to imitate whatever you happen to find in judicial opinions that appear in your casebooks. Opinions appear in casebooks for what they tell you about the law—not for what they tell you about how to write. In the last two or three decades, lawyers and judges have changed the way they think about writing. Verbosity, obscurity, arcaneness, and disorganization that were tolerated two generations ago are now considered unacceptable because they make the reader's job harder. Some of the opinions in your casebooks are hard to understand because they discuss difficult concepts. But some are hard to understand because they're badly written. Before you imitate something you've seen in an opinion, ask yourself whether you want to do so because you feel safer doing what a judge has done—which is *not* a good basis for a professional decision—or because it would actually accomplish your purpose.

---

[3] 33 N.W. 919 (Mich. 1887).

§22.3 Our Style and Yours

You might notice places in this book where our own writing can be improved. We can't say that our writing styles are perfect. No style is. The best a writer can hope for is an *effective* style—one that generally provides what the reader needs.

If in our writing you notice clarity, vividness, or conciseness, it might be worth emulating whatever we did to achieve that—*if* doing so would work well in the assignment you are working on. (That's a big *if*.) But please do *not* emulate the *informal* style of this book. Informality in a textbook can help students learn difficult skills. The writing you submit to senior lawyers and judges should be formal.

Our own memos and briefs contain no contractions (two words merged with an apostrophe). Contractions might be appropriate in an informal letter to a client, but they have no place in formal documents. In our memos and briefs, you would see far fewer dashes and italics than appear in this book. In a formal document, an occasional dash or italicized word or phrase might help make a point, but not often. Here are some guidelines for formal documents:

> contractions: *never*
> italics: *rarely* (and only when truly helpful)
> dashes: *infrequently* (and only when grammatically correct)

§22.4 How to Test Your Writing for Effective Style

While rewriting, ask yourself the following questions. They also appear on this book's website as a checklist, which you can print out.

1. Is everything crystal clear for the reader? Sometimes a phrase or a sentence will seem clear in a first draft. But when you read it again while rewriting, you're not so sure. You have an advantage the reader doesn't: *You* know what you're trying to say. Put yourself in the position of someone who doesn't know that. Will it be clear to that person? Try to read your draft like the supervisor who will read your office memo or the judge who will read your motion memo or brief. It's easier to think like that reader if you allow some time to pass before going back to your draft. A day or two doing something else will help you return to the draft refreshed. Try to read quickly like a busy person and skeptically like someone who must make a decision. Is everything clear? If not, fix the problem.

2. Have you used transitional words to show the relationships between ideas? Transitional words can help lead the reader through ideas by specifying their relationships with each another and by identifying the ideas that are most important or compelling.

when introducing new or supplemental material
 additionally
 and
 besides
 furthermore
 in addition (to)
 in fact
 moreover

when explaining how thoughts relate to each other
 finally
 first . . . second . . . third *(when listing reasons)*
 in fact
 not only . . . , but also
 on these facts
 specifically
 under these circumstances

when pointing out similarities
 analogously
 similarly

when introducing inferences or explaining how one thing causes another
 accordingly
 as a result
 because
 consequently
 for that reason
 since
 therefore
 thus

when pointing out differences, inconsistency, or lack of causation
 although
 but
 conversely
 despite
 even if
 even though
 however
 in contrast
 in spite of
 instead of
 nevertheless
 on the contrary
 on the other hand

when introducing examples
>   for example
>   for instance
>   such as

when explaining time relationships
>   after
>   afterward
>   at the same time
>   before
>   later
>   previously
>   then

Transitional words can be placed at the beginning of a paragraph, at the beginning of a sentence, or inside a sentence. Choose the spot that best makes the point without being awkward.

Some words work better than others at showing causation. *Because* and *since* are usually clearer than *as* and *so*. Both *as* and *so* can confuse a reader who sees them more often doing other things, such as joining contemporaneous events ("the muggles gasped as Harry flew past on his Nimbus 2000") or emphasizing abundance ("they were so astonished that . . .").

3. Have you replaced unnecessarily complicated verbs with simple ones? For example:

delete	*replace with*
entered into an agreement	agreed
gave consideration to	considered
had knowledge of	knew
was aware of	knew
is able to	can
is binding on	binds
made a determination	determined
made allegations of	alleged
made a motion for	moved for
made the argument that	argued that
made the assumption that	assumed that
took into consideration	considered

4. Have you streamlined unnecessarily wordy phrases? For example:

delete	*replace with*
because of the fact that	because
for the purpose of	to
for the reason that	because
in the case of	in
in the event that	if
in the situation where	where (or when)
subsequent to	after
with regard to	regarding
with the exception of	except

5. Have you deleted throat-clearing phrases (also known as "long windups")? Phrases like the ones below waste words, divert the reader from your real message, and introduce a shade of doubt and an impression of insecurity. It's acceptable to write them into first drafts to help you get your thoughts onto the page. But in rewriting, delete them.

> It is significant that . . .
> The defendant submits that . . .
> It is important to note that . . .

6. Have you used lists to express coordinated ideas? When you discuss several ideas collectively, you can lead the reader forcefully if you make that clear, perhaps through some sort of textual list introduced by a transition sentence ("The court rejected that position for four reasons . . ."), followed by sentences or paragraphs coordinated to the transition sentence ("First . . . Second" and so on).

7. When expressing a list, have you used parallel construction and made sure that every item in the list is consistent with the words that introduce the list? For example:

Martha Stewart was convicted of obstructing justice, making false statements to government investigators, and because she conspired with her broker to commit various crimes.

You can see the problems more easily when the sentence is tabulated

Martha Stewart was convicted of
(1) obstructing justice,
(2) making false statements to government investigators, and
(3) because she conspired with her broker to commit various crimes.

Parallel construction requires that each item in a list be worded in the same grammatical format as the other items. Martha Stewart's list is not parallel. The first and second items are similarly structured phrases ("obstructing justice" and "making false statements . . ."). But, unlike the others, the third is a dependent clause, with a subject ("she") and a verb ("conspired"). The third item is also introduced by "because," which is missing from and inconsistent with the way the others are structured. You would not say "because obstructing justice" or "because making false statements."

Consistency with words introducing the list: You can test each item in a list by ignoring temporarily the other items to see whether the sentence works when you leap straight from the introductory words to the item you are testing. Here, it doesn't: "Martha Stewart was convicted of . . . because she conspired with her broker to commit various crimes."

A reader unconsciously looks for parallelism and consistency to figure out where one item in a list ends and the next begins, like this:

> Martha Stewart was convicted of obstructing justice, making false statements to government investigators, and conspiring with her broker to commit various crimes.

8. Have you used terms of art where appropriate? When a term of art communicates an idea peculiar to the law, use that term. It conveys the idea precisely, and often it makes long and convoluted explanations unnecessary. Don't write "the court told the defendants to stop building the highway." A precise statement would be, "the court enjoined the defendants from building the highway." But use a term of art *only* to convey its exact meaning. If you use a term of art (perhaps because it sounds lawyer-like) but don't really intend to communicate the idea the term of art stands for, a reader can assume that you don't understand the term or the law. (See the next question.)

9. Have you edited out imitations of lawyer noises? Notwithstanding grievous misconceptions of what is fit and proper, said lawyer noises have, by undisclosed instrumentalities, been entirely expurgated, expunged, and otherwise eliminated from this textbook, both heretofore and hereinafter. (Translation: We kept that stuff out.)

The most influential memos and briefs are written in real English. For example:

just fine:	Elvis has left the building.
bad:	Elvis has departed from the premises.
worse:	It would be accurate to say that Elvis has departed from the premises.
meaningless:	Elvis has clearly and unequivocably left the building.
meaningful:	Uncontroverted evidence shows that Elvis has left the building.

Why is "clearly and unequivocably" meaningless? Elvis could not unclearly or equivocably leave the building. Either he has left, or he hasn't. Writing something like "clearly and unequivocably" pounds the table without adding meaning. But "uncontroverted evidence" says that some evidence shows that Elvis has left and no other evidence shows that he hasn't—which makes it easy for a court to decide that he has gone. We would expect to read in the next sentence about the 27 witnesses who can testify that they saw Elvis go through the stage door, step into a stretch limo, and disappear into the night.

It can take a while to learn how to distinguish between lawyer noises and true terms of art (see question 8, above). When you come across a word or phrase used exclusively by lawyers, ask yourself the following: Is it part of a rule of law you've read in a case or a statute—for example, in an element of a test? Is it the name of a concept that is part of the law, including the policies or the reasoning behind a legal rule? If either answer is yes, you probably have a term of art, although lawyer noises do appear in some statutes and older cases. If both answers are no, you probably have lawyer noise (although it might be a term of art). The answers don't produce 100% accuracy, but they increase the odds of correctly categorizing the word or phrase.

10. Have you placed modifiers so that they communicate exactly what you mean? When people talk, modifiers sometimes wander all over sentences, regardless of what they are intended to modify. But in formal writing, more precision is required. These sentences all mean different things:

> The police are authorized to arrest only the person named in the warrant.
> *[They are not authorized to arrest anyone else.]*

> The police are authorized only to arrest the person named in the warrant.
> *[They are not authorized to deport him.]*

> Only the police are authorized to arrest the person named in the warrant.
> *[Civilians are not authorized.]*

11. Have you avoided sexist wording? The English language uses the masculine pronouns *he, his,* and *him* to refer generally to people of either sex. English lacks a pronoun that would mean "any person," regardless of sex. Here are some solutions:

	To calendar a motion, an attorney must file his moving papers with the clerk.
replace pronoun with "the"	To calendar a motion, an attorney must file the moving papers with the clerk.

make actor plural	To calendar motions, attorneys must file their moving papers with the clerk.
eliminate actor from sentence	A motion is calendared by filing the motion papers with the clerk.

The solution you choose will depend on what you're trying to accomplish. Here, the last solution is the most concise one. But if you want to warn lawyers who carelessly forget to file their moving papers, that point is lost if lawyers are not mentioned.

12. Have you punctuated correctly? Punctuation is really grammar, not style, but we mention it here anyway. Correct punctuation is not decoration. It makes writing clearer and easier to understand—and it can affect your credibility. Many readers will question your analytical abilities if you do not observe the accepted rules of punctuation. (If you have trouble with punctuation, see Appendix F.)

Exercise. Style, Sentences, and Rewriting

Identify the problems in each passage. Then rewrite the passage. (This exercise tests both the skills explained in this chapter and the ones explained in Chapter 21.)

1. MySpace and Facebook are both being used more frequently by people in their twenties and thirties, which means that teenagers are being marketed to less by both websites.

2. Because the defendant made statements to the effect that the plaintiff was not able to have knowledge of the actual date of Michael Jackson's birth, the plaintiff brought suit against the defendant with allegations of defamation. The defendant made a motion for summary judgment and made the argument that the court should give consideration to the plaintiff's admission, in an earlier lawsuit, that he lacked knowledge of Michael Jackson's date of birth. After making a determination that the plaintiff had previously made an admission that he lacked knowledge of Michael Jackson's date of birth, the court made entry of judgment for the defendant and made provision for the defendant to obtain recovery of costs.

3. On the ground that the client's video is a violation of YouTube's user agreement, which makes prohibited material that is "unlawful, obscene, defamatory, libelous, threatening, pornographic, harassing, hateful, racially or ethnically offensive, or encourages conduct that would be considered a criminal offense, give rise to civil liability, violate any law, or is otherwise inappropriate," YouTube's management effectuated a removal

of the video from the website, and the client would like to know whether she has a cause of action against YouTube.

4. Jones was employed as a bouncer at Smith's nightclub. His job was to screen the people who were on line outside, admitting only those whose coolness was obvious. ("Coolness" and "cool" are business terms with specific meanings that are understood throughout the nightclub industry.) There were three reasons why Jones was fired by Smith. First, the people he admitted to the nightclub were not cool. Second, the people he left on the sidewalk were cool. Third, he was not liked by Smith.

Citing Authority

§23.1 When and Why to Cite

Cite authority:

1. when the authority does a good job of supporting something you say (according to the criteria in Chapter 8)

   or

2. when you quote words from the authority (see Chapter 24 on quoting effectively).

Legal writing has unique citation rules. A reader needs specific information about each authority you cite and needs it expressed precisely and succinctly in "citation language" that can be quickly skimmed and understood. A properly constructed citation conveys a large amount of information in a very small space. If your citation form is faulty, readers quickly notice that and might doubt the quality of your work in other ways.

Two manuals codify the most commonly followed rules of legal citation—the ALWD Citation Manual and the Bluebook. Your teacher has probably assigned one of these manuals. They address nearly identical citation issues, and in memos and briefs their rules usually produce identical citations.[1]

---

[1] The verb "bluebooking" does *not* mean using the Bluebook instead of the ALWD Manual. When a senior lawyer asks "Have you bluebooked your cites?", the lawyer just wants to make sure your cites are in proper form. It doesn't matter which book you use. Lawyers and judges cannot tell the difference between a cite

If you use the Bluebook, be careful about the relationship between the rules in the blue pages at the front and the rules in the white pages later. The white page rules are designed for cites in law review footnotes and might or might not be appropriate for memos and briefs. The blue pages have a separate but incomplete set of rules for citing in memos and briefs. Because the blue-page rules are incomplete, you will often need to check both the blue and white pages to solve a citation problem. (The ALWD Citation Manual does not have this problem because it provides a single set of citation rules for all types of writing.)

Don't imitate citation forms just because you see them in judicial opinions. Some courts and publishers follow their own citation rules, which are inconsistent with the rules in the ALWD Citation Manual and the Bluebook. And many Bluebook citation rules have changed over the years, which means that citations in older cases may be in a format no longer considered acceptable.

From a citation, a reader expects to learn where the authority can be found and some basic facts affecting the authority's value. These are communicated through *citation grammar:* words, abbreviations, and numbers that, when expressed in proper order, have precise meaning for the reader. This chapter explains some general principles of citation. For specific rules about citation details, see the manual your teacher has assigned.

§23.2 Citations to Cases

A case cite includes up to five components, which must appear in the following order:

1. the *case name*;
2. the *reporter* or *reporters* where the case can be found, with volume and page numbers;
3. the court that decided the case;
4. the *date* of the decision; and
5. *subsequent history* (if any).

Here is an example. (The numbers refer to the components above.)

---

created from the ALWD Manual and one created from the Bluebook. They can't tell because the two manuals generally produce identical cites, and because the Bluebook changes some of its own rules in each new edition. The verb "bluebooking" is an example of a brand name entering the language as a synonym for a *type* of product or service. Other examples are "a kleenex," meaning a tissue, regardless of whether it came from the Kleenex company or some other tissue manufacturer, and "a xerox," meaning a photocopy, whether it was made by a Xerox Corporation machine, a Canon machine, or some other company's machine. Lawyers and judges might also ask, "Have you shepardized your cases?" They want to know whether you've checked to make sure none of your cases have been reversed or overruled. It doesn't matter whether you use Key Cite on Westlaw or the Shepard's service on Lexis. The ultimate results are nearly always the same.

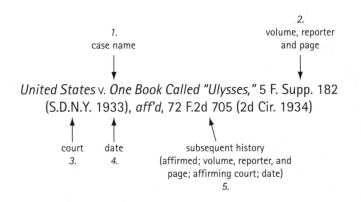

1.
case name

2.
volume, reporter
and page

United States v. *One Book Called "Ulysses,"* 5 F. Supp. 182
(S.D.N.Y. 1933), *aff'd,* 72 F.2d 705 (2d Cir. 1934)

court
3.

date
4.

subsequent history
(affirmed; volume, reporter, and
page; affirming court; date)
5.

The ALWD Citation Manual and the Bluebook both have detailed rules on how and what to abbreviate in case names; which reporter to use and how to refer to the court that decided the case. The appendices at the end of the ALWD Manual and the tables at the end of the Bluebook explain how to abbreviate. They also help you decode abbreviations, such as "S.D.N.Y." The date is the year in which the case was decided.

The subsequent history includes only the result of appeals from the decision cited to. Most decisions are not appealed and thus have no subsequent history. Where a case has a subsequent history, include the years of both lower and appellate decisions, if they are different. If both decisions date from the same year, put that year at the end of the entire citation.

§23.3 Citation to Statutes

A citation to a statute has at least three components:

1. the *codification*, such the United States Code;
2. *title* and *section* numbers, or other subdivisions, showing where in the codification the statute can be found; and
3. the codification or publication *date*.

If a statute is known not just by its title and section numbers, but also by a name under which it was originally enacted, such as the Civil Rights Act of 1965, the cite will include additional components:

4. the *name* of the statute as it was originally enacted and
5. the *section*, as numbered in the *original* enactment.

Here are examples of a statute that is not known by the name of its original enactment together with another statute that is. (The numbers refer to the components above.)

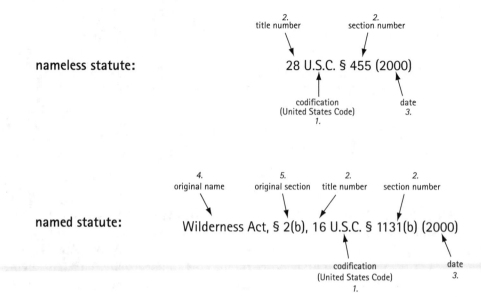

The United States Code is divided into 50 titles. State statutes are organized differently, but both the ALWD Citation Manual (in its Appendix 1) and the Bluebook (in its Table 1) show how to structure statutory cites for each state. Title 28 (the first example above) includes statutes on the judiciary and judicial procedure. Title 16 (the second example) includes statutes on conservation.

In a citation, use a section symbol ("§") and not the word "section." When you make a *textual reference* to a statute—by referring to it *outside* a citation—you can use either the section symbol or the word "section." But don't begin a sentence with a section symbol. Add a space between the section symbol and the number that follows. Even though the "§" symbol is not on your keyboard, readers will expect to see it in your writing. (In most versions of Word and WordPerfect, click on Insert, click on Symbol, find § in the pop-up dialog box, and click on it. The section symbol will then appear in your text.)

§23.4 Citations to Restatements, Treatises, and Law Review Articles

The rules on citing restatements, treatises, and law review articles are easier to understand than the rules on citing cases and statutes. Simply find the relevant section in the ALWD Citation Manual or the Bluebook and follow the directions you find there.

§23.5 Rules Governing All Citations

Full citations, short-form citations, and textual references: Authority can be referred to in three different ways. Here are some examples:

a full citation:	*Apple Computer, Inc. v. Microsoft Corp.*, 513 U.S. 1184 (1995).
a short-form citation:	*Id.* at 1199.
a textual reference:	In *Apple Computer,* the Supreme Court held . . . .

Use a full citation when you first mention an authority. At any point after you have done that, you may be able to use a short-form cite or a textual reference.

Citation sentences and clauses: A citation sentence includes one or more citations (and nothing else). A citation clause is a citation inserted into a *textual* sentence. A textual sentence is made up of words (like the sentence you are reading now). Where an authority supports an entire textual sentence, place the cite in a separate citation sentence:

> A defamation defendant enjoys an absolute privilege for expressions of mere opinion. *Gertz v. Robert Welch, Inc.,* 418 U.S. 323 (1974).

When an authority supports only part of a textual sentence, you can insert the cite into your sentence as a citation clause—although this is not always a good idea. The following textual sentence includes two citations:

> A defamation defendant enjoys an absolute privilege for expressions of mere opinion, *Gertz v. Robert Welch, Inc.,* 418 U.S. 323, 339-40 (1974), and whether a statement expresses fact or opinion is a question of law, to be determined by the court and not the jury, *Information Control Corp. v. Genesis One Computer Corp.,* 611 F.2d 781, 783 (9th Cir. 1980).

The sentence above is full of citation clutter, but it is one that many lawyers would write. You probably found it hard to climb over the *Gertz* cite so you could get to the rest of the sentence. If possible, write sentences with no cites inside them. Where a citation supports only part of a textual sentence, try breaking up the sentence:

> A defamation defendant enjoys an absolute privilege for expressions of mere opinion. *Gertz v. Robert Welch, Inc.,* 418 U.S. 323, 339-40 (1974). Whether a statement expresses fact or opinion is a question of law, to be determined by the court and not

the jury. *Information Control Corp. v. Genesis One Computer Corp.*, 611 F.2d 781, 783 (9th Cir. 1980).

A textual reference in a textual sentence is usually not a problem. But readers are distracted by a *complete* citation inside a textual sentence. They are also distracted by too many short-form cites in a textual sentence.

Pinpoint cites: A pinpoint cite directs a reader to a specific page in a case, treatise, or law review article. In this example, the pinpoint directs the reader to page 1201 in a case that begins on page 1184:

Apple Computer, Inc. v. Microsoft Corp., 513 U.S. 1184, 1201 (1995).

Every quotation requires a pinpoint cite. And where you refer to only part of an opinion—even without quoting—a reader often needs to know which pages you have in mind. Very few opinions are too short to need pinpoint citing.

String cites: A string cite is a list of authorities, all being cited for the same purpose. If you have found eight cases, all holding that in your state a contract can be voided for fraud, you might be tempted to use all eight cases in one string cite. But that is often a mistake.

The ideal case would settle the law on voiding contracts for fraud (such as a case from the highest court in the state) and would explain the rule's policy and how the rule works with facts like yours. If one of your eight cases does all that, use that one case, explain that case thoroughly for your reader, and ignore the others. More often, you might have to use two or more cases to show the reader that the law is settled and how the rule works. The important thing is to explain thoroughly the few cases that really matter. That is much more helpful to a reader than citing a lot of cases without much explanation.

In rare situations, a string cite can be helpful. If your state has no common law rule on the issue about which you are writing, and if your state's courts could adopt either of two competing rules (which we can call Rule A and Rule B), you might use a string cite to show how many states have adopted Rule A and another string cite to show how many states have adopted Rule B. But you should still explain a few Rule A cases and a few Rule B cases to show how each rule works.

Signals: If needed, your purpose in citing an authority can be communicated through signals—formulaic words or abbreviations that introduce the citation. Examples are *See, Accord*, and *Contra*. Never use a signal when the authority directly supports the idea you are citing it for, when you are using the authority as a source for a quote, or when your own discussion of the authority makes clear why you are citing to it.

In memos and briefs, signals might not help the reader. Signals help compress massive amounts of information in law review footnotes and in other kinds of scholarly writing, including the seminar papers you might write in the second or third year of law school. But in practical writing like memos and briefs, use signals only where they are truly necessary. Signals often do not communicate the type of precise information needed by your reader. A person who must make a decision based in part on your writing needs to know not only what an authority stands for but also *exactly how that is relevant to the decision to be made.* In memos and briefs, your own discussion of the authorities does that much better than signals can.

Parentheticals: Two types of parentheticals appear in legal citations. One is an *integral part of the cite* and provides required information, such as the court and year for a case or the year of a statute. The other type is an *explanatory parenthetical* that provides information you could express outside the citation but, for economy, want to compress into the cite. Sometimes that information is better compressed into the cite, and sometimes it's better expressed in text:

in the cite: *Carey v. Population Services Int'l,* 431 U.S. 678, 691-99 (1977) (plurality opinion).

in text: Although a majority of seven justices struck down that portion of the statute that prohibited distribution of nonprescription contraceptives to persons under the age of 16, only four justices supported the rationale now urged in this court. *Carey v. Population Services Int'l,* 431 U.S. 678, 691-99, 702-03, 707-08, 713-16 (1977).

You can run into trouble, however, if you go overboard trying to express the *substance* of an authority in an explanatory parenthetical:

Carey v. Population Services Int'l, 431 U.S. 678, 691-99 (1977) (holding that state statute prohibiting distribution of nonprescription contraceptives to persons under 16 years old is unconstitutional because sexual activity may not be constitutionally deterred by increasing its hazards).

This explanatory parenthetical is awkward and hard to read. And it oversimplifies and inevitably misrepresents the material in order to pack it into parenthetical form. If the material is complicated and important to the issue, explain it in your text. Use an explanatory parenthetical only for simple information that is not an important part of your discussion or argument. Don't use explanatory parentheticals to avoid the hard work of explaining complicated and important authority.

Typeface: Citation uses two typefaces, roman and italics. This sentence—and most of this book—is in roman. *The sentence you're reading now is in italics.* Case names and signals should be in italics. So should *id.*, *supra, infra*, and certain other terms specified by your citation manual.

If you use the Bluebook, be careful about the examples in the blue pages in the front. Before people wrote on computers, they had to underline rather than italicize because typewriters could not produce italics. The examples in the blue pages at the beginning of the Bluebook use underlining, even though virtually all law school and law office writing is now done on computers, which easily italicize. Italics look more professional than underlining.

Quoting Effectively

Quoting sources of law can be useful, but quotations can consume your writing if you're not careful. This chapter explains when to use a quote and how to satisfy the format requirements for quoting.

§24.1 When to Quote

Quotations help when they express *exactly* the idea you want to communicate to your reader. And the citation after the quote lets your reader know that this idea has some authority behind it. When your issue would be resolved by interpreting certain words, quote those words. With statutory issues, for example, quote the most essential words in the statute. Cases often are not as direct. Some statutes are like text messages, but a case is more like a novel. The language of a case resolves that case's issues, but it might not directly apply to other facts. Using phrases or words from a case may be the best way to communicate with a reader. Your reader doesn't need to know details from the precedent that are irrelevant to the current problem.

§24.2 Quote Sparingly or Not at All

Don't let quotes get out of control. They can eat up large chunks of your writing and your reader's attention. When that happens, many readers will refuse to read your quotes.

Keep your quotes limited to small, essential passages. Edit out the words that don't apply. For example, a statute or a case might set out the test that governs your facts, but not all of the elements of that test may be in dispute in the case about which you are writing. You can summarize or note the elements not in dispute, and you can highlight the contested one by quoting it. For example, if a criminal defendant's only argument is that she lacked purposeful intent, the other elements of the crime are much less important, and the only part of the statute worth quoting might be the part that requires purposeful intent for conviction.

Be very careful when you edit a quote. Make sure that your edited version accurately reflects the relevant meaning of the original. Sloppy editing may cost you your credibility.

Block quotations are especially troublesome. A block quote is a large quotation separated from the rest of your text, indented on the left and right sides, and single-spaced. A busy reader will skim over or refuse to read large quotations because their experience tells them that only a few of the quoted words will really matter, and it may take too much effort to find them. The more block quotes you use, the more quickly a reader may refuse to read any of them. Judges and supervising attorneys often believe your task is to find the essential words, isolate them, and concisely paraphrase the rest. When you throw many block quotations at a reader, you're asking the reader to do some of your work.

Don't use quotes as a substitute for your own analysis. Sometimes quoting an extended passage from a source of law helps the reader. But that is seldom true. *Experienced and effective writers quote less often, and their quotes tend to be shorter.*

§24.3 The Mechanics of Quoting

Legal readers will be looking not just at what you quote, but also at how you follow the format rules for quotations. The ALWD Citation Manual and the Bluebook both set out rules governing the format of quotations. Here are the most essential requirements:

Use brackets to enclose substitutions and additions that you place inside quotation marks, including the transformation of a lowercase letter into a capital or vice versa. Parentheses and brackets convey different messages, and you cannot substitute one for the other.

If you incorporate a quote beginning with a capitalized word into a sentence of your own, make the letter lowercase unless the capital denotes a proper name. For example:

wrong: The court held **that** "**Not** so long ago, in a studio far, far away from the policymakers in Washington, D.C., George Lucas conceived of an imaginary galaxy," but his trademark is not infringed when politicians refer to a proposed missile defense system as Star Wars. *Lucasfilm Ltd. v. High Frontier*, 622 F. Supp. 931, 932, 935 (D.D.C. 1985).

right: The court held **that** "[n]ot so long ago, . . ."

If you add or delete italics, or if you omit citations from a quote, note that in a parenthetical following the citation, like this:

> To obtain the names of a defamation defendant's confidential sources, a plaintiff must prove that she or he has "*independently* attempted to obtain the information elsewhere and has been unsuccessful." *Silkwood v. Kerr-McGee Corp.*, 563 F.2d 433, 438 (10th Cir. 1977) (emphasis added).

If you delete words from a quote, indicate that by an ellipsis of three periods ("..."). When you omit the last words of a sentence, place *four* periods at the end of the sentence—three for the ellipsis and one to end the sentence. But when you incorporate a quotation into a sentence of your own composition—as in the Star Wars and *Silkwood* examples above—do not place an ellipsis at the beginning or the end of the quotation. Incorporating the quote into your own sentence suggests that you might have omitted something at the beginning or end.

The ALWD Citation Manual requires that a quotation of 50 words or more or four lines of your typed text be placed in block-quote form. The Bluebook requires a block-quote for quotations of 50 words or more. A block quote should not begin or end with quotation marks. Blocking the words tells the reader that they are a quote. The citation to the quote's source does not appear in the quotation block. The cite goes instead in your text, at the beginning of the next line you write. The first example below is wrong on both counts:

wrong: The Seventh Circuit has explained the law's treatment of ligers:

> "As its name suggests, a 'liger' is a cross between a male lion and a female tiger. Ligers do not occur naturally, so all known ligers are in captivity. They apparently are a source of fascination in popular culture. *E.g.*, Napoleon Dynamite (Paramount Pictures, 2004) ('It's pretty much my favorite animal. It's like a lion and a tiger mixed . . . bred for its skills in magic.') As interspecies hybrids, ligers are not protected under U.S. wildlife laws." *U.S. v. Kapp*, 419 F. 3d 666, 670, n.1 (7th Cir. 2005).

Nor do the wildlife laws protect basilisks, boggarts, dementors, or phoenix birds.

right: The Seventh Circuit has explained the law's treatment of ligers:

> As its name suggests, a "liger" is a cross between a male lion and a female tiger. Ligers do not occur naturally, so all known ligers are in captivity. They apparently are a source of fascination in popular culture. *E.g.*, NAPOLEON DYNAMITE (Paramount Pictures, 2004) ("It's pretty much my favorite animal. It's like a lion and a tiger mixed . . . bred for its skills in magic.") As interspecies hybrids, ligers are not protected under U.S. wildlife laws.

> *U.S. v. Kapp*, 419 F.3d 666, 670, n.1 (7th Cir. 2005). Nor do the wildlife laws protect basilisks, boggarts, dementors, or phoenix birds.

§24.4 How to Test Your Quotations for Effectiveness

While rewriting, ask yourself the following questions. They also appear on this book's website as a checklist, which you can print out.

1. Have you quoted and cited every time you use the words of others? The words of others must have quotation marks around them and a citation to the source. If you do not do this, you may be treated as a plagiarist, even if you did it out of sloppiness and did not intend to deceive.

2. Have you quoted only the essential words? Generally speaking, quoted words should appear in your work when they fit into at least one of the following categories:

(a) words that must be *interpreted* in order to resolve the issue;
(b) words that—*with remarkable economy*—communicate the thinking of a court, legislature, or expert in the field; or
(c) words that are the *most eloquent and succinct conceivable* expression of an important idea.

The most convincing descriptions of authority are written almost entirely in your own words, punctuated with very few and very short quotations.

3. Have you followed the mechanical rules on quotations? Although they are summarized in this chapter, check the ALWD Citation Manual or the Bluebook.

4. Have you placed quotation marks exactly where they belong? The most common problems are (1) omitting the quotation marks that close a quotation (the reader wonders, "Where does the quote end?"); (2) omitting the quotation marks that open a quotation ("Where does the quote begin?"); and (3) where you have a quote within a quote, forgetting to change the double quotation marks of the original to single marks.

5. Have you quoted accurately? Suppose you see language in a case that you want to quote. You type it into your draft, but—although you don't realize it at the time—some of the words you type are different from those that appear in the case. It's only human to rewrite quotes unconsciously into our own style while copying them. The only way to prevent this is to proofread with the sources in front of you. If you printed out the sources, don't throw them away until after you've proofread.

Exercise I. The First Amendment

You are writing a memorandum involving the freedom of the press clause from the U.S. Constitution's First Amendment. You intend to quote the words to be interpreted. This is the text of the entire amendment:

> Congress shall make no law respecting an establishment of religion, or prohibiting the free exercise thereof; or abridging the freedom of speech, or of the press; or the right of the people peaceably to assemble, and to petition the government for a redress of grievances.

Using words from the Amendment, create a sentence that accurately quotes without including more than your reader needs.

Exercise II. Quoting Cases

Take a case you have read recently in any class. Write a one-sentence summary of the rule expressed in that case using these four different formats.

1. A sentence that quotes an entire sentence from the case.
2. A sentence that quotes a phrase from the case.
3. A sentence that quotes only one word from the case.
4. A sentence that paraphrases information from the case.

Which sentence was the easiest to write? Which sentence would make the rule easiest to understand for your reader?

VI

Informal Analytical Writing

Client Advice Letters

§25.1 Why and How Lawyers Write Client Advice Letters

Client letters are midway between a conversation with the client and an office memo. They record the essence of what you would say to the client in a meeting in your office. And often they summarize an office memo. A sample client letter appears in Appendix B.

The tone of a client letter should be professionally precise and should imply that you're supportive. If you sympathize explicitly, don't let it sound fake or forced. In choosing a tone, ask yourself these questions: What does the situation call for? What would this client want from a professional? What are you comfortable with in terms of your own style? And how do you want to present yourself to clients?

The second question—what this client would want from a professional—may be the most complex. Consider the client's level of sophistication (education, occupation, experience with lawyers). And consider the client's feelings. Is the client experiencing anxiety, grief, or anger? Even in positive situations, such as buying property, happiness can be mixed with anxiety. Or is this transaction pure business from the client's point of view? It probably is if the client is an organization or a business person, if the client considers the transaction or dispute to be routine, or if the client has a lot of experience with lawyers.

Contractions ("don't," "won't") are fine in a letter, though not in a memo or brief.

§25.2 Client Advice Letter Format

A typical structure is set out below. If the letter is complex, you might use head-ings to break some of it up. But adapt the wording in the headings to the client and the situation.

1. The beginning formalities: These include the letterhead, which is already printed on your law office's stationery; the date; the client's name and address; and the salutation ("Dear Ms. Lopez:"—always with a colon, never a comma).

2. One or two opening paragraphs, stating the problem about which the client has sought your advice and a brief summary of your advice: This corre-sponds to the issue and brief answer in an office memo. If you have bad news, this is where the client learns that it is bad. Think long and hard about the words you use to convey that bad news. Reading words on a page can be a cold experience for the client.

3. One or more paragraphs reviewing the key facts on which the advice is based, as the lawyer understands those facts: You might think it wastes words to tell the client the client's own facts, but there are several good reasons for doing so.

First, if you have misunderstood any of the facts and the client knows better, the client can correct you. Many lawyers add a sentence asking the client to do that ("If I have described any of the facts inaccurately, please call me").

Second, a fact recitation limits the advice in the future to the facts recited, and that can be important if the facts change. A tenant who does not have a claim against the landlord for a filthy lobby might have one next week if the lobby ceiling caves in.

Third, you might recently have learned of some facts the client does not yet know about. If so, describe the newly found facts in ways that tell the client they are new ("Since we last spoke, I have discovered that the 1986 deed was never properly recorded in the county clerk's office").

And finally, a fact recitation is a good, professional transition into the advice itself.

4. The advice, which can be structured in either of two ways: If the client wants to know how the law treats a certain situation—"Would I win a lawsuit against the airline?" or "Would my company violate the law if we were to import this product?"—you predict how a court would rule or you explain the client's or other people's rights and obligations.

On the other hand, if the client must make a decision, you counsel in the letter by suggesting the options from which the client can choose and, for each option, explaining the factors that might make it attractive or unattractive. List the options and explain their *advantages, costs, risks, and chances of success.* When you estimate risks and chances of success, you're making predictions.

Costs are not limited to money. The cost of suing includes not only legal fees and other litigation expenses, but also the time and energy the client would have to invest in the lawsuit and the stress many litigants suffer while the suit is in progress.

Be especially careful about the words you use to communicate how much confidence you have in the accuracy of your advice. When you write "we have a reasonably good chance of winning at trial," you might mean that you believe the client will probably win although the risk of loss is significant. But many clients would read those words to mean that victory is nearly assured. That's because it's only human for a client who has suffered a wrong to assume that forces of justice will correct it. Don't, through vagueness, imply unjustified optimism. Find ordinary, everyday words that the client will understand exactly as you mean them.

If the news truly is bad, don't cushion it so much that the client will not appreciate it. Don't say "our chances in litigation are problematic" if what you really mean is "we would probably lose if the other side sues."

A good client letter can be understood by a layperson in one reading. It takes much work on your part to accomplish that. Use as little lawyer talk as possible. If a legal term of art has a good equivalent in ordinary English, use the equivalent even if it doesn't convey 100% of the meaning of the term of art. (Eighty percent is good enough unless the missing 20% is relevant to the client's situation.) If you use a term of art, define it.

When you translate lawyer talk into ordinary English, do so respectfully. This isn't just good communication. It's also good business. Clients often feel uncomfortable with a stereotyped lawyer who speaks in legalese. But they can like and trust a genuine human being who does a good job of being their lawyer.

Write simply but don't oversimplify. If the law is unclear, point that out and explain why it's unclear ("courts disagree with each other on what the statute means"). Discuss authority only if it's central to the issue, such as a recent case that changes everything you have told the client in the past.

Reciting the law can be cold and confusing ("in this state, tax must be paid by the property owner on each lien against real property recorded in the county clerk's office"). But describing the law's effect on the client is warm, and it often eliminates the need to recite the law ("if you refinance the mortgage on your home, you will have to pay $1,250 in mortgage tax").

Unlike a supervising lawyer or a judge, your client assumes that you know the law, which means that you don't have to recite rules of law or cite and explain authority as thoroughly as you would in a memo or a brief. But you do have to know what you are talking about. Nobody is perfect at predicting. But if you are wrong because you don't understand the law, you'll lose clients and learn a lot about the details of malpractice law.

Organize the material in any way that will help the client understand it. Sometimes clients are confused by the CREAC formula described in Chapters 16 through 19. You aren't writing for the skeptical supervising lawyer or judge to whom everything must be proved. You're writing for a layperson who trusts your judgment, assumes you know the law, but probably won't understand a detailed and thorough legal explanation.

5. One or two closure paragraphs: Sum up your advice in two or three sentences. Specify what can or should be done next, who should do it, and when it should be done. If the client needs to make a decision, set the stage for that. Invite the client to telephone you or, if extended conversation might be needed, suggest that the client make an appointment to see you. On the other hand, if the advice is negative ("although your competitors behaved badly, they did nothing illegal"), closure might be limited to an offer to answer questions if the client would like to call.

6. The ending formalities: These are your signature over your typed name and under a closing like "Sincerely Yours" or whatever words are customary in your office. (Most readers never notice the closing or care about it, unless you say something completely inappropriate.)

Email Memoranda

§26.1 Why and How Lawyers Write Email Memos

An email memo may be appropriate where a supervisor needs analysis faster and more concisely than an office memo could provide. Speed is crucial. The supervisor needs an answer fast. The email memo has to be written quickly, and the supervisor needs to be able to read and understand it within moments of opening it.

As with every other kind of document, more time spent by the writer should result in less time spent by the reader. Compare the writing and reading times for two email memos:

	Email memo A	Email memo B
writing time	40 minutes	60 minutes
reading time	10 minutes	5 minutes

Assuming that both memos contain the same amount of analysis and that the only difference is how long it takes a reader to understand that analysis, supervisors in most situations would prefer memo B. That would be true of office memos, too, but it is dramatically true of email memos. They are written and read under time pressure, and a supervisor's time is more valuable than that of a recently hired lawyer.

Writing the memo inside your email system might actually be slower than writing it elsewhere and transferring it into an email message. Your word processor (Word or WordPerfect) was designed to help you write and rewrite. It might be more efficient to draft the memo in your word-processor and copy and paste it into an email message. But if you do that, save the word processed version in case something goes wrong while transferring it into email.

§26.2 Email Memo Format

Office memo format developed over decades, and lawyers generally agree on how an office memo should be structured. Email memos, on the other hand, have developed very recently, and there's no consensus about their format. An email memo might be structured somewhat like an office memo, or it might follow an entirely different format.[1]

Email memo format should be flexible. What works in one situation might not work in another. On Monday, a lawyer might send an email memo concerning a proposed jury instruction in case X. On Friday, the same lawyer might send an email memo to the same supervisor explaining the law concerning a discovery demand in case Y. These email memos might be structured in entirely different ways because the problems they address are different. The following is one way in which an email memo might be structured.

The email's subject line: Specify clearly and concisely what this memo is about ("Smith v. Jones, interrog. 6 in plaintiff's 2d set"). In the inbox on your supervisor's screen, it will appear with many other messages, and the subject line should identify the problem your memo addresses.

The memo's first sentence—or its statement of the issue: Say why you're sending the email memo. It will be read today, but it might be read again in a year's time. Both today's reader and next year's reader should be told exactly why you've written this memo. Here's an example:

> You've asked whether we're required to answer interrogatory 6 in the plaintiff's second set of interrogatories.

Worded this way, no heading is needed. But if you word it as an issue, use a heading:

> **Issue:**
>
> Are we required to answer interrogatory 6 in the plaintiff's second set of interrogatories?

---

[1] *See* Kristen Konrad Robbins Tiscione, *From Snail Mail to E-Mail: The Traditional Legal Memorandum in the Twenty-First Century*, 58 J. Legal Educ. 32-60 (2008).

The answer: State your answer, with the essence of why. This can probably be done in one or two sentences. Use a heading like "Answer" or "Brief Answer."

Answer
   No. That interrogatory seeks material protected by the attorney-client privilege.

An alternative way of beginning the memo: Instead of writing the two components above—the first-sentence/Issue and the Answer—you might combine them under a heading like "Summary":

Summary:
   We are not required to answer interrogatory 6 in the plaintiff's second set of interrogatories. That interrogatory seeks material protected by the attorney-client privilege.

If you do this, *omit* the first-sentence/Issue and the Answer.

The facts: Recite only the few facts that are crucial to your analysis. Your supervisor is working on the case right now and knows the facts generally. Don't recite the entire case story. You've been asked for a fast answer to a specific and narrow question. The only facts that matter are the ones that are essential to answering that question.

Your analysis: Explain why your answer is correct. This might take one paragraph or six paragraphs or something in between. You will need to determine what level of explanation will satisfy your supervisor's two needs: for speed and for confidence that you're right. Finding the right balance becomes easier with experience. If you're not sure how to do that now, err on the side of including more explanation. The heading for this part could be "Analysis," "Explanation," or "Discussion."

§26.3 Typography, Professionalism, and the Dangerous Send Button

Typography: In email, headings do not center well. You can place headings along the left margin, or you can indent them five or ten spaces from the left margin. Indenting makes them a little more obvious. Headings should be in bold print, unless your email system won't support bold. If it won't, the headings should be entirely in capital letters.

In a printed document, the first line of a paragraph is indented. But that is not true in emails, where a paragraph's first line starts at the left margin.

Professionalism: Even though an email memo is less formal than an office memo, it's still a communication between professionals and should be written in a professional tone and in precise language. It might be informal in some ways, but it is an office memo in miniature

The Dangerous Send Button: Email is so easy to send that it's (1) a marvel of convenience and (2) dangerous. If you accidentally put the wrong address into the "To" box, you might send confidential client information to someone who shouldn't have it. And even if you don't make that mistake, whatever you send can be forwarded to people whom you hadn't imagined would read it.

Check *everything* before you hit Send. Don't let the demand for speed trick you into a painful mistake. Take a long moment and be sure that every detail is exactly as it should be.

VII

The Shift to Persuasion

What Persuades a Court?

What could you write to persuade a judge to give you what you're asking for? What persuades?

§27.1 A Compelling Theory and Theme Persuade

A *theory* is a way of looking at the controversy that makes your client the winner. A *theme* is a sentence or two or even just a phrase that summarizes the theory. You're already familiar with theories and themes in a commercial sense. Think of the businesses or products to which you are loyal. Each of them has been marketed with a theory and theme—sometimes implied rather than stated openly—that has persuaded you to spend money. Here are a few examples:

> iPod and iTouch—so much inside; take it anywhere with all your tunes
> jetBlue—fly on an airline that's fun
> Amazon—stop driving to stores: just click, and it's delivered to you

In law, a persuasive theory is a view of the facts and law—intertwined together—that *justifies* a decision in your favor and that *motivates* a court to render that decision. A persuasive theory

1. relies on the supportive facts;
2. explains why the adverse facts should not prevent a decision in your favor;
3. has a solid basis in law and overcomes your adversary's interpretation of the law;
4. appeals to a judge's sense of fairness and good policy; and
5. can be summarized in one or two easily remembered sentences or a vivid image (the theme).

Unfocused writing can make a judge feel as though she's drowning in detail without a clear idea of how all the detail adds up to a coherent view of the case. Judges complain about lawyers who write that way. *A judge needs a clearly stated theory and a memo or brief sharply focused on proving that theory.*

§27.2 A Compelling Story Persuades

The client's story makes the theory *come alive.* It can do that because—although in a scientific world we expect ourselves to think logically—deep down inside, we think also in terms of stories. You've already experienced something like this. Suppose you're in an audience. Someone is speaking from a podium in the front of the room. For half an hour, that person talks about the logical connection between the Heisenberg uncertainty principle and the invention of chocolate. Your eyelids grow heavy, and you contemplate sleep. Then, the speaker stops talking about logic. To illustrate some point, he tells about a family of ducks who start crossing a busy highway at rush hour—the mother at the head of a long line of ducklings, the father who-knows-where; brakes screeching; Officer O'Leary rushing up waving his arms in air. Suddenly, you are sitting upright on the edge of your seat. Why are you listening differently now? It can't be that chocolate bored you. Instead, the tension in the story has gripped you. Never mind about Heisenberg and his uncertainty. Will the cars hit the ducklings? Will all that slamming of brakes cause a huge chain collision, followed by drivers standing on the pavement and swearing at each other? Will Officer O'Leary be able to prevent all this harm?

Nearly all good stories have tension. The stories lawyers tell courts have tension because they involve conflict. When we start to hear or read a story like that—and if the story is told well—we naturally start asking questions like these: Who's the good person? Who's the bad person? What bad thing did the bad person do? How did it affect the good person? (We're worried.) What happens next? How will the story end?

Every case has a story. You've been reading them in the casebooks in other courses. Actually, every case has at least two stories, one for each side. The one you read in the court's opinion is the winning story. Sometimes, you read the losing story in a dissenting opinion.

How do we know judges are persuaded by stories? The judges say so, in the opinions they write. Judges often tell us, by the way they explain the facts of a case, *how* they have been influenced by a story. For example, here are the first two paragraphs of *BMW v. Gore*,[1] a U.S. Supreme Court case.

> The Due Process Clause of the Fourteenth Amendment prohibits a State from imposing a "grossly excessive" punishment on a tortfeasor. [citation omitted] The wrongdoing involved in this case was the decision by a national distributor of automobiles not to advise its dealers, and hence their customers, of predelivery damage to new cars when the cost of repair amounted to less than 3 percent of the car's suggested retail price. The question presented is whether a $2 million punitive damages award to the purchaser of one of these cars exceeds the constitutional limit.
>
> In January 1990, Dr. Ira Gore, Jr. (respondent), purchased a black BMW sports sedan for $40,750.88 from an authorized BMW dealer in Birmingham, Alabama. After driving the car for approximately nine months, and without noticing any flaws in its appearance, Dr. Gore took the car to "Slick Finish," an independent detailer, to make it look "snazzier than it normally would appear." [citation omitted] Mr. Slick, the proprietor, detected evidence that the car had been repainted. Convinced that he had been cheated, Dr. Gore brought suit against petitioner BMW of North America (BMW), the American distributor of BMW automobiles. Dr. Gore alleged, *inter alia*, that the failure to disclose that the car had been repainted constituted suppression of a material fact. The complaint prayed for $500,000 in compensatory and punitive damages, and costs.

Dr. Gore is going to lose this appeal. We know it already—even though the court hasn't even begun to analyze the law. Here are the clues from the way the court begins:

- Dr. Gore paid about $40,750 to buy the car.
- It took a specialist to notice that the car had been damaged and repaired, and Dr. Gore didn't know about it until the specialist told him.
- He sued for $500,000 in compensatory damages and was awarded $2 million in punitive damages.

The plaintiff's story, which the court rejected, appears in these words in one of the dissents:

> Dr. Gore's experience was not unprecedented among customers who bought BMW vehicles sold as flawless and brand-new. In addition to his own encounter, Gore showed . . . that on 983 other occasions . . . , BMW had shipped new vehicles to dealers without disclosing paint repairs costing at least $300, [and] at least 14 of the repainted vehicles . . . were sold as new and undamaged to consumers in Alabama.[2]

---

[1] 517 U.S. 559 (1995).
[2] *Id.* at 608.

§27.3 Compelling Arguments Persuade

Arguments provide the logical reasons to accept the theory. They're based on the interpretation of statutes and judicial precedent as well as public policy. In all your courses, you've been immersed in arguments since you started law school.

§27.4 How Arguments and Stories Work Together

Suppose you're being asked to believe the last sentence in the paragraph below:

> Almost 80% of the people of India live on less than $2 a day, according to the World Bank, and a typical work day might be 12 or 15 hours long. Millions of Indians are self-employed as farmers or other small producers or as sellers or resellers. *A self-employed Indian in these circumstances can earn dramatically more income and reduce work hours substantially simply by owning a cell phone.*

Assume that you're a government official with a budget. You're besieged by people and organizations asking you to spend money on projects they consider important. For every request you agree to, you will have to turn down a hundred more. You're asked to spend a million dollars in a seed program to get cell phones into the hands of Indian farmers, fishermen, sellers, and resellers. A logical argument in support of this plan appears in the left column below. Read it and ask yourself whether it persuades you and, if so, how *deeply* you are persuaded ("this might work," "it probably will work," or "absolutely will it work!"). Then read the story in the right column.[3]

A Logical Argument

In economics, a market is any system in which buyers and sellers can transact business with each other. In an *efficient* market, all information is available to everybody so that each buyer or seller can make rational decisions. If all information is available to everybody, each person gets the most value out of the market, and waste is minimized. Developing countries are

A Story

Devi Datt Joshi sells fruit and vegetables on the street in New Dehli. He has no store and no refrigerator. He has only a three-wheeled cart and a regular spot on the street where his customers know to find him.

Well before dawn, he goes to a fruit and vegetable wholesale market and buys as much produce as he thinks he can sell that day. That pre-dawn

---

[3] The details in both columns come from Kevin Sullivan, *Dialing Up a Sea of Change*, Wash. Post, Oct. 15, 2006, at A01, and Kevin Sullivan, *Cell Phone Turns Out To Be Grocer's Best Buy*, Wash. Post, Oct. 14, 2006.

plagued by inefficient markets, where people don't have access to the information they need, and where buyers and sellers have a hard time even finding each other.

The smallest and cheapest medium for transmitting information instantly is a cell phone. It is cheaper than a Blackberry or a laptop and does not require telephone wires or a wifi infrastructure. All it requires is cellular transmitting towers, which are being built anyway throughout the world to satisfy the wealthy. A cell phone also does not require any education. A person who does not know how to read or write can operate a cell phone.

Although the U.S. cost of buying a cell phone and paying the monthly service charges would consume most of an average Indian worker's income, costs in India are lower than in the United States. Cell phone air time in India costs less than one U.S. cent per minute.

Cell phone subscribers in India have grown from 1.6 million in 2000 to 125 million in 2006 (when cell phones in India outnumbered land lines by three to one).

"One element of poverty is the lack of information," according to C.K. Prahalad, a professor in the business school at the University of Michigan, who has studied how cell phones can help people escape poverty. "The cell phone gives poor people as much information as the middleman."

Therefore, if small businesses in India start using cell phones, their owners, employees, and customers will all be better off.

decision of how much to purchase—based on his prediction of how much his customers will want to buy by afternoon—is crucial to whether he will make any money at all that day and how hard he will have to work to make it. Without refrigeration in a hot climate, if he buys more than he can sell, he will have to throw away most of the excess because it will not be fresh the following day. If he buys too little, he loses sales and risks also losing frustrated customers to some other produce seller.

Making this kind of gamble, he used to earn an average of $3 a day for more than 12 hours of work. Once his morning customers had bought what they wanted, he would have to wander through the streets looking for buyers for the produce that was left.

Everything changed when he got a cell phone.

Customers call him the night before to place their orders. He knows how much to buy, and they can depend on him to supply what they need. He buys a little extra for customers who do not call ahead, and he sells that, too—without having to wander in the streets.

"The mobile phone has more than doubled my profits," he told an American newspaper reporter. He now earns $8 a day for about eight hours of work. He still gets up before dawn but his work day ends before lunch. He has been able to hire an assistant and put his children into better schools.

And the food he buys rarely goes to waste.

Again, you're the government official with a budget. Suppose you hear the story above without the logical argument. The story makes you interested, even excited, about the idea, but you don't yet have confidence that this is a good use of development money. Now you hear the logical argument, which gives you the confidence you didn't have before. The story provided motivation, and the logical argument finished the job by justifying with logic.

The story and the logical argument work together. Neither alone would be sufficient. The story touches us and motivates us to act. The logical argument explains why the story is valid and provides a justification a decision-maker can rely on to explain the decision to someone else. Persuading thus requires telling a good story *and* making an argument that *work together*.

§27.5 Overcoming Your Weaknesses Persuades

Which cases and statutes favor your adversary? Which facts work to your adversary's advantage? What are your adversary's strongest arguments? And what will your adversary say to fight against your arguments? The answers to these questions identify your weaknesses.

Hiding from these problems will not make them slink away in the night. You have to confront and defeat them. "Be truthful in exposing . . . the difficulties in your case," an appellate judge has written. "Tell us what they are and how you expect to deal with them."[4] If you fail to mention your weaknesses, and if you fail to explain why they do not undermine your case, the court probably will hold them against you.

Acknowledging your challenges can preserve your reader's trust in you. Tell the reader the bad news with your spin on it. Think of inviting a friend to your apartment for an impromptu study session. If the apartment is a mess, you might explain—sheepishly and before you bring the guest in—that your place is usually cleaner. Then your guest could still think well of you, despite your mountains of dirty laundry.

§27.6 Solving Judges' Problems Persuades

Make it easy for the judge to rule in your favor.

Imagine an office with a desk, a side table, and book shelves. On the desk and side table, many files are piled up. Each file is very thick and represents a motion or appeal the judge must decide. The judge behind the desk has a huge docket of cases. To decide each of them, the judge must read what the lawyers have submitted—page after page after page of reading—and for most judges there are too few hours in the day to read all that.

---

[4] Roger J. Miner, *Twenty-five "Dos" for Appellate Brief Writers*, 3 Scribes J. Leg. Writing 19, 24 (1992).

Most writing seen by judges has a high word-to-meaning ratio: Many words are used to express a given amount of meaning. If your writing has a low word-to-meaning ratio—no wasted words, every word carrying weight—your work will be more persuasive simply because for the judge it solves a problem instead of creating one. You may have spent days writing a motion memo or brief, but the judge needs to be able to read it—and *completely understand it*—in minutes. To persuade, you will spend more time writing so the judge can spend less time reading.

Think about the other problems a judge might have with your memo or brief, and solve them, too, so that judges find your writing a pleasure. For example, the font should be easy to read, and the headings should look like genuine headings (and not like part of the text). A visually inviting document is more likely to be read with care. See Appendix H.

§27.7 Professionalism Persuades

Professionalism generates trust. Judges respect lawyers who hold themselves to high professional standards. One mark of professionalism is to produce memos and briefs that are sharply focused on the issue, carefully reasoned, thoroughly researched, precisely written, and diligently proofread, with careful attention to details.

Writing a Motion Memorandum

§28.1 Persuasive Writing in Trial Courts

A motion is a request that a court do something. If you move for summary judgment, for example, you're asking the court to issue a summary judgment in your client's favor. With your motion, you will submit a memo explaining why your client should be granted summary judgment. Your memo might be titled "Memorandum in Support of Defendant's Motion for Summary Judgment." (Most summary judgment motions are made by defendants.) Your adversary will submit an opposing memo, perhaps titled "Plaintiff's Memorandum in Opposition to Defendant's Motion for Summary Judgment." Similar documents might be called trial memoranda or trial briefs.

The judge (and the judge's law clerk) may look at a memorandum more than once. The judge may read some of the memorandum in preparation for a hearing or oral argument on the motion, a second time while deciding the motion, and a third time while writing an opinion. You cannot assume that a memorandum will be read from front to back or at one sitting.

And you cannot assume that a long memorandum will be read in its entirety. Most trial court judges are overwhelmed by their workload and have very little time—perhaps 15 minutes or less—to spend on your memo. If you don't make your point very quickly and well, you risk losing your audience.

§28.2 Motion Memo Format

The format of a motion memo (or a trial memorandum or trial brief) is often more flexible than that of an office memo or an appellate brief. Few court rules govern the content of motion memos, and customs among lawyers differ from one jurisdiction to the next. A typical motion memo might include these:

1. a cover page (or, if there is no cover page, a caption at the top of the first page)
2. a Preliminary Statement, also called an Introduction or a Summary
3. a Statement of the Case, also called Statement of Facts or, simply, Facts
4. an Argument, which may be broken up by headings
5. a Conclusion

See the motion memo in Appendix C.

The **cover page** includes a caption and title, which correspond to the memorandum heading at the beginning of an office memorandum. The caption identifies the court and the parties, specifying their procedural designations (plaintiff, defendant, etc.). In a criminal case, the prosecution is called, depending on the jurisdiction, "State," "Commonwealth," "People," or "United States," and no procedural designation follows those terms in the caption. (The prosecution is not a "plaintiff.") The title identifies the memorandum and the purpose of its submission (for example, "Memorandum in Opposition to Defendant's Motion to Dismiss").

The **Preliminary Statement**—or **Introduction** or **Summary**—briefly sets out the case's procedural posture by identifying the parties, to the extent necessary; explaining the nature of the litigation; and describing the motion before the court and the relief sought through the motion. If it can be done very concisely, the Preliminary Statement might also summarize the parties' contentions, emphasizing the writer's theory of the motion. The point is to tell the judge why the matter is before the court and to define the type of decision the judge is being asked to make. For example, a Preliminary Statement might begin:

> This motion seeks an order preliminarily enjoining the defendant from marketing its product, which infringes 19 separate patents held by the plaintiff. This memorandum explains how the plaintiff will prove its patent infringement claims and why the defendant has no defense to them.

The next few sentences can name the parties and supply other details needed to understand how this motion got before the court. It might seem illogical to summarize the theory before introducing the parties, but the two sentences quoted above will quickly get a judge's attention. The whole Preliminary Statement is often shorter than a page.

The **Statement of the Case** or **Statement of Facts** corresponds to the Facts in an office memorandum, but there are differences in substance and in drafting technique. Chapters 29 through 31 explain how to write a Statement of the Case.

The **Argument** corresponds to the Discussion in an office memorandum, but here again the goal is to persuade as well as to explain. The Argument is divided up by point headings and subheadings. Chapters 32 and 33 explain how to write an Argument.

In a motion memorandum, the **Conclusion** reminds the judge of what you want the court to do, together with a quick summary of your theory. The Conclusion should not be longer than one reasonably sized paragraph. A Conclusion will not persuade if it is cut to the bone. Compare the following:

Conclusion

For all these reasons, this court should preliminarily enjoin the defendant from marketing its Thimble Camera.

Conclusion

The defendant's Thimble Camera fits over the end of a finger. In the three weeks it has been on the market, the defendant has sold 170,000 Thimble Cameras. Each of them infringes 19 patents held by the plaintiff, nearly ruining sales of the plaintiff's cameras. To prevent irreparable harm that would drive the plaintiff out of business, this court should enjoin sales of the Thimble Camera.

The second example does a much better job of reminding the court, in just a few sentences, not only of what the writer wants but also of why it should be done.

§28.3 Writing the Memorandum

Lawyers differ about which part of a motion memorandum they draft first. But most lawyers modify their work habits somewhat from document to document, simply because a practice that works well in one instance might not work well in another.

Many lawyers start by working with the Statement of the Case. Telling a story in a persuasive way can be a productive place to start.

Some lawyers write the Argument first because that shows them what to do with the facts. Other lawyers might write the Argument and the Statement of the Case simultaneously. Some might outline the Statement of the Case while writing the Argument, or the reverse.

Some lawyers write the point headings and subheadings before starting to write the Argument. Others might write an outline of the Argument and gradually convert the outline into headings and subheadings.

There's no one "right" place to start writing. The best place is what works quickly for you.

The Conclusion is usually done last. The cover page can be done at any time.

§28.4 Handling the Procedural Posture

Because most of a legal education focuses on the substantive law of Torts, Contracts, and so on, you might tend to view issues in the abstract ("should the plaintiff win?"). But judges see issues in terms of the *procedural posture* in which the issues have been raised. The procedural posture is the procedural event—usually a motion—that places an issue before the court.

Each type of motion is governed by rules that dictate how the motion is to be decided. If you move for summary judgment, for example, your motion will be granted only if you satisfy the test for summary judgment. And the issues the judge will see are the elements of the test for summary judgment—whether there's a material dispute of fact and whether the plaintiff is entitled to judgment as a matter of law. Your arguments should be designed to satisfy that test, and the procedural posture also determines how you discuss the facts.

§28.4.1 Types of Procedural Postures

Trial court motions fall into four categories:

1. motions that challenge the quality of an adversary's allegations in a pleading;
2. other motions that challenge the manner in which the litigation began;
3. motions that challenge the quality of a party's evidence; and
4. case management motions.

Motions that challenge the quality of a party's allegations: In a civil action, a defendant can, before answering a complaint, move to dismiss it for failure to state a claim on which relief can be granted. You might already have studied this in the course on Civil Procedure, where it's called a Rule 12(b)(6) motion. Because this motion tests the sufficiency of allegations (and nothing more), the "facts" are limited to the allegations contained in the complaint. The question is not whether either party has proved anything. Instead, the court assumes—for the purpose of the motion only—that the factual allegations in the complaint can be proved, and the court then decides whether those allegations would amount to a claim. If the court concludes that they could not, it strikes the claim from the pleading. If the court strikes all the claims pleaded in a complaint, the court dismisses the entire complaint, and the litigation ends unless the plaintiff can serve and file an amended complaint with additional or reformulated allegations that would survive a motion to dismiss.

Because, at this stage, no evidence has been submitted, lawyers do not describe the "facts" alleged in the pleadings as events that actually happened. Until a court receives evidence later in the case, it has no idea whether the alleged "facts" happened, and the "facts" therefore are described purely as allegations:

> Although the plaintiff has alleged that the defendant struck him from behind with a stick, he has not alleged that the defendant intended to cause him injury.

In this procedural posture, you cannot accurately write the following:

> Although the defendant struck the plaintiff from behind with a stick, the defendant did not intend to cause the plaintiff injury.

We will find out later—after evidence has been produced—whether the defendant struck the plaintiff or intended to cause injury.

Other motions that challenge the manner in which the litigation began: A defendant might move to dismiss on the ground that the court lacks jurisdiction over the subject matter, or that it lacks personal jurisdiction over the defendant, or that venue is improper, or that the summons did not include all the information required, or that it was improperly served, or that somebody who should have been made a party has not been—all of which are defenses provided for in Rule 12(b) of the Federal Rules of Civil Procedure.

These motions are not limited to the contents of the complaint. In fact, the contents of the complaint might be irrelevant to the motion. If the defendant asserts that the summons was improperly served, for example, the court would hear testimony from the process server and from the defendant about how the summons was delivered to the defendant.

Motions that challenge the quality of a party's evidence: These include

- motions for summary judgment made *before* trial under Federal Rule 56 or a state equivalent;
- motions for judgment as a matter of law (also called motions for directed verdict) made *at* trial under Federal Rule 50(a) or a state equivalent; and
- renewed motions for judgment as a matter of law (also called motions for judgment notwithstanding the verdict) made *after* trial under Federal Rule 50(b) or a state equivalent.

All of these motions require the court to decide whether a party has carried a burden of production. If a party has the responsibility of carrying a burden of production, that party must produce enough evidence to allow a jury to decide the case. Each of these motions is decided according to the same logic. The motion should be granted if (1) there is no genuine issue of material fact because the party with the burden of production has failed to carry it and (2) under the law defining the claim and its defenses, the movant is entitled to a favorable judgment. The second element of this test incorporates the substantive law at issue. For example, if you move for summary judgment in a negligence case, the second element incorporates the relevant parts of the law of negligence.

Case management motions: These move the case along toward trial. Examples are motions for preliminary injunctions, discovery motions, and suppression motions in criminal cases.

§28.4.2 Researching to Find the Law Governing the Procedural Posture

First, identify the procedural posture you must deal with. What kind of motion was made? What has the court been asked to do?

Then find the *procedural* law that governs how the court decides the motion. You are looking for—

- the test for granting the motion, such as: "Summary judgment is appropriate if there is no genuine issue of material fact and if the moving party is entitled to judgment as a matter of law."
- rules on how the court must evaluate the record when deciding that particular motion, such as: "In deciding a motion for summary judgment, the court views the evidence in the light most favorable to the party opposing the motion."

You may find what you are looking for in court rules, statutes, or case law. Often you can find both the test and the evaluative rules in a judicial opinion, right after the court has recited the facts and just before the court begins the legal analysis. This is typical of what you might find there:

> Summary judgment is appropriate "if the pleadings, depositions, answers to interrogatories, and admissions on file, together with the affidavits, if any, show that there is no genuine issue as to any material fact and that the moving party is entitled to judgment as a matter of law." Fed. R. Civ. P. 56(c); *see also Celotex Corp. v. Catrett*, 477 U.S. 317, 322-23 (1986). "The moving party bears the initial burden of showing the absence of a genuine issue of material fact." *Plant v. Morton Int'l, Inc.*, 212 F.3d

929, 934 (6th Cir. 2000). Once the movant has satisfied its burden, the nonmoving party must produce evidence showing that a genuine issue remains. *Id.*[1]

This is from a Court of Appeals case. Because of the hierarchy of authority (Chapter 8), you will want to cite Rule 56(c) because it is the ultimate authority for the test. And you will want to read the Supreme Court case (*Celotex*) because it may be the ultimate interpretation of that test.

§28.4.3 Writing within the Procedural Posture

Because the procedural posture and the rules governing it control the way the judge will make the decision, you must show the judge how to decide within those procedural rules. How can you do that in writing?

First, remember that in a motion the core rule is *not* the rule of substantive law that provides rights, obligations, or remedies. The core rule is the one defining the procedural test.

Several procedural tests contain an element that incorporates the underlying substantive rules on which the litigation as a whole is based (claims, affirmative defenses, and so on). In the test for a summary judgment, that happens through the element requiring entitlement to judgment as a matter of law. In the test for a preliminary injunction, it is done through the element requiring likelihood of success on the merits. In these situations, the court makes a procedural decision, but part of that decision is substantive.

Third, organize your CREAC variations around the procedural test. If the procedural test incorporates a substantive test, the substantive test operates as a sub-rule. (See Chapter 18.)

Finally, do not go overboard in citing to authority for the procedural test. Most procedural tests are so commonly invoked that judges know them by heart. A conclusory explanation of the procedural test is usually sufficient.

---

[1] *In re Rodriguez*, 487 F.3d 1001, 1007 (6th Cir. 2007).

Telling the Client's Story

The Statement of the Case in a Motion Memo or Appellate Brief

§29.1 How a Statement of the Case Persuades

It may sound paradoxical, but most contentions of law are won or lost on the facts.

—*Justice Robert H. Jackson*

In a persuasive memorandum or brief, the judge learns about the facts in the Statement of the Case (also called a Statement of Facts or just Facts). In the Statement, you must include every fact that you mention elsewhere in your memo or brief. You must also include in the Statement all facts on which your adversary relies. This is the one place in the document where all the legally significant facts can be seen together in the context of your client's story. And you lose credibility if you omit unfavorable facts.

In the Statement, you are not allowed to argue, analyze law, draw factual inferences, or even characterize the facts. It is called a *Statement* of the Case because the facts are *stated* there and analyzed elsewhere. Inferences and characterizations of facts belong in the Argument. You are, however, allowed to report the inferences witnesses drew and the characterizations they made while testifying.

If you cannot argue in a Statement of the Case, how can you persuade there? Persuade by *telling the story in a way that emphasizes facts that support your theory while saying nothing that the adversary could reasonably claim to be inaccurate.* Consider the two examples below. Assume that the plaintiffs are suing a backcountry hiking guide for negligence after the guide led them into disaster. (Citations to the record have been deleted.)

On July 2, the plaintiffs asked in Stove Pipe Springs whether a backcountry guide might be available to lead them through certain parts of Death Valley. After some discussion, they hired the defendant to take them on a full-day hike the next day.

When they started out, the defendant carried a compass and map. Each plaintiff carried sunglasses, a large-brim hat, and a quart of water.

A climatologist testified about the climate in Death Valley. Occasionally, winter temperatures fall below freezing, but there is no water to freeze. Spring and fall temperatures approximate summer temperatures elsewhere. July is the hottest month, with an average high of about 116° and an average low of about 87°. The highest temperature ever recorded in Death Valley was 134°. (The highest recorded on earth was 136°.) Average annual rainfall is about 1½ inches, and the number of days on which precipitation falls in an average year is eight.

The climate in Death Valley is one of the hottest and driest known. The highest temperature recorded each summer reaches at least 120° and in many years at least 125°. The highest temperature recorded in Death Valley—134°—is also the second highest recorded on earth. (The highest was only two degrees hotter and was recorded in the Sahara desert.) Rainfall is only 1½ inches per year, the lowest in the Western Hemisphere, and in a few years no rain falls at all.

In the summer sun in Death Valley, a person can lose, on average, about four gallons of perspiration per day. After about two gallons are lost, that person can become delirious and, if the lost water is not quickly replaced, die of dehydration.

The defendant advertised himself as a professional and experienced backcountry guide. Relying on that, the plaintiffs hired him. He then took them into Death Valley for a full-day hike in July with a quart of water each.

After reading the example on the right, you can believe that this hike was madness and that the guide was responsible for it. But in early drafts, many beginners instinctively produce a Statement like the one on the left, which tells the story, but not in a compelling way. How does the example on the right persuade?

First, in the example on the right the writer selected a very few facts that would illustrate the theory: You can lose four gallons of water a day in such a place. After losing two gallons, you can become delirious, and if the water is not replaced, lives will be in danger. This was a full-day hike. The plaintiffs had a quart of water each. The defendant claimed to be a professional and experienced guide. As each of these facts is added, the logic of the theory unfolds.

Second, the example on the right is free of factual clutter—marginal facts, such as the temperatures in other months, that can obscure critical information. It focuses instead on the facts crucial to the persuasive story.

Finally, the example on the right gives the kind of vivid details that make a theory come alive—the delirium, for example, and the comparison to the Sahara desert.

But the example on the right *appears* to be nothing more than a description of the relevant facts. An adversary cannot reasonably challenge anything in it as untrue. Each fact is objectively verifiable in the record. And—most importantly—the writer never expressed any inferences from the evidence. *You drew all the inferences yourself.*

Sometimes a reader can think, "I can't tell whether this Statement was written by the plaintiff's lawyer or by the defendant's." That confusion is a sure sign that the Statement fails to persuade. Is it true of either of the Death Valley excerpts? If so, which one?

§29.2 The Record

The record might include any or all of the following:

- the pleadings
- evidence in the form of testimony, affidavits, and exhibits
- prior court orders, judicial opinions in the same case, and, on appeal, the judgment below

A Statement of the Case can describe *only* facts that are before the court through the record. Other facts must be ignored, a process called *limiting the Statement to the record.* But you can point to the *absence* from the record of a particular allegation or piece of evidence—"no witness identified the defendant," for example—if the absence shows that the opposing party has failed to satisfy a relevant legal test.

In the Statement, describe the facts in terms of the type of record where they can be found. If the record includes testimony, explain what the witnesses testified to. But if the "facts" are allegations in a pleading,[1] don't describe those allegations as events that actually happened. Section 28.4.1 explains how to describe this kind of record and why.

For every fact you mention, courts require that you provide a cite to a specific page or paragraph in the record—not only when you recite the fact in the

---

[1] Allegations are most often at issue when the pleading is challenged through a motion to dismiss for failure to state a claim. *See* Rule 12(b)(6) of the Federal Rules of Civil Procedure.

Statement of the Case, but also when you analyze it in the Argument.[2] This provides an easy method of checking what you say. Court rules aside, cites to the record have a persuasive effect of their own. Careful cites give the reader confidence that every fact on which you rely is fully supported in the record. Spotty or missing cites arouse a court's skepticism. Both the ALWD Citation Manual and the Bluebook explain how to cite to the record. In either book, look in the index for "record" or "records."

§29.3 Fact Ethics

It is unethical for a lawyer to "knowingly ... make a false statement of fact ... to a tribunal."[3] Even if it were not unethical, factual misrepresentation never fools a court and hurts only the misrepresenting lawyer and that lawyer's client. Misrepresentations are quickly spotted by opposing attorneys, and once a misrepresentation is pointed out to a court, the entire memorandum or brief will be treated with deep suspicion. And afterward the court will mistrust the misrepresenting lawyer.

---

[2] *See, e.g.,* Rules 28(a)(7) and (e) of the Federal Rules of Appellate Procedure.
[3] ABA Model Rules of Professional Conduct, Rule 3.3(a)(1).

Developing a Persuasive Story

When I was an attorney . . . , I realized after much trial and error that in a courtroom whoever tells the best story wins.
> —*John Quincy Adams (fictionally) in the movie* Amistad

§30.1 The Power of Stories

Robert McKee[1] has taught many of the best screenwriters in Hollywood how to write stories. So many screenwriters are in his debt that he was actually portrayed in that role in the movie *Adaptation*. Nicholas Cage plays a screenwriter who consults McKee about writer's block.

McKee also teaches business people how to persuade by telling stories. In a typical business situation, a young start-up company has developed a valuable idea, such as a drug that will prevent heart attacks, and the company needs investment bankers to lend money or buy stock so the company can finish the job and put the drug on the market. This situation resembles the one lawyers face when asking a court for relief: A person who wants something (a lawyer or a company's executives) tries to persuade a decision-maker (a judge or an investment banker) who has very rational criteria for making the decision (legal rules or the math that would predict whether an investment will make a profit).

---

[1] The quotes from McKee and the material about him are from *Storytelling that Moves People: A Conversation with Screenwriting Coach Robert McKee*, Harv. Bus. Rev., June 2003, at 51.

If the company's chief executive officer meets with the investment bankers and makes only a logical presentation with Powerpoint slides, based on statistics and sales projections, the "bankers would nod politely and stifle yawns while thinking of all the other companies better positioned" to bring this drug to market. But suppose the CEO tells a compelling story about how the company overcame obstacles to develop the drug, get it patented, and get regulatory approval, and now has to overcome one final hurdle—financing—to bring the drug to market. That causes "great suspense" and the possibility that "the story might not have a happy ending. The CEO has the bankers on the edges of their seats, and he says 'We won the race, we got the patent, we're poised to go public and save a quarter-million lives a year.' And the bankers just throw money at him."

Why? Nothing should be more rational than finance. If the numbers on the spreadsheets and Powerpoint slides show that this project will produce a profit without too much risk, the bankers should invest in it. But they won't unless they feel enthusiasm—unless they have been captured by the story. If you challenge McKee on this, he will say, "I know the storytelling method works, because after I consulted with a dozen corporations whose principals told exciting stories to Wall Street, they all got their money."

§30.2 How Stories Persuade

In a law school classroom, making the best logical argument is everything. That is as it should be. Legal argumentation is difficult to master, and legal education devotes a lot of effort to teaching students how to argue.

But in the real world, when you make purely logical arguments to decision-makers like judges, as Mckee points out, "they are arguing with you in their heads"—because logic and argument naturally arouse skepticism—and "if you do persuade them, you've done so only on an intellectual basis. That's not good enough because people are not inspired to act by reason alone." A story, he says, persuades "by uniting an idea with an emotion."

A story also persuades by letting the reader decide—on her own—to agree with you *before* you have asked her to agree. In an argument, you start by telling the reader what you want her to believe, and then you set out the steps of logic to prove that position. With a story, you tell what happened. If you develop a good story and if you tell it well, the reader's decision *comes from her* while reading the story, and she is therefore more committed to it. She's motivated to act for two reasons. First, she saw the point before you told her what it was. (If you tell her the point during the story, it isn't a story any more. It's an argument.) And second, stories move us in ways that logic can't.

Some litigation stories can be told only to juries. They have too much emotion, and if you were to tell those stories to judges, they would feel that you have insulted their sense of professionalism. A story told to a judge can succeed only by simultaneously addressing both the legal issues and the judge's basic human sense of right and wrong.

§30.3 Building the Story—Generally

In a Statement of the Case, the story should

1. "ignite action"—motivate by making a judge care enough to act
2. "communicate who you are"—actually, communicate who your side is by defining your client and supporting witnesses favorably
3. communicate who the other side is by defining the opposing party or the harmful witnesses or some combination of them unfavorably
4. "neutralize bad news" by explaining why facts that at first seem bad for your case should not be held against you (more about this in Chapter 29).[2]

These are the four goals in storytelling. Most stories have a simple, three-part structure:

1. The story starts in a state of equilibrium. Things might not be wonderful, but they are at least okay.

2. Bad things happen to disrupt the equilibrium. If you represent the plaintiff or the prosecution, the disruption is whatever the defendant did wrong. If you represent the defendant, the disruption is the lawsuit or prosecution itself, which puts the defendant under stress and at risk.

3. The protagonist struggles to restore equilibrium. Unless you're the prosecutor, the protagonist is probably your client. Because prosecutors have no client, they often cast the victim as a protagonist. If you represent a plaintiff, equilibrium could be restored by a judgment awarding your client an injunction or damages. If you represent the prosecution, equilibrium could be restored by convicting and sentencing the defendant. If you represent the defendant in either kind of case, equilibrium could be restored by dismissing the lawsuit or prosecution and freeing the defendant from the unjust burden of being an involuntary litigant in fear of losing.

Next time you watch a movie, ask yourself whether the plot in the movie has this structure—equilibrium, disturbance, struggle to restore equilibrium. Most do. Sometimes you will tell your client's story in exactly this sequence, and sometimes you will tell it differently.

---

[2] The quotes are from Stephen Denning, *Squirrel Inc.* 44, 47 (2004). See also Stephen Denning, *The Springboard: How Storytelling Ignites Action in Knowledge-Era Organizations* (2001).

This structure also works when the issue isn't who should win in the end, but instead some smaller part of the litigation. For example, if you represent a party resisting discovery before trial in a civil case, the equilibrium is your client's possessing private information that your client reasonably wants to keep secret. Disruption is the other side's demand for this information through interrogatories or a deposition. The struggle to restore equilibrium is your attempt to persuade the judge to grant a protective order that would prevent discovery of this information.

The judge is a hidden character in the third phase of the story, the struggle to restore equilibrium. Will the plaintiff win an injunction? Will the defendant win a dismissal? Will the party resisting discovery win a protective order? That is all up to the judge. If you build a good story and tell it well, the judge should *want* to restore equilibrium.

Once you have determined the inner structure of the story, the most important components are characters and imagery.

§30.4 Characters

Character cannot be described. You can't say, "My client is a really nice person, extremely conscientious and responsible." Nobody will believe you. You have to imply character by reciting things your client has or has not done. You'll do the same, if you can, with witnesses and with other parties.

> Take, for example, a rear-end collision that caused a lot of soft-tissue and nerve damage to the driver. At first glance, it seemed like a routine personal injury case. The at-fault driver was a business woman coming home from work who had been talking on her cell phone when the accident occurred. What really established her character was the fact that she continued talking during the accident and for another five minutes afterward [which defined her] as callous.[3]

§30.5 Imagery

> If you want to win a case, paint the Judge a *picture* and keep it simple.
> —*John W. Davis*

Imagery has a powerful effect in stories.

A truck runs off the highway, through a farmer's fence, and into the farmer's cow. The truck driver's insurance company wants to pay as little as possible for this cow, and the farmer, of course, wants more.

The insurance company's lawyer will tell a story in which the cow is "a unit of livestock" or "a farm asset," as though the issue is how much money the farmer

---

[3] Joel ben Izzy, *Character Development*, L.A. Daily J., Oct. 26, 1999, at 8.

should get to replace a machine-like object that consumes grass as fuel to produce milk and an occasional calf. This story will focus on numbers from the farmer's books that show the productivity of this object, its acquisition costs, depreciation, useful life remaining at the time of its destruction, etc. The insurance company's lawyer will use this story because the numbers show the cow to be an unexceptional object.

The farmer's lawyer looks for a different story to tell. "Tell me about the cow," she asks the farmer. "That wasn't just any cow," replies the farmer,

> That was Bessie! She was the only Guernsey cow left in this county. She didn't give that thin milk you get out of a Holstein that people buy in the grocery store. She gave the thickest, most flavorful milk you ever tasted. We didn't sell it to the dairy. They wouldn't pay a decent price for it anyway because dairies care about quantity, not quality. We drank it ourselves and made the best butter and cheese out of it. And Guernseys are smaller cows. They're friendly, like pets, and Bessie was part of our family.

Imagery you can "see" in your mind creates the persuasive weight of each of these stories. The farmer's lawyer wants us to see a big pair of eyes in a Guernsey head nudging the farmer with affection—a loss to the farmer's family that exceeds the loss of a grass-to-milk machine. The insurance company's lawyer, on the other hand, wants us to see the farmer's balance sheet, where a certain item of livestock is carried as an asset valued at a certain number of dollars.

If you develop an eye for revealing detail, your stories will much more quickly come to life as vivid and compelling. Vividness not only helps the reader remember the story, but it makes the story more believable. Imagery makes a story real.

Word choice is critical. The right words help the judge see the image.

§30.6 Finding the Story

Facts are not the story. They are the raw materials for the story.

A client sits in your office, describing in detail a problem that the client wants you to solve. The facts are these details. The client is not telling you a persuasive story. Clients usually don't know how to do that. They hire lawyers to do it for them. The client can tell you only facts—"I got this letter in the mail," "Smith told me the company was going bankrupt," "I can't pay my bills." In a law school writing assignment, you might get these details as part of your assignment.

Regardless of how you get the facts, they are not yet a story. The story is *hidden* in the facts. You have to find it there. Look for the equilibrium, the disturbance, and the struggle to restore equilibrium. Look for details that reveal character. Look for details that lend themselves to persuasive imagery. Assemble these into a story that fulfills the four purposes of storytelling—to motivate the judge to act, to communicate who your client and witnesses are, to communicate who the other side and their witnesses are, and to neutralize the unfavorable facts.

Try telling the story to a friend or relative whose intelligence and judgment you respect and who does not know the case you are working on. Telling the story orally helps you refine it and test it out before you start writing it. *Saying* it helps you understand it and how to improve it. Then ask how your friend or relative feels about the story. Does it motivate? Do the characters seem realistic? And so on.

§30.7 Two Last Questions

You've discovered the story. Now step back and ask yourself two questions.

First, can you summarize the essence of it persuasively in one or two sentences? If you can do that persuasively, those sentences are your theme (see §27.1). If you can't, either the story is too complicated or you haven't identified the core facts. If the story is too complicated, your reader will get lost. If you don't know the core facts, you won't be able to focus on them when you tell the story. You will need to focus on them at the very beginning of the Statement of the Case. The Statement of the Case should begin with a paragraph that summarizes these very facts (see Chapter 31).

Second, will the judge care? If not, the story won't work because it doesn't motivate.

Telling the Story Persuasively

§31.1 Selecting Facts to Tell the Story

Here's how to select the facts for the Statement of the Case:

Step 1: Identify the facts that show how the relevant legal tests have or have not been satisfied. Make a list of the facts that show either how you have satisfied the governing legal tests or how your adversary has not. Some lawyers do this by making an elements-facts-witness/evidence chart. For example, you might make the chart on the next page if you represent the plaintiff and must show that you have satisfied the test for negligence concerning an auto accident witnessed by two pedestrians, Smith and Jones, both of whom corroborate the plaintiff's story (π = plaintiff; Δ = defendant).

The chart helps you see what the dispute is all about. The elements of duty, injury, and proximate causation are easily satisfied. The real issue is breach. Three witnesses say the defendant ran the stop sign, and one says the defendant did not. The chart helps you realize that your factual theory should be that the two disinterested witnesses (Smith and Jones), as well as the plaintiff, testified that the defendant ran the stop sign, and that only the defendant testified that he stopped before entering the intersection. Why is that a good theory? The plaintiff and defendant testified consistently with their own interests. But Smith and Jones are credible because they are disinterested.

Elements, Facts, Witnesses/Evidence Chart

Elements	Satisfied?	Facts	Witnesses/Evidence
1. duty owed by Δ to π	yes	π driving on street that has no stoplight or stop sign—Δ driving on cross street with stop sign	testimony of π, Δ, Smith, and Jones
2. Δ's breach of that duty	probably yes	Δ drove through stop sign without stopping	testimony of π, Smith, and Jones
			contradicted only by Δ
3. injury to π	yes	π's medical injuries	testimony of π, doctor, and paramedic; x-rays
		damage to π's car	testimony of π, mechanic, Smith and Jones; photos
4. proximately caused by Δ's breach	yes (if Δ breached)	the front of Δ's car hit the side of π's car	testimony of police officer, mechanic, π, Smith, and Jones; photos of damaged cars

When you write the Statement of the Case, include everything in the Facts column together with the supporting proof from the Witnesses/Evidence column. For example, find the duty element in the chart. Look at the facts that satisfy that element and the witnesses who testified to those facts. Now you know what to say in the Statement of the Case concerning that element:

> All the witnesses, including the defendant, testified that the intersection did not have a traffic light; that the plaintiff entered the intersection from the north on State Street, where there was no stop sign; and that the defendant entered from the east on Maple Lane, where a stop sign required him to stop.

In the Statement, you will *not* mention the duty element or say it was satisfied. That is legal analysis, which you will do in the Argument. In the Statement, you will only mention the substantiating facts and whatever proved them.

The defendant's lawyer might make her own version of this chart to identify the facts and proof she will need to mention in the Statement.

If several tests are involved, you might make a chart for each test. For example, suppose the defendant in the auto accident case has pleaded the affirmative defense of comparative negligence. Now two tests are in the case. The plaintiff must prove that the defendant was negligent. And the defendant must prove that the plaintiff was comparatively negligent. The facts relevant to each test can be identified by making a chart for that test.

Step 2: Identify additional facts that help tell your client's story persuasively. Include facts that accomplish the storytelling goals explained in §28.3, such as facts that communicate who your client and witnesses are, as well as similar facts about the other side. Who is an innocent victim, who is predatory, who is careless, and so forth? Only by understanding what each fact *reveals* about people and events can you tell the client's story in a compelling way. Also include facts that a reader would need to understand the story, facts that hold the story together.

Step 3: Identify facts that hurt your case and facts on which your adversary will rely. If you do not include unfavorable facts, your Statement of the Case will lack credibility. Treat an unfavorable fact as an opportunity rather than a threat. If you include the unfavorable fact, you can try to neutralize it. The next section in this chapter explains how (see question 6 there). If you don't include the unfavorable fact in your Statement, you can't neutralize it—and it really will be a threat.

Step 4: Eliminate factual clutter. Too much information distracts from the story. Identify a witness by name only if the reader really needs to know. In the example above, the names of Smith and Jones are needed because they testify to so many different things, and because their testimony is crucial to the disputed element. But the doctor, paramedic, mechanic, and police officer can each be identified by their role instead ("the emergency room doctor who treated the plaintiff testified that . . .").

Specify dates, times, and places only if they are essential to the story or your theory. Specifics about them can be seductively concrete while you are writing. But to a reader they can also obscure what really happened. It isn't necessary to say that the witnesses agree that the accident occurred at 1:25 p.m., that an ambulance arrived at 1:40, that at 1:53 the ambulance delivered the plaintiff to the emergency room at Highview Memorial Hospital, or that at 1:55 a doctor there began to treat the plaintiff. Just say, "Thirty minutes after the accident, the plaintiff was treated by a hospital emergency room physician." Unless the hospital is being sued or its identity is otherwise significant, naming it gets in the way of telling the story. The exact times also get in the way.

§31.2 How to Test a Statement of the Case for Persuasiveness

While rewriting, ask yourself the following questions. They also appear on this book's website as a checklist, which you can print out.

1. Have you correctly decided which facts to include in the Statement? See the first section of this chapter.

2. Have you chosen a method of organization that tells the story persuasively? Set out the facts in a sequence that persuades and can easily be understood. Sometimes, the most effective sequence is chronological. But more often, a topical organization works better because you can use the way you organize the facts to imply the logical relationships between them. In some cases, you might try a topical organization that breaks into a chronological narrative where it's important for the reader to understand the sequence in which events happened. Use headings to break up the Statement and show how you have organized it.

3. Have you started with a punch? Begin the Statement with a short passage—one or two paragraphs—summarizing your most compelling facts and perhaps neutralizing the most unfavorable facts so that the judge understands the heart of your theory. This functions as an introduction to the story, although you don't need to call it that. For example:

> The defendant drove through a stop sign and into the plaintiff's car, putting him in the hospital for a week and disabling him from working for seven months. Every witness except the defendant testified that he entered the intersection without stopping. Although the plaintiff was driving an uninsured car with an expired registration, there was no evidence that these infractions caused the accident or contributed to the plaintiff's injuries.

Then, in the rest of the Statement, tell the story—describing in detail the facts you summarized at the beginning.

The opening passage is the most important part of the Statement. If written well, it puts the judge in a receptive frame of mind, tells the judge what facts to look for later; and creates a lasting impression. The opening passage is also one of the hardest parts of the Statement to write. But the extra time and effort are worth it. Never begin the Statement with neutral facts or unimportant facts. You can include the most unfavorable facts to neutralize them (as in the last sentence of the example above) but the introductory paragraphs are not always the best place to do this.

4. Have you reflected your theory throughout the Statement? Tightly focus the Statement on facts that advance your theory. If the Statement wanders aimlessly through the facts, the reader will not grasp your theory and may not even understand the story. Throughout the Statement, the reader should be aware of whom you represent from the way you tell the story. If the reader wonders about that, even for a paragraph or two, your Statement probably is unpersuasive. Every word should be selected to make the theory more clear. If you focus the Statement in this way, it can be surprisingly short.

5. Have you emphasized favorable facts? You can do that through organization. Readers tend to be most attentive at the beginning, least attentive in the middle, and attentive to a middling degree at the end. You can also describe the most favorable facts in detail while omitting marginal facts that would cloud the picture you want the reader to see. If a favorable fact is undisputed, you can point that out:

> Every witness, including the defendant, testified that the stop sign could easily be seen by a driver in the defendant's position (T. at 14, 35, 62, 68, 97, 132.)

You can also point to things that are missing from the record, where that helps you:

> No evidence suggested an emergency or other situation that might have justified disregarding a stop sign.

6. Have you neutralized unfavorable facts? The most effective method is to juxtapose an unfavorable fact with one or more favorable facts that show why the unfavorable fact should not hurt you. Juxtaposition is placing two things side by side. Effective juxtapositions often use "although" or "even though" contrasts. For example:

> Although the plaintiff was driving an uninsured car with an expired registration, there was no evidence that these infractions caused the accident or contributed to the plaintiff's injuries.

An unfavorable fact cannot be neutralized by tucking it away in an obscure part of the Statement. Hiding it will not make it go away.

7. Have you humanized your client? Be careful about how you refer to the parties. You could write "the plaintiff" and "the defendant" in a civil case or, in a criminal case, "the defendant" and "the State" (or "the People," "the Government," or "the Commonwealth"). More still can be conveyed by using some generic factual designation related to the issues: "the buyer" and "the seller" in a commercial dispute or "the employer" and "the employee" in a discrimination case. All those are clear enough for a reader to understand.

But how you refer to the parties can also have a persuasive effect. Many lawyers try to humanize their clients by referring to them by name while depersonalizing the opposing party ("the insurance company" or "the university").

Sometimes that works, and sometimes it doesn't. If the parties are both people, for example, it can be confusing and look unfair to call one party "Ms. Falco" and the other "the defendant."

In an appellate brief, a reader will be confused if you refer to the parties continually as "appellant" and "appellee." These designations identify only who lost in the court below. In many appellate courts, you are not allowed to use these designations inside a brief, although they appear on the cover page.[1]

Exercise I. Storytelling

Using a case you have read in another course, develop the facts of the case into a story. Do not change or embellish the facts. Stay strictly faithful to the *substance* of what you read in the case. But develop a story that would move a listener or reader to feel or think that one party or the other should win. Use the techniques described in this chapter and in Chapter 30. Then tell the story to another student and ask that student to suggest improvements.

Exercise II. Factual Inferences

You work at the local prosecutor's office and need to determine whether to charge a defendant with a basic crime (battery) or an aggravated version of that crime (domestic battery). Domestic battery is punished more severely. A local resident, Victor Tyne, was punched in the face by A.A. Bragenkrantz, who is the boyfriend of Victor's cousin, Anna Canelli. You already know you can charge battery. Can you also charge domestic battery (which would require Bragenkrantz to be a "household member" of Tyne's)?

Bragenkrantz and Canelli stayed overnight at Tyne's house every Sunday through Thursday during the summer so they could attend summer classes at the university. Bragenkrantz and Canelli slept on a fold-out futon in Tyne's spare bedroom. They each kept clothing in a drawer of a dresser in the spare bedroom. Bragenkrantz had registered for summer classes using Tyne's address as his home address in order to qualify for in-state tuition. Bragenkrantz and Canelli spent their weekends at Canelli's parents' home, about two hours drive away. Bragenkrantz has kept most of his possessions in a storage locker since his recent divorce.

Use the diagram below to determine whether Bragenkrantz is a member of Tyne's household. Add facts from the paragraph above this one if relevant inferences can be drawn from them. If a fact tends to show Bragenkrantz was a household member, add the inference you draw from that fact in the column on the far right. If a fact tends to show he was not a household member, add your inference in the column on the far right. If the fact could go either way, add inferences in both columns. (To help you get started, we've inserted a fact that could go either way.)

---

[1] *See, e.g.,* Rule 28(d) of the Federal Rules of Appellate Procedure.

Facts and Inferences

Inference?	Facts tending to show he was a household member	Facts that could go either way	Facts tending to show he was *not* a household member	Inference?
clothes indicate a permanent connection to the household		clothes in the drawer		not many clothes—so this is probably not his household

If the clothes in the drawer tended to show *only* that Bragenkrantz was a member of the household, the inference on the left would appear in the diagram, and no inference would appear on the right. If, on the other hand, the clothes tended to show only that he was *not* a household member, the only inference would be on the right. Both inferences appear here because the clothes can be used to support each of them.

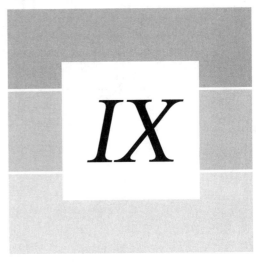

Making the Client's Arguments

The Argument in a Motion Memo or Appellate Brief

§32.1 Arguments

Monty Python's Flying Circus was a British comedy group that created television shows and movies. In their Argument Clinic sketch, a man walks into an office and announces that he'd like to have a good argument. A second man, sitting at a desk, contradicts everything the first man says. After several minutes of this, the first man complains that what's happening is not an argument. "Yes it is," replies the man at the desk. "An argument isn't just contradiction," says the first man. *"An argument is a connected series of statements intended to establish a proposition."* "No it isn't," contradicts the man at the desk, and things go downhill from there.

In a motion memo or appellate brief, an argument—"a connected series of statements intended to establish a proposition"—is expressed in the section of the document called the Argument. An Argument section often contains several arguments. Often, you need to establish several propositions. For example, you might have to show that

- the wording of a controlling statute supports your position,
- the courts have interpreted that statute consistently with its wording, and

● that interpretation is consistent with the reasons the legislature enacted the
statute (the policy behind the statute).

Each of these propositions must be supported by its own argument or arguments.
Sometimes it takes several arguments to prove a proposition.

Writing the Argument is a process of (1) identifying the propositions you
must prove, (2) developing persuasive arguments to support each of them, and
(3) finding the words to articulate those arguments.

§32.2 Understanding the Judicial Audience

Ask yourself, "What will make the court *want* to agree with me?"

Proving that you're right is not enough. Before starting law school, most of
us have already had a fair amount of experience justifying our own beliefs. But
that is not the same as getting inside another person's thinking and persuading
her or him to *want* to do something. To motivate, we need to learn not only a
new argument style, but also a new process of creating arguments. That is because
the process of justifying our own position is different from the process of
persuading others to agree with us. Here's how one student began to learn the
difference:

> [In a college course, Kathleen wrote a paper on the] question "Is American Sign
> language (ASL) a 'foreign language' for purposes of meeting the university's foreign
> language requirement?" Kathleen had taken two years of ASL at a community college.
> When she transferred to a four-year college, the chair of the foreign languages depart-
> ment at her new college would not allow her ASL proficiency to count for the foreign
> language requirement. ASL isn't a "language," the chair said summarily. "It's not
> equivalent to learning French, German, or Japanese."[1]

Is this really why the department chair rejects Kathleen's request? If yes, Kathleen
will be able to change his mind if she can prove that ASL is a real language,
equivalent to French, German, or Japanese. But if this is not really why he refuses,
it is only a rationalization for his decision—a statement he can use to justify saying
no. If it is only his rationalization, then his motivation—the true cause of the
refusal—remains hidden. If he is rationalizing, he might not even be aware of
his own motives. We'll see in a moment whether what he has stated is a rationalization or his true motivation.

---

[1] The quotes in this section are from John D. Ramage & John C. Bean, *Writing Arguments: A Rhetoric with
Readings* 10-11 (4th ed., Allyn & Bacon 1998).

Kathleen was not satisfied with what the department had said, and in a different college course she decided to write a paper on this issue.

> While doing research, she focused almost entirely on subject matter, searching for what linguists, brain neurologists, cognitive psychologists, and sociologists had said about the language of deaf people. Immersed in her subject matter, she was [not] concerned with her audience, whom she thought of primarily as her classmates and the professor [who taught the class in which she was writing the paper. They] were friendly to her views and interested in her experiences with the deaf community. She wrote a well-documented paper, citing several scholarly articles that made a good case to her classmates (and the professor) that ASL was indeed a distinct language.
>
> Proud of the big red A the professor had placed on her paper, Kathleen returned to the chair of the foreign language department with a new request to count ASL for her language requirement. The chair read her paper, congratulated her on her good writing, but said her argument was not persuasive. He disagreed with several of the linguists she cited and with the general definition of "language" that her paper assumed. He then gave her some additional (and to her fuzzy) reasons that the college would not accept ASL as a foreign language.

Kathleen has now addressed the concerns the department chair expressed before. But rather than reflect sympathetically on her argument, he nitpicks it and offers new reasons that he hadn't mentioned before. Something else—which he hasn't specified—must be motivating him. Because Kathleen has not discovered the real cause of his refusal, she inadvertently made an argument that only challenged his rationalizations instead of one that addressed his true motivations.

What has happened to Kathleen is a common experience when *an advocate justifies her position rather than trying to influence the person making the decision.* The decision-maker ignores the ideas that made sense while writing and sounded wonderful to colleagues. It makes no difference whether that person is a college administrator (as here) or a judge.

To persuade, figure out how a judge would react to the issues. Proving you're right and persuading the judge sound like the same thing, but they aren't. Think about the person you're trying to persuade and what would matter to *that person.*

It would be easy for Kathleen to dismiss the chair of the foreign language department as a numskull, but for two reasons she cannot and should not. First, she can't get around the fact that, like a judge, he has the power of decision. The only way she can get her ASL work to count for the foreign language requirement is to *change his mind.*

Second, he might have sincere concerns that deserve to be addressed. Does Kathleen know what they might be? At this point, she doesn't. Imagining only a friendly audience, she had not considered how a skeptical audience might react.

But that audience—the department chair—has the power to decide. The skeptical audience may seem frustrating, but if we want action, we have to *concentrate* on that audience.

How can Kathleen find out what the department chair's concerns might be? How can she address them?

> Spurred by what she considered the chair's too-easy dismissal of her argument, Kathleen decided . . . to write a second paper on ASL—but this time aiming it directly at the chair of foreign languages. [She] once again immersed herself in research, but this time it focused not on subject matter (whether ASL is a distinct language) but on audience. She researched the history of the foreign language requirement at her college and discovered some of the politics behind it (an old foreign language requirement had been dropped in the 1970's and reinstituted in the 1990's, partly—a math professor told her—to boost enrollments in foreign language courses). She also interviewed foreign language teachers to find out what they knew and didn't know about ASL. She discovered that many teachers [inaccurately] thought ASL was "easy to learn," so that accepting ASL would allow students a Mickey Mouse way to avoid the rigors of a real foreign language class. Additionally, she learned that foreign language teachers valued immersing students in a foreign culture; in fact, the foreign language requirement was part of her college's effort to create a multicultural curriculum.

Now Kathleen has begun to understand what's *really* going on. She has gained insights into what the department chair is worried about, and she can write arguments that might genuinely influence him.

> This new understanding of her target audience helped Kathleen totally reconceptualize her argument. She condensed and abridged her original paper. . . . She added sections showing the difficulty of learning ASL (to counter her audience's belief that learning ASL was easy), and literature (to show how ASL met the goals of multiculturalism), and showing that the number of transfer students with ASL credits would be negligibly small (to allay fears that accepting ASL would threaten enrollments in language classes). She ended her argument with an appeal to her college's public emphasis (declared boldly in its mission statement) on eradicating social injustice and reaching out to the oppressed. She described the isolation of deaf people in a world where almost no hearing people learn ASL and argued that the deaf community on her campus could be integrated more fully into campus life if more students could "talk" with them [in their own language]. Thus, the ideas included in her new argument, the reasons selected, the evidence used, the arrangement and tone all were determined by her primary focus on persuasion.

This second paper was good lawyering. She got inside the decision-maker's thinking and showed him that what he cared about would actually benefit from doing what she wanted.

Judges tend to be skeptical, but they know less about your case than you do. "Audience sense" is a writer's ability to understand the needs and outlook of a reader.

Judges are *skeptical.* Until you have proved a proposition, they do not believe it. The job simply requires that frame of mind. You earn a favorable decision only by proving—with persuasive arguments and good storytelling—that your client deserves it.

Judges *know less about your case than you do.* In most courts, judges are generalists rather than specialists. Although they know a great deal about rules of procedure (which they use constantly), they usually know much less about individual rules of substantive law (which come up less often). Thus, judges often do not know as much as you do about the law governing your case.

Judges want you to *teach* them your case. Think of an Argument as a *manual on how to make a particular decision.* If you show the court how the decision should be made, laying out all the steps of logic, you stand a much better chance of winning. If done in a respectful tone, this is not as presumptuous as you might think. A really good Argument shows the court how to write the judicial opinion that justifies a decision in your favor.

Truly persuasive writing speaks to each reader directly. How can you do that if you'll meet judges for the first time when you appear in court for oral argument—*after* you've written and submitted your trial court memo or appellate brief?

An experienced lawyer has usually developed an instinct for how judges generally make decisions and view their responsibilities. And to some extent, the lawyer can research an individual judge by reading the judge's past opinions and talking to other lawyers who have appeared before the judge in past cases.

As a student, you might write to an imagined judge. Think of someone whose intelligence, wisdom, and judgment you deeply respect. Write to persuade this person, as though she or he were a judge with the power to decide for or against your client. Do that in your first draft. In later drafts, continue to write to this person. Rework your rewriting to improve its capacity to persuade your imagined judge and to satisfy the professional standards expected in your legal writing course.

§32.3 How to Test Your Arguments for Effectiveness

While rewriting, ask yourself the following questions. They also appear on this book's website as a checklist, which you can print out.

1. Have you tried to persuade a judge rather than just prove that you're right? See the second section in this chapter.

2. Have you focused on what is most likely to persuade and summarized or cut out the rest? A boy opens the door to his bedroom and finds it filled to the ceiling with manure. With a shout of joy, he gets a shovel and starts cleaning out the room. Asked why he is so happy, the boy says, "With all that manure, there must be a pony in there somewhere." On its website, the North Dakota Supreme Court warns that judges "don't like to have to look for the pony."[2] Your best arguments may be in your writing *somewhere*, but judges don't have time to dig to find them.

Start by asking the question asked earlier in this chapter—"What will make the court want to agree with me?" Focus on your strongest contentions. Develop them fully. Leave out the weak ones. That creates a document that is more compact but explores more deeply the ideas that will most influence the court.

You might be tempted to throw in every good thing you can think of about your side of the case and every bad thing about your adversary's side. But don't hide the pony. Include only contentions that have a reasonable chance to persuade.

3. Have you organized persuasively? First, present the issues on which you are most likely to win. Within issues, make your strongest arguments first, and use your best authority first.

Early impressions tend to color how later material is read, and, like most people, a judge might read most carefully at the beginning. In addition, because judges are so busy, they expect the strongest material first. If they find themselves reading weak material early, they assume that nothing better follows and might stop reading altogether. Sometimes, however, the logic of the dispute requires that the strongest material be delayed to avoid confusing the court. Some arguments are simply hard to understand unless preceded by less punchy material. In these situations, weigh your need for clarity against your need to show merit from the start.

---

[2] http://www.ndcourts.gov/_court/filing/tips.htm (Appellate Practice Tips).

In the Argument, the CREAC formula can be varied for persuasive reasons. For example, lawyers sometimes summarize the most compelling facts for a given issue before stating the rule. Normally, the CREAC formula puts the facts almost entirely in rule application. But if the most compelling facts are summarized before the rule, a judge can read the legal analysis in a frame of mind aroused by the story. Those same compelling facts would appear again in rule application to show how they combine with the rule to produce the conclusion.

4. Does your discussion of each issue begin with a roadmap briefly summarizing your argument? Insert the roadmap at the beginning of your analysis of the issue. For example,

> The defendant is subject to the jurisdiction of this state. Courts in other states have generally held that a defendant who maintains an interactive website is subject to the jurisdiction of any state where residents can access the website and interact with it. The defendant maintains a website that meets this test. The plaintiff, a resident of this state, ordered a $15,000 motorcycle and paid for it with a credit card—all through the defendant's website.

This paragraph lays out a roadmap, showing the reader that in the following pages you will prove each of these propositions. To find where you prove a particular proposition, a reader can look at your point headings and subheadings (Chapter 33), which should reflect what you promise in the roadmap.

5. Have you given the court a precise statement of the rule or rules on which the case turns? In an appellate court, a judge may ask, "Counselor, what rule would you have us enforce?" The judge may be wondering how—if you win—the court should word the rule component of the CREAC formula when it writes the opinion. If the court will be making law, it wants to know exactly what rule you want it to adopt, and exactly how to phrase that rule for maximum clarity. In your brief, state the rule in the words that most precisely express it.

6. Have you handled authority well? Use the hierarchy of authority (Chapter 8) to choose the best authority. Focus on the cases and statutes that really matter. A judge does not have time to read an exhaustive explanation of every case you found. But if you cite and explain too little, the judge will not be persuaded. How do you steer a middle course between underciting and overciting and between underexplaining and overexplaining?

Predict the amount of citation and explanation a skeptical but busy judge would need. Then carefully study the available authorities. Place in a "major authority" category those that will probably *influence* the court and in a "peripheral" category those that are merely related to the issue. If you had to make the judge's decision, which authorities would be most likely to have an effect on you (including those adverse to your position)? The potentially influential authorities are the ones you must discuss. Peripheral authorities can be discarded unless they would fill holes in your argument not settled by the major authorities.

With case law, choose the few cases that most clearly make your argument. Concentrate on them and explain them thoroughly. Use other cases to settle odds and ends related to the issue. For a given issue, don't be afraid to spend 75% of your words on a few cases (for example, three) and 25% on the other cases (for example, ten). Taking a judge deeply into a compelling precedent can be very persuasive. Two, three, or four cases, thoroughly explained, can fill a judge with confidence in your argument. Thirty cases, each with no more than a sentence of explanation each, are background noise.

Your goal is to give the court confidence that you're right without trying the court's patience.

7.   Have you made persuasive policy arguments? Have you explained the benefits of a decision in your favor and the harm that would result from a decision in your adversary's favor? Explain how the parties have been affected by the dispute, how they would be affected by the relief you seek, or how in some other way what you seek is fundamentally fair. And go further to show that what you want will produce the best result in future cases as well, remembering that the decision could become precedent. If a court must choose between competing rules, for example, explain how the rule you urge is better than others. If you win, the decision will stand for that rule. Lawyers often introduce policy-based arguments with wording like the following:

> This court should reject the rule urged by the defendant because it would cause . . .

> Automobile rental companies [or some other category of litigants] should bear the risk of loss because . . .

> Not only is the order requested by the plaintiff not sanctioned by this state's case law, but such an order would violate public policy because . . .

To learn how to make policy arguments in appellate briefs, see Chapter 37.

8. Have you attacked your adversary's authority and arguments? Hiding from your weaknesses and your adversary's strengths does not work. Your odds of winning are greatly increased if you confront them openly and boldly. Is a statute or case inconsistent with your argument in a troubling way? Adverse authority will not go away just because you ignore it. The court will know about it, and if you fail to argue against it, the court may assume that you have no defense to it.

If the adverse authority is a statute, show that the provision was not intended to govern the controversy, or that it was intended to govern it but without harm to your client. Use the tools of statutory interpretation explained in Chapter 10.

If the adverse authority is precedent, distinguish it or use other techniques explained in Chapter 9. If none of those techniques will work, you might need to attack the precedent head-on, challenging its validity on the grounds that it is poorly reasoned or that changes in society or in public policy have made it unworkable. But in general, don't ask a court to overrule mandatory authority if you can win through distinguishing, reconciliation, or some other skill of precedent analysis. Judges simply prefer distinguishing and reconciling precedent to overruling it.

Make your *own* arguments first. You will win more easily if the court's dominant impression is that you deserve to win, rather than that your adversary deserves to lose. A defensive tone can undermine an otherwise worthwhile argument. And your theory will be more easily understood if you argue it before you attack opposing arguments.

How much should you emphasize an attack on an adverse argument or authority? Give it as much emphasis as necessary to convince the judge not to rule against you. Little treatment is necessary if the point is minor and if the argument or authority is easily refuted. Say more if the point is significant or if your counteranalysis is complex.

Students sometimes have difficulty writing the transition and thesis sentences that introduce attacks on opposing arguments. Begin your counterargument in the very sentence in which you introduce the other side's argument:

> The plaintiff misconstrues §401(d)(1). Four other circuits have already decided that §401(d)(1) provides only for compensatory damages and not, as the plaintiff contends, for punitive damages as well. *[Follow with an analysis of the circuit cases.]*

Argue affirmatively and not defensively. These are much weaker than the example above:

> The plaintiff has argued that §401(d)(1) provides for punitive damages, but . . .

> The plaintiff might argue that §401(d)(1) provides for punitive damages, but . . .

A dependent clause can be useful in thesis and transition sentences:

> Although the House Judiciary Committee report notes that its bill would have provided for punitive damages, §401(d)(1) more closely tracks the bill drafted in the Senate Judiciary Committee. Both that committee's report and the conference committee report flatly state that §401(d)(1) does not provide for punitive damages.

9. Will a judge be able to understand your Argument quickly and easily? Think about the judge's limited time and heavy caseload. Have you written the Argument so that a busy judge will not have to struggle to understand what you're trying to say?

§32.4 Argumentation Ethics

The law of professional ethics—which in nearly all states is the Model Rules of Professional Conduct—places limits on what you're permitted to do in argument.

First, and most importantly, you may not "knowingly make a false statement of fact or law" to a court.[3] Imagine what courts would be like if lawyers were free to lie to judges.

Second, a lawyer must inform a court of "legal authority in the *controlling jurisdiction* known to the lawyer to be *directly adverse* to the position of the [lawyer's] client and not disclosed by opposing counsel."[4] Imagine what courts would be like if lawyers were free to hide the law from judges. But you can inform the court of the adverse authority and at the same time try to neutralize it. To learn how, see question 8 in the preceding section.

Third, you may not advance a "frivolous" theory or argument, although you may make a "good faith argument for an extension, modification or reversal of existing law."[5] In a legal system like ours, where "the law is not always clear and never is static," the rules of ethics permit a lawyer to advance theories and arguments that take advantage "of the law's ambiguities and potential for change."[6] But a frivolous theory or argument—one that stands little chance of being adopted by a court—is unfair to courts and to opposing parties because it wastes their time, effort, and resources.

---

[3] Model Rules of Professional Conduct, Rule 3.3(a)(1).
[4] Model Rules of Professional Conduct, Rule 3.3(a)(2) (emphasis added).
[5] Model Rules of Professional Conduct, Rule 3.1. See also Rule 11 of the Federal Rules of Civil Procedure and Rule 38 of the Federal Rules of Appellate Procedure. Both are printed in the rules supplement used in most Civil Procedure courses.
[6] Drafters' Comment to Model Rules of Professional Conduct, Rule 3.1.

Point Headings and Subheadings

No, for three reasons:

    A. I'm not that lucky,

    2. We have smoke detectors, and

    D. We live on the most boring street in the United States of America.

—*Buzz McCallister in* Home Alone

§33.1 What Point Headings Do

How do you know what you're about to read right now? The title of the book and the chapter heading give a general idea about the broad topic, and a short section heading like "What Point Headings Do" provides a specific idea of what you will read about in this and the next three paragraphs. Written Arguments use a similar structure. Point headings and subheadings are short guides to readers about what they can expect to read.

A point is an independent unit within your Argument. Your reader will be better able to understand a lengthy Argument if it is divided into logical parts. The points could be several alternative ways in which your client could win. For example, where your client wants to escape contractual obligations, you may argue that the contract is void for lack of capacity or lack of consideration. Either point could win the case for your client. Or, the points might be a list of things that must be proved for you to win—for example, the elements listed in a criminal statute that must be proven by the prosecutor.

For clarity, an Argument should strike a balance between too many and too few points. Too many separate points can make it challenging for a reader to connect the points into a whole. But bunching up a complex argument into only one point can also make your reader work too hard. Crafting point headings can be a good way to check for an effective structure. If two point headings resemble each other, you might have only one point to make. And if a point heading seems impossibly complicated, you might be tackling too much at once and might need to divide the point into two or more points.

Point headings should help to persuade your reader. The point heading plants an idea that you hope the reader will agree with after reading that section of the Argument. Find a middle ground between the neutral, which does nothing for your client, and the too aggressive, which could cause your Argument to lose credibility. The middle ground is a *forceful reasonableness* that shows why the judge should have confidence in your Argument.

§33.2 What Each Point Heading Should Contain

An effective point heading includes all of the following:

- at least one essential fact
- an allusion to a legal issue
- the conclusion you want the court to draw or the action you want it to take

Choosing an essential fact for a point heading is like finding the determinative facts in cases that you read for class. What fact makes your case different or hard to decide? What fact makes your side a winner in this part of your Argument?

Describing the legal question resembles finding and describing issues in the cases you read for other courses. What kind of legal question is involved or what element is required?

Identify the conclusion you want the court to reach or the action you want it to take. For example:

conclusion:	**The Complaint Is Legally Insufficient Because It Fails to Allege Any Facts That Could Be Construed as an Offer.**
action:	**The Complaint Should Be Dismissed Because It Fails to Allege Any Facts That Could Be Construed as an Offer.**

Identical arguments could follow these headings. The only difference is that the first one specifically asks the court to draw a conclusion (legal insufficiency) while implying the action the writer wants (dismissal), while the second does the reverse, specifying the action and implying the conclusion.

Don't go too far in defining the action you want. Sometimes a point heading can ask for all the relief your client desires in a motion or appeal. If this section of your Argument, standing alone, will justify granting or denying a motion or reversing a trial court decision, go ahead and ask for one of those things. But often the point you are working on will be just one of several building blocks in your Argument and not enough by itself to win the motion or appeal. For a point like this, the heading should be more limited. For example, "The Defendant's statement was made at a police substation, a custodial situation, satisfying the first requirement for suppression of the evidence."

§33.3 Subheadings

Unless a point in your Argument is short, you can make things clear for the reader by subdividing it with subheadings. Each subheading can identify a step in logic necessary to support the proposition in the point heading. Under the subheading, you can develop that step in logic. But don't go overboard with subheadings. A lot of subheadings with only two or three paragraphs under each makes your reasoning look thin.

§33.4 How to Test Your Point Headings for Effectiveness

While rewriting, ask yourself the following questions. They also appear on this book's website as a checklist, which you can print out.

1. Do your headings and subheadings lay out a complete and persuasive outline of your Argument? Many judges read the point headings *before reading any other part* of a memo or brief. In an appellate brief, a judge can read them collected in the brief's table of contents. In a motion memo, a judge can read the headings by leafing through the Argument. With good headings, you can introduce and outline your theory. Some lawyers draft the headings before writing the Argument. Others write the headings and the Argument together. When you compile the headings and subheadings in a table of contents, you may find that you have to redraft them because only then might you discover gaps or inconsistencies not apparent when the headings are scattered around in the Argument.

2. Do you have an appropriate number of point headings and subheadings—neither too many nor too few? Too many headings overwhelm the reader. Too few don't give the reader an accurate outline of your Argument. See the definition of a point at the beginning of this chapter.

3. Is each heading or subheading a single sentence that a reader can immediately understand? Readers will ignore headings that are too big and dense. Be brief. Because you have to include an essential fact, a legal question and a request for relief, a point heading can swell up so much that it's unreadable—unless you find the most concise wording available. A heading doesn't *make* an argument. It *introduces* the reader to what you will say next. A heading that is too long can discourage your audience from reading either the heading itself or the text that follows. An effective point heading is short and complete, priming your reader for persuasion.

4. Does each point heading identify the conclusion or action you want? In point headings, don't leave a judge wondering, "What do you want me to do or decide?" (See the second section in this chapter). In point headings, this is required. In subheadings, it isn't, although you might do it anyway.

5. Does each point heading allude to the legal issue? You don't need to state the issue completely in a point heading. Often it's enough to allude to the legal concept involved. But be specific. If this part of your argument discusses only whether an offer was made, use the word "offer" rather than a broader term like "contract formation," which could include other legal concepts. In point headings, this is required. In subheadings, it isn't, although you might do it anyway.

6. Does each point heading include at least one essential fact? See the second section of this chapter. In point headings, this is required. In subheadings, it isn't, although you might do it anyway.

7. Are your headings appropriately numbered? Use Roman numerals, letters, and numbers as you would in a formal outline. If you have only one point, do not give its heading a number. Never use only one subheading under a point heading. If you find yourself with a subheading "A" but no "B," look again at how you have organized that point. You can either come up with at least two subheadings for the point, or if the point is short enough, you can eliminate subheadings there.

8. Are your headings appropriately typeset? Traditionally, lawyers have used all capital letters for point headings. Decades ago, when people wrote on typewriters, all-capping was the only way to make a heading stand out. Today, many lawyers still all-cap point headings. Many others use **bold** print instead of all-caps. Similarly, subheadings were once underlined because typewriters could not emphasize them in any other way. Today, lawyers either use *italics* or underlining for subheadings. When headings and subheadings appear in a table of contents, however, they are not italicized or bolded, although the point headings might be all-capped if they were all-capped in the Argument.

In subheadings, and in headings that are not all-capped, capitalize the first letter of each significant word. Always single space point headings. See Appendix H.

Exercise I. *Hamdan v. Rumsfeld* and *Bush v. Gore*

Below are point headings from two Supreme Court briefs, as they appeared in the table of contents. Did the brief-writers make the right choices in balancing completeness against brevity? Would these point headings have helped to persuade you if you were on the court?

First, from a brief in *Hamdan v. Rumsfeld*[1]:

I. The Detainee Act Does Not Strip the Court of Jurisdiction Over This Case

    A. *Congress Must Use Specific and Unambiguous Language to Effect a Repeal of Federal Court Jurisdiction Over Pending Claims.*

    B. *The Language of the Act Shows That Its Jurisdiction-Stripping Provisions do not Apply to Pending Claims.*

    C. *The Legislative History Confirms That the Jurisdiction-Stripping Provisions do not Apply to Pending Claims.*

    D. *Any Uncertainty About the Application of the Jurisdiction-Stripping Provisions Should Be Resolved Against Applying Them to Pending Claims.*

II. If the Detainee Act Divests the Court of Jurisdiction Over This Case, the Act Violates the Suspension Clause and Is Unconstitutional.

Second, from the petitioner's brief in *Bush v. Gore*[2]:

I. The Decision of the Florida Supreme Court Violates Article II of the Constitution.

    A. *The Decision Below Overrides Numerous Provisions of Florida Election Law.*

    B. *Article II Precludes the Florida Supreme Court's Exercise of Jurisdiction.*

    C. *The Florida Supreme Court's Decision Is Improperly Predicated on Its Now-Vacated Opinion of November 21, Perpetuating Its Article II Errors.*

---

[1] The entire brief is at 2006 WL 53983 (U.S.), and the Court's decision is at 126 S. Ct. 2749.
[2] The entire brief is at 2000 WL 1810102 (U.S.), and the Court's decision is at 121 S. Ct. 525.

   II. **The Florida Supreme Court's Decision Conflicts with 3 U.S.C. §5.**

   III. **The Florida Supreme Court's Decision Violates Equal Protection and Due Process Guarantees.**

     A. Equal Protection.

     B. Due Process.

Exercise II. Creating a Point Heading

For a memo or brief that your teacher has assigned, pick out one point that you have written about or will be writing about. Before writing the heading for that point, identify words or phrases for the following chart:

_____

essential facts

_____

key legal issue

_____

relief requested

_____

supermarket tabloid headline for this point
(think short & dramatic, like "Baby Hijacks Commuter Train!")

Now shuffle and combine these words and phrases in several different orders to see which produces the best point heading. (If in the future you find it hard to write a point heading, this method might be a good way to start.)

Appellate Briefs and Oral Argument

Appellate Practice

§34.1 Introduction to Appeals

A *judgment* (or, in equity, a *decree*) is the document through which a court terminates a lawsuit and determines the parties' rights and obligations. The judgment might award damages to one party or grant an injunction to the other. An *order*, on the other hand, is a court's command during the lawsuit that something be done or not be done while the litigation is still in progress. Usually, an appeal is from a judgment, although sometimes it is from an order.

The appellate process performs two functions. One is correcting errors made by trial courts. The other is making new law and clarifying existing law through the precedents created by appellate decisions. A lower appellate court tends to view its job largely as error correction, although it necessarily engages in some law formation and clarification because appellate decisions are precedents. Higher appellate courts, on the other hand, generally view their work primarily as making and clarifying law.

The party who appeals will be called the *appellant* or the *petitioner*, and the opposing party will be called the *appellee* or *respondent*, depending on local court rules and the type of appeal. Before writing a brief, check the court's rules for the terms appropriate to your type of appeal. If you cannot find the answer, see how the parties are referred to in a reported case in the same court that *procedurally* resembles your own.

§34.2 The Roles of the Brief and the Oral Argument

The brief and oral argument perform different functions. Each is crucial, but in a different way.

In a brief, you can tell the client's story and make the client's arguments in persuasive detail. A successful brief not only persuades the judge that your client should win, but it can also be used as a manual explaining to the judge how to make the decision and how to justify it in an opinion. A judge may use the brief when preparing for oral argument, deciding whether to reverse or affirm, preparing for the conference with other judges, and writing the opinion.

The oral argument can do two things better than the brief: First, in oral argument you can more immediately motivate the court by focusing on the most important ideas—the few facts, rules, and policies—that most make your case compelling. Second, in oral argument you can try to discover, through the bench's questions, each judge's doubts. And, on the spot, you can explain exactly why those doubts should not prevent a ruling in your favor. Oral argument, in fact, is your only opportunity to learn directly from the judges the problems they have with your arguments. But oral argument also has a significant disadvantage: It lasts only a few minutes, and memories of it can fade. The brief, on the other hand, has permanence. It is always among the judge's working materials, and it "speaks from the time it is filed and continues through oral argument, conference, and opinion writing."[1]

There's another important difference between the brief and oral argument. Detail is communicated best in writing, which can be studied. But the spontaneity of conversation during oral argument encourages dialogue and lends itself to the broad sweep of underlying ideas.

§34.3 How Judges Read Appellate Briefs

In a single month, an appellate judge might hear oral arguments and confer with colleagues on several dozen appeals. For each appeal, the judge will have to read at least two briefs or, in multiparty cases or public-interest cases, perhaps a half-dozen briefs or more, together with portions of the record. The judge will have to write majority opinions in a proportion of the appeals not summarily disposed of. On a five-judge court, for example, each judge is assigned one-fifth of the majority opinions. In addition, the judge may feel obligated to write several concurring or dissenting opinions. The judge will also have to read opinions drafted by other judges and at times will write memoranda to colleagues suggesting changes in those opinions. And the judge will spend a fair amount of time reading some of the cases and statutes cited in all these briefs and draft opinions.

With all this work, the typical appellate judge would find it a luxury to spend as much as an hour reading the average brief. The time available is often no more than half an hour. That's why briefs, although large, must be written carefully to persuade with the least possible time and effort from the reader.

---

[1] Herbert Funk Goodrich, *A Case on Appeal—A Judge's View*, in *A Case on Appeal* 10-1 (ALI-ABA 1967).

How does a judge read a brief? The answer may vary considerably from judge to judge, but the following is not unusual:

> Usually I first read both parties' statements of the questions presented; then I read the appellant's statement of the general nature of the controversy. Then I look at his outline of argument to see what points he makes. Then I look at the appellee's outline of argument to see what he is going to do in reply. . . . Then I read the appellant's statement of the facts and the appellee's statement. Thereafter I examine the two briefs one point at a time, first the appellant's and then the appellee's, on the first point; then both briefs on the second point, etc. If the point is an obvious one, or if one side or the other seems to be wholly without strength on it, I do not spend too much time on that point in my first study. On the really contested points I study both sides, read the cases, and, if facts are critical check the record references.[2]

Other judges might read the parts of a brief in a different sequence—perhaps reading the point headings before anything else—and a given judge might vary the sequence from case to case. But several things are true regardless of the judge's work habits.

First, you must write for several different readers. Depending on the court, an appeal might be decided by anywhere from three to nine judges. And briefs are also read by law clerks or research attorneys who assist judges by studying the briefs and recommending decisions.

Second, briefs—like memos—are not necessarily read from beginning to end at a single sitting. They are read in chunks, at different times, depending on the needs of the reader. You probably read an appliance or automobile owner's manual in pretty much the same way, and a good brief is a manual for making a decision.

Finally, a brief is read for different reasons at different times, depending on who is reading and when. The judges will read or at least scan it in preparation for oral argument. Afterward, they will read the brief again to decide how to vote. One judge will be assigned to write the court's opinion, and that judge will reread various portions of the brief several times, looking for the detail needed to justify and explain the decision. And all along the way, the judges will be assisted by law clerks who check the details of the brief while the judges focus on the broader principles. Each segment of the brief must be written to satisfy all of these purposes.

---

[2] E. Barrett Prettyman, *Some Observations Concerning Appellate Advocacy*, 39 Va. L. Rev. 285, 296 (1953).

Writing the Appellate Brief

§35.1 Appellate Brief Format

Although rules on format differ from court to court, the required structure would commonly include the following. Some courts require additional material, such as a statement specifying how the court acquired jurisdiction over the appeal in question.

1. a cover page
2. a Table of Contents (sometimes called an Index)
3. a Table of Authorities
4. the words of a constitutional provision, statute, administrative regulation, or court rule—if the appeal rests on interpreting those words
5. a Preliminary Statement (also called Proceedings Below or Nature of the Proceedings)
6. a Question Presented or Questions Presented (also called Statement of the Issues)
7. a Statement of the Case
8. a Summary of Argument
9. an Argument, broken up with point headings and subheadings
10. a Conclusion

See the briefs in Appendices D and E.

The **cover page** includes the caption, followed by the document's title—such as "BRIEF FOR APPELLANT"—and the name, address, and telephone number of the lawyer submitting the brief. The caption includes the name of the appellate court, the appellate court's docket number, and the names of the parties and their procedural designations (appellant, appellee, etc.) in the appellate court. The cover page does not have a page number.

The **Table of Contents** begins on the page after the cover page. It lists all of the components of the brief (except the cover page and the Table of Contents itself); reproduces the point headings and subheadings from the Argument; and sets out the page on which each component, point, or subpoint begins.

The **Table of Authorities** appears on the first page after the Table of Contents. It lists the cases, statutes, and other authorities cited in the Argument together with every page number in the brief where each listed authority is cited.

The **Constitutional Provisions, Statutes, Regulations, and Court Rules Involved** specifies any enacted law that's crucial to the appeal and quotes the section at issue. A provision is crucial to the appeal if the parties disagree about its meaning and *if the court cannot dispose of the appeal without resolving the disagreement.* A court rule that merely provides for the type of motion made below is not critical to the appeal unless the parties disagree about the rule's meaning and the appellate court has been asked to resolve the disagreement. Phrase the heading of this section of the brief to fit its content. If the First Amendment—and nothing else—is at issue, the heading would read "Constitutional Provision Involved" with no mention of statutes, regulations, or court rules.

The **Preliminary Statement** briefly sets out the appeal's procedural posture by explaining who the parties are, listing the relevant procedural events, and describing the judgment or order appealed from. (If a party is a government or a large, well-known organization, you don't need to explain who that party is.) The Preliminary Statement can also describe the reasoning of the court below and identify the grounds on which it is challenged on appeal. The Preliminary Statement should tell the court why the appeal is before it and specify the type of decision you want the court to make. That can usually be done in less than a page. Many lawyers add a paragraph summarizing their own arguments.

This portion of the brief goes by different names in different courts. Where it is not titled "Preliminary Statement," the heading might read "Proceedings Below," "Nature of the Proceedings," or the like. In some courts, the Preliminary Statement is called the "Statement of the Case" (and the client's story is told elsewhere in the brief in a "Statement of Facts").

A persuasive **Question Presented** is explained in Chapter 38.

The **Statement of the Case** is explained in Chapters 29 through 31.

A **Summary of the Argument** is what its name implies. The point headings and subheadings, as they appear in the Table of Contents, *outline* the Argument. The Summary, on the other hand, *condenses* the Argument into a few paragraphs—perhaps one paragraph per issue—with more explanation than will fit into headings. The Summary should not merely repeat the point headings.

The **Argument** is explained in Chapters 32 and 33.

Although some lawyers use the **Conclusion** to reargue and resummarize the theory of the appeal, it's better to limit the conclusion to a one- or two-sentence reiteration of the relief you want together with the ground on which that relief would be based. For example:

> For all the foregoing reasons, the Circuit Court's order dismissing the complaint should be affirmed because the complaint does not state a cause of action.

The primary purpose of the Conclusion is to remind the judges of exactly what you want them to do.

Every court has rules governing the contents of briefs and other submitted documents. The rules are designed to make briefs easier for judges to use, and judges understandably become exasperated when the rules are ignored. Egregious violations of court rules can result in the court's striking the brief, in financial penalties imposed on the lawyer, and even in dismissal of the appeal.

§35.2 Three Brief-Writing Suggestions

1. Start writing before you finish the research: "I can't start writing yet," you might say. "I haven't found *all* the cases." But waiting until you find all the cases can feed procrastination. And if you don't start writing, you won't know what kind of cases you should be looking for. Researching like a vacuum cleaner is inefficient. Research takes less time and effort if you know what you're looking for. A good way to find out what you should be looking for is to start writing before you finish the research. Start writing as soon as you have enough research to know roughly what your theory will be. Because writing and thinking are inseparable, the act of writing will show you where you need more authority. When you go back into research, you will focus on exactly what you have discovered you need.

2. Start practicing oral argument while you're writing the brief: It might seem illogical to spend time on oral argument when you're up against a closer deadline with the brief. But many students discover that when they *talk* about a complicated subject, they say surprisingly interesting and perceptive things, because talking helps them understand more deeply. Many people learn not just by reading and listening, but also by talking and doing. The best reason for practicing oral argument early is to help you write a better brief.

Suppose you disregard this advice. You submit your final draft brief, rest for a few days, and then start developing an oral argument. As you practice, you come up with some terrific wording and wish you could put it in the brief—but by then it's too late.

3. Think of brief-writing as a collection of small tasks—rather than as one huge task: A huge task can be intimidating. But a lot of small tasks can be organized and then done one by one. "The secret to good brief writing is to write small pieces."[1] You have not been given one big assignment. You have been given several smaller ones—a Question Presented, a Statement of the Case, and so on. You can write all these things separately—as separate word processing files, if you prefer—and then stitch them together into a single document. Even the Argument can become two or more smaller jobs. If you have two points, writing each of them is a separate task. But be careful to coordinate all these smaller tasks, so that the eventual brief becomes coherent and internally consistent.

§35.3 What Part of the Brief to Write First

Just as a judge does not read a brief from beginning to end, neither does a lawyer write it that way. The Table of Contents and Table of Authorities are always done last (see the last section in this chapter for why). The order in which the other parts are written differs from lawyer to lawyer and from appeal to appeal because one lawyer's work habits are not necessarily effective for someone else and because an effective lawyer adapts to the individual task at hand. Eventually, you will settle into a range of work habits that work for you. Your first brief is an opportunity to begin to understand yourself in that way.

To help you start, consider two very different methods of writing a brief.

Sequence in Which a First Draft Might Be Written

Model I	Model II
1. point headings	1. Questions Presented
2. Argument	2. Statement of the Case
3. Statement of the Case	3. point headings
4. Questions Presented	4. Argument
5. rest of brief	5. rest of brief

---

[1] John T. Graubatz & Taylor Mattis, *The Moot Court Book: A Student Guide to Appellate Advocacy* 41 (3d ed. 1994).

A lawyer who uses Model I writes point headings and subheadings first as a way of outlining the Argument. This lawyer might draft the Statement of the Case after writing the Argument on the ground that writing the Argument reveals which facts have the most legal significance. The Questions Presented would be written afterward because the lawyer identifies the most essential facts—the ones recited in the Questions—while working out the Argument and the Statement of the Case.

But a lawyer using Model II would begin the first draft by writing the Questions Presented in the belief that the other parts of the brief will be more focused if the issues are first precisely defined. A lawyer who uses this model writes the Statement of the Case next, using it to work out the details of the theory of the appeal (which the Model I lawyer does while writing the Argument). Both lawyers draft the point headings before the Argument because the Argument is easier to write in segments (which the headings create).

A lawyer with flexible work habits might use Model I in an appeal where the authority and legal issues are difficult and complex and Model II in a more fact-sensitive appeal. Some lawyers write the Question Presented and the Statement of the Case (and sometimes even the Argument) simultaneously.

§35.4 The Last Step: Creating the Table of Contents and the Table of Authorities

Why you should create the Tables last: For pagination purposes, a brief is broken down into two parts. The two Tables (sometimes called the "front matter") are paginated together in lowercase roman numerals ("i," "ii," "iii," and so on). The rest of the brief (the "body") is paginated separately in arabic numbers, beginning with "1," on the first page immediately following the Tables.

This might seem odd. But it has a very practical purpose. Because the Tables must include page references to the body, *any* change in the body—even a change of only a few words—can alter the page breaks and require changes in the Tables. And because you cannot know how many pages the Tables will occupy until you are ready to print them, the body must begin on page 1. The only efficient solution is to use two separate paginations: lowercase roman numbers for the Tables and arabic numbers for the body. (The same thing is done for the same reasons in your textbooks, including this one.)

What the Table of Authorities should look like: Although the Table of Contents is easy to visualize and put together, the Table of Authorities is more complicated. In the Table of Authorities, list a complete cite for every authority, with an asterisk to the left of those authorities that form the core of your theory. In a footnote, identify those citations as "authorities chiefly relied on" or similar words to the same effect.

The Table of Authorities is broken down into at least three sections headed "Cases," "Statutes," and "Other Authorities." List cases in alphabetical order. If constitutional provisions, court rules, administrative regulations, or legislative histories are cited in the brief, you can add one or more extra sections for them. Regulations, court rules, and legislative histories might be grouped under one heading. Sometimes legislative histories are included with statutes instead. Some lawyers include constitutional provisions with statutes. Others put them in a separate section. The heading should reflect where they are. "Other Authorities" is reserved for secondary authorities, such as restatements, treatises, and law review articles (which are listed there in that order).

Handling Standards of Review

Appellate judges cannot reverse merely because they don't like what the lower court did. Instead, they can reverse only when the relevant standard of review lets them do so. The standard of review controls the appellate court's decision. For that reason, appellate judges become annoyed when lawyers write and speak as though standards of review don't exist.

§36.1 The Three Main Standards of Review

The type of ruling made by a trial court determines the standard of review. The three main standards of review are

1. *de novo* review for issues of law
2. *clear error* review for issues of fact
3. *abuse of discretion* review for discretionary issues

Other standards of review exist, but these are the most important ones.

Issues of Law—de novo review: A trial court decides an issue of law when it interprets the law or decides what the law is. For example, when a trial judge instructs the jury at the end of a trial, the judge explains to the jury the elements of the legal rules the jury must follow in reaching a verdict. When deciding what to say to the jury, the judge decides a pure issue of law. If the jury instruction accurately states the law, the trial judge has not committed error. But if the

265

instruction is wrong, the judge has erroneously decided an issue of law and could be reversed on appeal.

In reviewing a trial court's ruling on an issue of law, an appellate court measures error simply by asking whether it would have interpreted the law in the same way the trial court did. *De novo* is the term used in federal courts for this standard of review. In Latin, it means to do "from the beginning" or "as though new." Some states use other phrases, such as "independent and nondeferential review." They mean the same thing. If the trial court interpreted the law incorrectly, an appellate court can reverse.

When you're assigned to write an appellate brief, look first for the type of decision the trial court made. If it is one of the following, you have an issue of law:

- an order dismissing a plaintiff's complaint or other pleading
- a summary judgment
- a directed verdict or, in federal court, judgment as a matter of law
- a jury instruction
- a judgment notwithstanding the verdict or, in federal court, judgment as a matter of law
- a decision denying a motion or request for any of the above

Many other trial court decisions resolve issues of law, but these are the big ones.

Most, but not all, law school appellate brief assignments involve de novo standards of review. If that's true of your assignment, you probably won't have much difficulty arguing within the standard. A de novo standard is neutral, like a pane of glass through which light passes without distortion. The other standards (explained below) are like filters and lenses that modify the image because they defer to the trial court, which a de novo standard does not.

With a question of law there's no reason to defer in any way to the trial court. An appellate court can decide an issue of law at least as well as a trial court can, and the appellate court might do a better job because an appeal is decided by several judges as opposed to a single judge in the trial court.

Issues of fact—review for clear error: An issue of fact is a question about what happened factually between the parties. For example, was the defendant's gun loaded or unloaded at the time of the crime? Which witness should be believed: the one who testified that the defendant loaded the gun with bullets just before the crime, or the one who testified that the defendant instead emptied the gun of bullets?

Although these fact issues and many others would typically be decided by a jury, some fact issues are decided by a trial court judge. When a law school appellate brief assignment includes a fact issue, it usually involves a bench trial or a pretrial motion. A bench trial is one where a judge decides the facts without a jury.

A pretrial motion asks the judge to make a procedural decision before the trial begins. For example, if a criminal defendant moves to suppress his confession, the defendant is asking the judge to exclude the confession from the evidence admitted at trial. If the defendant claims that he confessed only because a police officer threatened to beat him up, the judge would decide whether the police really did that—which is a fact issue.

Don't confuse a fact issue with a law issue. Suppose the defendant claims that the police officer bragged that he is an amateur boxer who is so good at punching opponents that he almost qualified for the U.S. boxing team at the last Olympics.

fact issue: Did the police officer brag in the defendant's presence?

law issue: Does that kind of bragging violate the defendant's Fifth Amendment right against forced confessions?

When a trial judge's findings of fact are challenged on appeal, the appellate court will reverse only if the trial judge's decision was "clearly erroneous."[1] It's not enough that the trial court was wrong. A deeper level of error is required for reversal.

Typically, courts say that they will reverse only if they "are left with a definite and firm conviction that a mistake has been made."[2] The Seventh Circuit has put it more bluntly: "To be clearly erroneous, a decision must strike us as more than just maybe or probably wrong; it must . . . strike us as wrong with the force of a five-week-old, unrefrigerated, dead fish."[3] Other courts use less vivid language to express the same idea.

However you express it, this is a very difficult standard for an appellant to satisfy. Appellate courts defer to the trial court's factual determinations because the trial judge saw and heard the witnesses testify while appellate courts can only read the trial court's transcript, which appellate judges describe as a "cold record."

Discretionary issues—review for abuse of discretion: Many procedural issues permit a trial judge to exercise discretion. Here is a typical appellate court formulation of what that means:

> When we say that . . . a district court has discretion to grant or deny a motion, we do not mean that the district court may do whatever pleases it. The phrase means instead that *the court has a range of choice, and that its decision will not be disturbed as long as it stays within that range.* . . . An abuse of discretion, on the other hand, can occur . . . when a relevant factor that should have been given significant weight is not considered; when an irrelevant or improper factor is considered and given significant weight; and when all proper factors, and no improper ones, are considered, but the court, in weighing those factors, commits a clear error of judgment.[4]

The most important words here are "the court has a range of choice, and . . . its decision will not be disturbed as long as it stays within that range." How do you know what that range is? You have to read your jurisdiction's case law, where you'll find general definitions that might (or might not) resemble the one above.

---

[1] See, *e.g.,* Rule 52(a) of the Federal Rules of Civil Procedure.
[2] *United States v. Brown,* 156 F.3d 813, 816 (8th Cir. 1998).
[3] *Parts & Electric Motors, Inc. v. Sterling Electric, Inc.,* 866 F.2d 228, 233 (7th Cir. 1988).
[4] *Kern v. TXO Prod. Corp.,* 738 F.2d 968, 970 (8th Cir. 1984) (emphasis added).

The abuse-of-discretion standard—like the clear-error standard for fact decisions—reflects appellate deference to the trial court. Appellate courts reason that the trial judge is closer to the problem and might have a better view of how to solve it. As long as the trial judge chooses a decision within the permissible range, that decision will be affirmed.

Some decisions involve a combination of discretionary and other types of issues. For example, suppose a plaintiff moves for a preliminary injunction alleging that the defendant is infringing the plaintiff's trademark by selling a product called a Hyper Blob Blaster. (A preliminary injunction is a court's command to a party to do or not do certain things before trial.)

Some appellate courts will divide up the issues like this:

fact issue:	Is the defendant selling a product called a Hyper Blob Blaster?
law issue:	What rules of trademark law govern this dispute?
discretionary issue:	Is a preliminary injunction an appropriate remedy in this situation?

With this view of the issues, an appellate court will reverse for clear error in fact-finding, or for an erroneous interpretation of the law (de novo), or for abuse of discretion in choosing or rejecting a preliminary injunction as a remedy.

Mixed issues of law and fact: Sometimes a fact issue can't be separated from a law issue. For example,

fact issue:	What factually happened between the parties?
law issue:	What's the governing legal test?
mixed issue:	How does the legal test apply to these facts?

It's hard to generalize about how appellate courts handle mixed issues of law and fact. If you have a mixed issue, find the case law on issues like the one in your assignment and read carefully to see how the courts in your jurisdiction analyze the issue.

§36.2 How to Determine Which Standards of Review Govern Your Issues

Look at what the appellate court is being asked to decide. Suppose the trial court determined what the facts are, decided what the law is, and chose a discretionary remedy. Suppose also that the losing party appeals only on the ground that the trial court misinterpreted the law.

In this example only the trial court's law decision has been appealed. The fact and discretion issues have been left behind and are not before the appellate court. (Most, but not all, law school assignments are pure issues of law.)

Law issues usually don't have labels on them that say "Law Issue Right Here." Instead, you might be told something like "The appellant contends that the trial court misinterpreted §1331." That's an issue of law, which can be resolved entirely by deciding what the law is and how it should be applied to the facts.

Look also at how the analogous case law discusses your issue. Standards of review are usually found in case law, although they might partially be addressed in court rules. Look for cases that tell you not only what the standard is, but also what it means and how it works. When a court mentions the standard of review in a decision, it usually does so right after reciting the facts and just before beginning the legal analysis. Here's an example of the type of language you will find:

> We review *de novo* the district court's dismissal of a complaint for failure to state a claim under Rule 12(b)(6). In reviewing such a motion, we accept all material allegations of fact as true and construe the complaint in a light most favorable to the non-moving party. We have consistently emphasized, however, that "conclusory allegations of law and unwarranted inferences" will not defeat an otherwise proper motion to dismiss. Dismissal for failure to state a claim is appropriate only "if it appears beyond doubt that the non-moving party can prove no set of facts in support of his claim which would entitle him to relief."[5]

Here we learn what the standard of review is (de novo). The court explains how the standard works by describing how the lower court should have made its decision ("Dismissal for failure to state a claim is appropriate only ... ").

Occasionally, you'll come across an issue that is subject to more than one standard of review. Each portion of this test for laches has a different standard of review:

> Our standard of review on the laches issue has various components. We review factual findings such as length of delay and prejudice under the clearly erroneous standard; we review the district court's balancing of the equities for abuse of discretion; and our review of legal precepts applied by the district court in determining that the delay was excusable is plenary [meaning de novo].[6]

§36.3 How to Use Standards of Review in a Brief

In federal appeals, the appellant's argument "must contain ... for each issue a concise statement of the applicable standard of review (which may appear in the

---

[5] *Vasquez v. Los Angeles County*, 487 F.3d 1246, 1249 (9th Cir. 2007) (citations omitted).
[6] *Bermuda Express, N.V. v. M/V Litsa*, 872 F.2d 554, 557 (3d Cir. 1989) (citation omitted).

discussion of each issue or under a separate heading placed before the discussion of the issues)."[7] The appellee can omit this statement "unless the appellee is dissatisfied with the statement of the appellant."[8]

When you tell the court the standard of review, it often helps to explain, at the same time, the procedural posture below and the procedural test that governs it. And—if it can be done succinctly—tell the court how the standard justifies reversal (if you're the appellant) or how it doesn't (if you're the appellee). For example, from an appellant's brief:

> The plaintiff appeals from a summary judgment, which is reviewed de novo in this court. [Citation omitted.] Summary judgment should be granted only where there is no genuine issue as to any material fact and the movant is entitled to judgment as a matter of law. [Citation omitted.] In this case, the defendant should not have been granted summary judgment because he was not entitled to judgment as a matter of law.

This passage tells us that the standard is de novo, and that appellant will argue that the second element of the test for summary judgment was not satisfied. In the paragraphs that follow, the writer will have to explain thoroughly why the appellee was not entitled to judgment as a matter of law.

Set out the relevant standard of review at or near the beginning of the Argument section of the brief. Or, if you have more than one point, each with a different standard of review, a point's standard can be set out shortly after the point heading. Cite to authority to prove the standard of review. A conclusory rule explanation (Chapter 17) is usually sufficient because appellate courts are generally familiar with the applicable standards of view.

If the standard is de novo, you can state it at the beginning and ignore it afterward because it's a neutral standard. But if the standard is one of the deferential ones—clear error or abuse of discretion—you have to argue in terms of the standard. For example, if you're appealing from a decision committed to a trial court's discretion, show exactly how the trial court abused its discretion. If you're the appellee in such a case, show the opposite. With a deferential standard, weave it into your argument.

If you're unsure of how to do any of these things, take a look at several opinions in which the court to which you're writing has handled the same standard of review in appeals involving the same procedural posture as in your case. Look for a definition of the standard. Try to learn its relationship to other procedural rules. And get a feel for the court's expectations about how the standard should be used.

---

[7] Fed. R. App. P. 28(a)(9)(B).
[8] Fed. R. App. P. 28(b).

Making Policy Arguments

§37.1 Why Policy Is Especially Important in an Appeal

Policy matters in an appellate court for two reasons. First, when a court enforces a rule of law, it tries to do so in a way that accomplishes the policy behind the rule. In any court—trial or appellate—your odds of winning increase if you can show that the decision you want would achieve important public goals.

Second, a substantial part of an appellate court's work is clarifying ambiguous law and making new law. The higher up you go in the appellate system, the more that is true. Clarifying the law and making new law are virtually the only things the U.S. Supreme Court does. When a court makes law in this way, it tries to do so consistently with policies that are already accepted in the law (or should be).

When you appear before a court in a law-making case, judges will naturally ask questions like this: What rule of law would a decision in your favor stand for (remembering that it would become binding precedent)? In what words would that rule be most accurately expressed? If the court does as you request, how would the law in the future treat facts that are similar to—but not exactly the same as—yours? What would be the practical effects in the courts, in the economy, and in society as a whole? Why is the rule you advocate better than the one your adversary urges?

In your brief, make policy arguments that would answer these questions persuasively.

§37.2 Types of Policy Arguments

The following article will help you choose public policies and argue them.

TEACHING STUDENTS TO MAKE EFFECTIVE POLICY ARGUMENTS IN APPELLATE BRIEFS
Ellie Margolis
9 Perspectives 73 (2001)

... While there are several different types of policy arguments, all policy arguments share the common attribute of advocating that a proposed legal rule [or a proposed interpretation of a statute or constitutional provision] will benefit society, or advance a particular social goal (or conversely, that the proposed rule [or interpretation] will cause harm and should not be adopted). ... Thus, all policy arguments involve an assessment of how a proposed rule will function in the real world. ...

A. Judicial Administration Arguments

... These are arguments about the practical administration of the rule by the courts. The goal at the heart of these arguments is a fair and efficient judicial system. ...

The dual goals of fairness and efficiency are sometimes at odds, however. This tension gives rise to the first type of judicial administration argument, the "firm vs. flexible rule" argument. The argument for a firm rule is that a clear, specific standard will be easy for the court to administer, and therefore promote efficiency. A firm rule also promotes fairness by leaving little room for judicial discretion and leading to more consistent application, which makes it easier for [the public] to understand the rule and act accordingly [because of the] adoption of a clear, precise rule. The "flexible rule" argument, on the other hand, focuses more heavily on fairness. The argument for a flexible rule is that flexibility will allow the court to ... take into account the individual circumstances of each case[, which would be] more responsive and fair ....

There are three other judicial administration arguments that focus primarily on efficiency. These can be made individually or combined with the firm/flexible rule arguments. The first is the "floodgates of litigation" argument.[*] This argument asserts that a proposed rule, if adopted, will inundate the court with lawsuits. ...

The second of these arguments is the "slippery slope" argument [which] asserts that if the proposed rule is adopted, the court will not be able to prevent

---

[*] This argument is much overused and used inappropriately. Over the years, I have seen many student briefs making "floodgate" arguments because the students knew they should make some kind of policy argument and this was the only one they could think of. While this argument still has value it should be used selectively, and only where truly appropriate.

its application to a broader and broader set of cases. First it will be applied to one new circumstance, then another, leading the court to hear a whole range of cases it had never intended to entertain [—and may additionally] lead to a large number of frivolous claims. . . .

The final judicial administration argument asserts that a proposed rule, even if firm, is so complex that it will be impossible to administer efficiently[,] . . . making it difficult [for the public] to understand and comply with the law [and] undermin[ing] judicial efficiency by requiring a large number of judicial resources in order to resolve claims under the rule.

B. Normative Arguments

. . . Although there is a significant overlap between different types of normative arguments, they can be broken down into roughly three categories: moral arguments, social utility arguments, and corrective justice arguments. Normative arguments tend to appear more "political" in nature because, in today's complex society, there is rarely widespread social consensus on issues of morality or other social good. As a result, the goal of a normative policy is not always as obvious or easy to establish as the goal in a judicial administration argument.

Moral arguments generally take the form of asserting that a particular rule should be adopted because it is consistent with generally accepted standards of society. . . .

. . . Under [a social utility] argument, the advocate asserts that a proposed rule will serve a social good and benefit society, or conversely, that it will undermine a social value and harm society [—because it] either deters or encourages conduct that affects . . . public health, public safety, economic health, [or] national security. Social utility arguments are particularly useful in tort law cases. . . .

[A] corrective justice argument . . . centers on the goal of fairness and asserts that as between two innocents, the one that caused the damage should be responsible. . . . In common law cases of first impression, [when] the court is being asked to establish a new cause of action, [especially in torts,] corrective justice arguments could be very useful.

C. Institutional Competence Arguments

. . . These are arguments about which branch of government (generally the judiciary or the legislature) should address a particular issue. . . .

[Although a legislature is the primary creator of new law, u]nder the common law method, judges have the power to fill in gaps in the law and formulate new rules . . . creating the potential for arguments over whether an issue is better suited to the courts or the legislature.

An argument that an issue is better suited for the courts focuses on the nature of courts as institutions set up for resolving individual disputes . . . . The argument would emphasize the court's ability to [act on the facts before it when the legislature has not acted and to learn facts from] witnesses and make objective determinations of credibility. . . .

The argument that the legislature is better suited . . . asserts that the courts are not competent to resolve the issue because . . . the legislature [is better able] to reflect changes in public opinion, and to hold hearings and gather complex and varied facts that may not be relevant in the [narrow] context of litigation. . . .

D. Economic Arguments

. . . One form of economic argument focuses on the efficient allocation of resources. . . . For example, a rule might be desirable because it spreads loss over a large segment of the population. On the other hand, a defendant trying to avoid liability in a products liability suit might argue that the cost of such liability will be passed on to the public, ultimately punishing those the rule was designed to benefit.

Another form of economic argument asserts that a cost-benefit analysis dictates that a rule should be adopted. Under this analysis, the arguer must show that the economic benefits of a rule outweigh the costs of implementing it. . . . The key to a cost-benefits analysis is the determination of the factors going into the cost. In addition to obvious costs, such as the monetary costs of fixing a defective part, costs such emotional damage can be factored in. . . .

A third type of economic policy argument is that the proposed rule will have a positive or negative effect on economic efficiency and affect the operation of the free-market economy[, asserting, for example,] that a proposed rule would either promote or inhibit competition. . . .

§37.3 How to Make a Policy Argument

The preceding section of this chapter describes the most frequently used policies. Look at the cases and statutes you have found in your research. What policies do they enunciate? When you write the brief, make policy arguments in three steps:

Step 1: Identify one or more public policies that a decision in your favor would further. Tell the court exactly which policy or policies you want the court to be guided by.

Step 2: Persuade the court that the policy or policies you have identified are valuable. Your adversary will urge competing policies. Show that yours are more important. It's not enough just to say yours are worth more. Prove it with argument.

Step 3: Show exactly how a decision in your favor will further the policy or policies you have identified. Don't assume that the court will understand how. Explain it *specifically*.

Policy arguments are much stronger if supported by authority. If the policy you urge has already been recognized by the courts in other cases, cite and explain those cases. If the legislature has adopted the policy in enacting statutes that are not directly related to your case, cite those statutes and explain how they reflect the policy you are urging. If you have only a few cases or statutes, try to find secondary authority, such as treatises and law review articles, that explain policies that should govern your case. You might also cite and explain nonlegal sources that show a genuine public need. For example, if you argue that the courts should adopt strict tort rules assigning liability for contamination with industrial chemicals, you can cite scientific studies showing the presence of PCB's and other toxic chemicals in the food supply.

When a court is being asked to clarify the interpretation of a statute, the court is not free to attach to the statute any policy the court likes. Instead, the court must use the policy the legislature adopted when it enacted the statute. Sometimes that policy is expressed in the statute or the legislative history. If not, the court (with your assistance) must figure out what policy the legislature probably adopted.

When making a policy argument, use the terminology you find in the cases and statutes in preference to the terminology used in this chapter. You will be able to recognize a normative policy when you see one in a case or statute. But when you argue that policy to a court, refer to it in the way the cases or the statutes do. Or simply say in plain language what you mean: "This rule would be consistent with standards of behavior generally accepted throughout society. Specifically, . . ." The terms "normative argument," "social utility argument," and "corrective justice argument" rarely occur in the case law, although many statutes and thousands of cases have adopted policies that can be categorized as normative, social utility, or corrective justice. Courts and law school teachers sometimes use different words to refer to the same policies. When writing for a court, use the wording that judges use.

You might also avoid telling a court that it is a less competent institution than a legislature. It would be more diplomatic to say that the legislature is "in a better position" to decide whether to adopt the rule of law urged by your adversary, or that the decision is a type that "should be reserved to" the legislature. (Then show why.)

Questions Presented

§38.1 The Purpose of a Question Presented

An effective Question Presented does two things. First, it defines the decision the court is being asked to make. And second, within limits, it persuades by framing the decision within the most essential facts of your theory. If the Question defines the decision objectively, it does not perform the second function of persuasiveness. And if it argues the case, it does not fulfill the first function. The solution is to persuade through juxtaposition and careful word choice, just as you do in a Statement of the Case—but much more concisely.

A Question Presented combines

- an inquiry,
- a reference to the legal test or concept that will govern the result, and
- a list of the few most essential facts.

These three ingredients can be put together in either of two ways—a traditional format and an alternative format.

§38.2 Traditional Format

Here's an example of the traditional format:

Question Presented:	Is the manufacturer of an electronic keyboard liable under an implied warranty of fitness for purpose to a purchaser in whose hands the keyboard exploded the first time it was plugged in?
inquiry:	Is the manufacturer of an electronic keyboard liable
legal test:	under an implied warranty of fitness for purpose
essential facts:	to a purchaser in whose hands the keyboard exploded the first time it was plugged in?

The essential facts and the reference to the governing test or legal concept define the issue so that it becomes the question "presented" by the situation. "Is a manufacturer liable to a purchaser?" may be a question, but it is not a Question Presented.

The inquiry can begin with whatever verb is most appropriate to the issue:

Is the manufacturer of an electronic keyboard liable . . . ?

Does the First Amendment allow . . . ?

In many briefs, you will see Questions Presented that begin with the word *whether*, even though the result is not a grammatically complete sentence:

Whether the manufacturer of an electronic keyboard is liable . . .

Whether the First Amendment allows . . .

Try to avoid this, if you can. A "whether" Question Presented can seem artificial and harder to read. A Question that begins with a verb—like most other examples in this chapter—is easier to understand because it looks like a question in ordinary English.

Facts that do not fit naturally into the inquiry can be attached at the end in clauses beginning with "where." The manufacturer's lawyer might have written this:

Is the manufacturer of an electronic keyboard absolved of liability under an implied warranty of fitness for purpose where a consumer bought it in pieces from a street vendor and attempted to reassemble it himself even though the words "Do Not Open or Attempt to Repair This Product" were engraved on the outside?

The list should appear at the end because the facts make sense only after the reader knows the inquiry. The following, for example, are not easy to understand:

facts before inquiry:	Where a consumer bought an electronic keyboard in pieces from a street vendor and attempted to reassemble it himself even though the words "Do Not Open or Attempt to Repair This Product" were engraved on the outside, is the manufacturer absolved of liability under an implied warranty of fitness for purpose?
facts interrupting inquiry:	Is the manufacturer of an electronic keyboard, which was bought from a street vendor by an ordinary consumer who attempted to reassemble it himself even though the words "Do Not Open or Attempt to Repair This Product" were engraved on the outside, absolved of liability under an implied warranty of fitness for purpose?

§38.3 Alternative Format

In some cases, a reader would drown in a series of "where" clauses because even the most essential facts are so complicated that they cannot be reduced to a short list. Lawyers sometimes use a different format, expressing the essential facts in an introductory paragraph, and then posing the Question or Questions Presented.

[paragraph stating the essential facts that are common to most or all of the issues]

1. [issue, including an inquiry and a reference to the legal test]
2. [second issue, if you have one, stated the same way]
3. [third issue, if you have one, stated the same way]

See the Question Presented in the Appendix C brief. This format works especially well when you have several issues, but it can also be effective when you have only one. If you have two or more issues and if a particular fact relates to only one of them, that fact can be listed in the statement of that issue rather than in the preceding paragraph. If you have only one issue, all the facts essential to that issue should be in the preceding paragraph.

Don't use this format as an easy fix when your list of facts is long and complicated. First, try to compress the list. Are all the facts you've listed truly essential? Have you stated each fact concisely? Then, choose the format that works best.

§38.4 How to Write a Question Presented

Given the relatively few words involved, drafting a Question Presented can be one of the more difficult tasks in legal writing. Start by creating the raw materials. Write out the inquiry and the allusion to governing law. Separately make a list of the facts that you believe to be most essential to that issue. Then work out a concise phrasing of the fact list and merge it into the inquiry. Many lawyers write the Question Presented after writing a first draft of the rest of the brief.

§38.5 How to Test Your Questions Presented for Effectiveness

While rewriting, ask yourself the questions in bold print beginning on the next page.[1] They also appear on this book's website as a checklist, which you can print out.

The examples in this section are drawn from these facts: A stockbroker grew tired of his work and decided to do something artistic. He persuaded a gourmet bakery to take him on as an apprentice baker. The bakery has perfected a secret method of adding a citrus taste to its croissants, which have become a trendy food for that reason. The bakery requires its employees to sign a covenant not to compete with the bakery for three years in either of the two urban counties in an otherwise rural state. After a short time, the stockbroker quit and formed his own company to bake and sell gourmet baked goods. The bakery where he apprenticed has sued for an injunction to prohibit that.

In the state where this arises, a covenant not to compete is enforceable if the prohibition on competition is "reasonably limited" in duration and geographic area, if it "does not exceed that reasonably necessary for protection of the employer's business," if it "is not unreasonably restrictive" of the employee's rights, and if it does not violate public policy.[2]

The bakery's attorney might draft this Question Presented:

> **Should a successful stockbroker entering the baking business be enjoined from violating a three-year covenant not to compete as a baker where he was trained as a baker by the plaintiff, had access to the secret recipe for the plaintiff's biggest-selling product, and has now set himself up in business as the plaintiff's only competitor in a specialized two-county gourmet baked goods market?**

From the other side might come a very different Question:

> **Is it inequitable to enjoin an apprentice baker from working "in any baking capacity" for three years in an area that includes three-quarters of the state's population, where**

---

[1] Some of the bold-printed questions are reworked from Frank E. Cooper, *Writing in Law Practice* 80 (1963).
[2] *American Credit Bureau v. Carter*, 462 P.2d 838, 840 (Ariz. Ct. App. 1969).

the plaintiff's only fear of potential injury is that, in starting his own business, the apprentice might use a croissant recipe?

1. Have you kept conclusions of law or fact out of the Question Presented?

In the following Question Presented, the "facts" are really *conclusions of law*, which must be proved later and cannot be assumed here:

> Should a defendant bakery apprentice be enjoined from violating a covenant not to compete where the covenant is reasonably limited in duration and geographic area, where its prohibitions are reasonably necessary to protect the employer's business, where it does not unreasonably restrict the employee's rights, and where it does not violate public policy?

This Question asks whether the defendant should be enjoined when the applicable legal test has been satisfied. Of course the answer to that will always be yes. But that's not the issue before the court. The issue is *whether* that test has been satisfied. Factual inferences and conclusions of law—such as "the covenant is reasonably limited in duration and geographic area"—cannot be posited as factual givens. Conclusions and inferences cannot be assumed. They must be proved in the Argument. If you posit conclusions as facts, judges will ignore your Question Presented.

If you find conclusions in your Question Presented, cut them out and *replace them with the facts that would make them true.* For example, which facts make this restraint reasonably necessary to protect the bakery's business? Those facts belong in the Question Presented, and the conclusion of law should come out.

2. Is each fact in the Question Presented stated so that your adversary cannot deny its accuracy?

A Question Presented persuades only if based on undeniable facts. The Questions Presented at the beginning of this section persuade by listing facts that the opposing attorney cannot claim to be untrue or missing from the record, and by describing those facts in words the opposing attorney cannot reasonably claim to be inaccurate. Moreover, neither attorney has pretended that the other side's strongest facts do not exist. The apprentice's lawyer must concede that his client suddenly created a competing company, but he does so in words that suggest that the bakery will not suffer much as a result ("the plaintiff's only fear of potential injury is that, in starting his own business, the apprentice might use a croissant recipe"). The bakery's attorney can hardly ignore the fact that the state's population is concentrated in the two counties covered by the covenant, but she mentions that in a phrase showing why the covenant ought to address that area ("a specialized two-county gourmet baked goods market"). As in a Statement of the Case, juxtaposition is the key to neutralizing unfavorable facts.

3. Will a judge be able to understand the Question Presented without reading it twice? List only the most essential facts and eliminate unnecessary details. Use the most concise wording that would not sacrifice clarity. Finding the right level of compression is not easy. Consider this:

> Should this court enjoin the violation of a covenant not to compete, which applied only to the baking industry and included a prohibition on competition that lasted three years, where the defendant was a baking apprentice who has made a considerable income as a stockbroker and continues to derive passive income from his partnership in a brokerage house, where he was trained as a baker by the plaintiff and has never received any other instruction or experience in the field, where he had access to the plaintiff's hitherto secret recipe for a unique form of croissant embodying citrus flavors, where he has now set himself up in business as the plaintiff's only competitor in this field, and where the parties compete in a specialized gourmet baked goods market that extends over two adjacent counties, each of which includes a major city?

Can you understand this in one reading? Can you tell immediately what facts are important? Compare it—phrase by phrase—with the bakery's Question Presented at the beginning of this section. There's no difference in meaning. The only difference is that the Question Presented above adds unnecessary details and uses too many words to say no more than the other Question says.

It's often concise and clear to refer to the parties generically—"a malpractice insurer," "the employee," and so forth. Procedural terms can be confusing. "Appellant" and "appellee" tell the court virtually nothing. Sometimes (but not always) "plaintiff" and "defendant" do not make clear the parties' roles in the controversy. In a criminal case it's rarely confusing to refer to one party as the defendant. The other party is always the prosecution. Although a busy judge can be confused when the parties are referred to by name only, it may be tactically wise to try to personalize a party beset by an institutional opponent, if the context will make clear who's who.

It takes a lot of rewriting to make a Question Presented both concise and understandable.

4. Does the Question Presented clearly define the decision the court has been asked to make? Many judges read the Questions Presented before they read any other part of the brief. Don't ask a Question that *assumes* the reader already knows the case:

> Should the violation of a covenant not to compete be enjoined, where the defendant is actually a successful stockbroker who was trained entirely by the plaintiff, who had access to the plaintiff's hitherto secret recipe, and who has now set himself up in business as the plaintiff's only competitor?

If you had not already read about this case at the beginning of this section, the Question Presented above would make little sense. Did the plaintiff train the defendant to be a *stockbroker*? Is this a suit to enjoin competition *in the stock brokerage industry*? What does a recipe have to do with this? Remember that the reader might not yet have read the Statement of the Case and certainly has not yet read the Argument.

5. Do you have the right number of Questions Presented? You should have a Question Presented for each big, encompassing issue—but not more than that. The bakery example has lots of issues—whether the covenant not to compete reasonably limits the employee in time and geography, whether it limits the employee no more than reasonably necessary to protect the employer, and so on. But these are all really sub-issues inside one big, encompassing issue—whether the covenant should be enforced.

Too many Questions diffuse the reader's attention. Below, the bakery's lawyer has carved up one big, encompassing issue into three Questions Presented, none of which is complete:

> 1. Did the Superior Court properly enjoin the violation of a covenant not to compete, which was limited to a three-year period in a two-county area?

> 2. Did the Superior Court properly enjoin the violation of a covenant not to compete, where the enjoined former employee had access to the plaintiff's hitherto secret bakery recipe and has now set himself up as the plaintiff's only competitor?

> 3. Did the Superior Court properly enjoin the violation of a covenant not to compete, where the former employee is a successful stockbroker who does not depend on baking for his livelihood?

6. Does the Question Presented persuade? A persuasive Question Presented causes a skeptical judge to think, "This lawyer has the winning side" or at least "On these facts, I do not want to rule against this lawyer." The Question should overcome a judge's natural tendency to ask "So what?" or "Is this really so bad that I should use the power of the court to interfere?"

Draft the Question Presented in a positive tone to invite the answer you seek. The answer you want is always "yes."

Oral Argument

§39.1 Three Goals at Oral Argument

First, you want to engage the judges' attention by getting them *interested* in your case and *motivated* to rule in your favor. They will hear many other arguments on the same day, and they will read many other briefs in the week they read yours. You want to touch their natural desire to do the right thing.

Second, you want to focus the judges' attention on the *few aspects of your case that are most determinative*—the fundamental one or two issues, the most prominent facts in your story, and the most compelling policy considerations. Judges expect oral argument to help them find the heart of the dispute. Oral argument works best when it concentrates on a few important ideas, while details are best left to the briefs.

Third, you want *access to the judges' thinking.* You want to discover each of their doubts about your theory and any way in which they're confused about your case—so you can dispel their doubts and clear up their confusion. Listening to the judges' questions is the only way you can get access to their thinking. And the most effective thing you can do in oral argument is to answer their questions well. Usually when judges interrupt you with questions, they're not trying to debate with you. They're telling you what troubles them and asking you to help them make the decision. Thus, an experienced oral advocate goes into the courtroom *for the purpose of being interrupted.*

§39.2 Structure of an Oral Argument

You will (1) introduce yourself and the case, (2) summarize the client's story and identify the core issue or issues raised by the story, (3) make a legal argument, and (4) conclude.

If you represent the appellant, you will argue first. Begin by introducing your client and yourself and identifying the decision below from which you have appealed. Here are two examples of effective openings:

> Good morning, Your Honors. I am [lawyer's name], representing [client's name], the appellant here and the plaintiff below. A jury verdict in her favor was overturned when the trial court granted a post-trial motion for judgment as a matter of law.

> May it please the court, representing [client's name], I am [lawyer's name]. The jury returned a verdict in favor of [client's name], but the trial court granted a post-trial motion for judgment as a matter of law—a decision she now asks you to reverse.

Next, summarize the story and identify the core issue or issues. If you will use the issues to introduce the story, identify the issues first. Otherwise, tell the story and identify the issues afterward as a bridge into your legal argument.

Focus on the most essential facts so the judges don't get lost in marginal details. Think carefully beforehand about how you will tell the story and what words you will use. One of the most successful Supreme Court advocates once said that "in an appellate court the statement of the facts is not merely a part of the argument, it is more often than not the argument itself. A case well stated is a case far more than half argued."[1] You must mention the facts that hurt you, but you can minimize their effect through juxtaposition, just as you did when you wrote the Statement of the Case. Some courts study the briefs carefully before argument, and they might consider a fact recitation to be a waste of time. In those courts, lawyers are discouraged—either informally or through the courts' rules—from opening with the facts.

If you represent the appellee, your opening may be similar to the appellant's, except that you should explain how your positions differ from the appellant's. For example, rather than tell your version of the story, you might point out the ways in which the appellant has not given a full or accurate picture. Suppose a group of plaintiffs won a judgment against the owner of a dam that collapsed; the owner has appealed; and the owner's lawyer has opened oral argument by stressing that the plaintiffs had reason to know the dam had weakened. The plaintiffs' lawyer can respond like this:

> The key fact is *not* that slowly rising waters in a creek could have alerted nearby residents that something might be wrong, but that the defendant's dam burst, sending a wall of water seven feet high down the valley where the plaintiffs lived. Slowly rising water cannot be considered a warning of that.

You can begin your legal argument with a statement of the rule or rules most essential to your position. If you're arguing two or more issues, you might have to

---

[1] John W. Davis, *The Argument of an Appeal*, 26 A.B.A. J. 895, 896 (1940).

do this separately for each issue. On each issue, your argument can resemble the CREAC structure. Persuade the judges that they should adopt and enforce the rule you urge, explain how the rule works, and apply it to your facts.

If you represent the appellee, listen carefully to the appellant's oral argument. When your turn comes, you will respond to the appellant's contentions. You may have anticipated most of them when you read the appellant's brief and when you planned your argument. But if the appellant surprises you during oral argument by saying something new that truly might hurt, you will need, on the spot, to find a way of neutralizing it.

Appellate advocates distinguish between a "hot" bench, which erupts with questions, and a "cold" bench, which listens impassively. If the bench is hot, the judges may ask so many questions that you will be surprised to find that your time is about to run out, or already has. Your time is up when the presiding judge says, in a firm tone, "Thank you, counselor." Then conclude with *one short* sentence in which you specify the relief you seek ("Therefore, the judgment below should be affirmed. . . ."). If you're in the midst of answering a question when your time runs out, ask for permission to finish the answer. If your request is granted, finish quickly. If the judges continue to ask you questions after your time expires, answer them fully: The court has implicitly enlarged your time. If you finish your argument before your time expires, conclude anyway, pause to see whether you will be asked further questions, and, if not, sit down. Whatever the situation, you can signal your intent to finish by using an introductory phrase such as "In conclusion, ..."

An appellant's lawyer sometimes reserves a minute or two for rebuttal by saying so after the introductory sentences. The time reserved is subtracted from the time allowed for the appellant's main argument. After the appellee has argued, the appellant can use the reserved time to reply. But a court considers rebuttal time wasted if an appellant uses it to reiterate arguments already made or to raise new arguments for the first time. Use rebuttal only to correct significantly inaccurate or misleadingly incomplete statements made by the appellee, and preferably not more than one or two of those. If the appellee's misstatements are trivial, an appellant looks petty correcting them. If it turns out that there's no need for rebuttal, an appellant makes a confident impression by waiving it.

§39.3 Questions from the Bench

Listen carefully to the question and understand it before answering.
Answer the question when it is asked.
Don't evade.
If you don't know the answer to a question, say so.
If the premise of a question is wrong, politely say so.
If a Justice throws you a life preserver, don't bat it away.

Justices ask hypothetical questions because they are concerned about how the decision in your case may affect other cases. What are the limits of the principle you advocate?

— *North Dakota Supreme Court*
Appellate Practice Tips

Some questions are neutral requests for information. Some are challenges, asking you how you would overcome an adverse case or a policy contrary to your argument. Some are expressed as concerns: the judge asks how a particular problem in the case can be resolved. Some questions are openly friendly, asking you to focus on an aspect of your case that the judge believes to be particularly persuasive. And some questions are prompts, suggesting that whatever you're discussing at the time can be dispensed with in favor of something else the court cares about more. Some questions are asked because the answer is crucial to the judge's thinking. Others grow out of the spontaneity of the moment, and the answer may have little or no impact on the decision.

When you hear a question, listen to it carefully. Don't be afraid to pause for a moment to think before answering. Never interrupt a question. Try to figure out the question's purpose and exactly what's troubling the judge. Then craft your answer to satisfy the skepticism or curiosity implied by the question. In your answer, don't say too little or too much. Don't give a one-sentence reply to a question that a judge plainly considers to be the crux of the case. And don't spend three minutes resolving a straightforward request for simple information.

Don't leap to assumptions about a judge's predispositions from the questions the judge asks. A neutral judge might ask challenging questions just to see whether your theory will hold up. A friendly judge might ask challenging questions to cause you to argue matters that the judge believes might persuade others on the bench. And an adverse judge might ask friendly or neutral questions out of politeness and a sense of fairness.

Answer the question on the spot. Don't promise to get back to it later at a place in your outline where you had already planned to discuss the subject. Other questions might prevent you from getting that far, and your answer will be most persuasive immediately after the question is asked. Even if a question asks you to discuss an entire issue earlier than you had planned, do it and rearrange the order of your presentation to accommodate the judge's needs. Later, when you reach the spot where you had intended to discuss the issue, simply skip what you have already covered.

Answer the question you've been asked, not one you would rather have been asked. You can persuade only by facing the problems raised by the question and by showing the judge why those problems should not prevent a decision in your favor. In every fully litigated case, each side has points of weakness. If your side had none, your adversary would have given up long ago. When a judge has truly identified a point of weakness, face it and give a realistic counterargument. Here are three ways to begin:

> I agree, Your Honor, that in that hypothetical the police would have had probable cause, but the facts of the hypothetical are not the facts of this case. For example, ...

> Yes, *Soares* did so hold, but later rulings of this court have impliedly undermined *Soares.* For example, ...

> Certainly, the record does reflect two isolated events that might be construed as evidence of good faith by the defendant, but the record also includes many, many events, stretching over several years, that show exactly the opposite. For example, ...

During the answer, build a bridge to the rest of your argument. If you do this smoothly, it may be hard for a listener to tell where your answer has ended and your planned presentation has picked up again. Bridge-building helps you redirect the argument back to your theory of the appeal so you can show the court how your theory, as a coherent whole, satisfies each concern raised from the bench.

If you're asked a question to which you do not know the answer, the best thing to say is exactly that. Judges know you're human, and, unless the point is a big one, you gain credibility by admitting that you can't answer. Moreover, judges are skilled interrogators, and if you try to fake your way through an answer, they will realize what you're doing. If you knew the answer when you prepared but can't remember it now, you might feel a little better saying something like "I'm sorry, Your Honor, but I don't recall." In real appeals (not in law school assignments), a lawyer might offer to file a supplemental brief or memorandum if the lawyer fears that the unanswered question might be crucial to the decision. Courts usually refuse these offers, which may suggest that the point isn't critical after all.

If you're not sure you understand the question, signal that indirectly so the judge can correct you, if necessary:

> If your Honor is asking about the possibility that the issue has not been preserved for review—and please correct me if I've misunderstood—trial counsel objected to the evidence and moved for . . .

Or do it directly:

> I'm sorry, Your Honor. Are you asking whether the order appealed from is final?

Except for the kinds of examples above, it's not a good idea to ask the judges questions.

In many legal writing courses, students are assigned to coauthor briefs, usually in teams of two, and to split the oral argument between them. If you're working with another student, you may be asked questions about material that your colleague intends to argue. Don't respond by saying that your colleague will answer the question. That can disconcert judges because they expect you to know enough of the other student's material that you can give at least a summary answer. If you're arguing first, your colleague can elaborate on your summary later.

§39.4 Affect, Delivery, and Style

The most effective way to present arguments is in a tone of what has been called "respectful intellectual equality."[2]

> [I]f the lawyer approaches a court with . . . awe, perhaps verging on fear, he will not be able effectively to stand up to the court's questioning. . . . It is just as important, however, not to talk down to a court. . . . The only proper attitude is that of a respectful intellectual equality. The "respectful" part approximates the quantum and type of respect that a younger [person] should show when speaking to an older one. . . . Counsel must stand up to the judges quite as he would stand up to the senior members of his own firm. If he permits himself to be overawed . . . then he—and his case—are well on their way to being lost.[3]

Although the judges have the power to decide your case, their *need* to decide the case causes them to look to you for intellectual leadership.

What works best in this situation is not a speech, but a *conversation* in which you take the initiative, talking *with* the judges—not at them. It's an unusual kind of conversation, limited by the formalities of the occasion and by a focus on the decision the bench must make, but it is a conversation nonetheless. Try to create for yourself a *persuasive presence* that helps you reach and engage the bench.

Think of nervousness as a fact of life. Even the most experienced lawyer is nervous before making an oral argument. But that anxiety tends to disappear once the lawyer becomes engaged in the conversation. For beginners, the *moment of engagement*—when you're so caught up in the work that you forget to be nervous—might not come for several minutes into the argument. But with each succeeding performance that moment will move closer and closer toward the opening, until eventually it coincides with the words "May it please the court" or "Good morning, Your Honors."

Look straight at the judges throughout the argument, preferably making eye contact. Look at your notes only to remind yourself of the next subject for discussion and, even then, get your eyes off your notes and back to the bench as fast as possible. Whenever you look away from the judges, their attention can wander to other thoughts, partially tuning you out. And judges can become impatient with lawyers who read their arguments to the court.[4]

Speak loudly enough that the judges do not have to strain to hear you. If you're soft-spoken by nature, breathe in deeply before you begin and exhale while

---

[2] Frederick Bernays Wiener, *Oral Advocacy*, 62 Harv. L. Rev. 56, 72-74 (1948).
[3] *Id.*
[4] *See* U.S. Sup. Ct. R. 28.1 ("Oral argument read from a prepared text is not favored") and Fed. R. App. P. 34(c) ("Counsel must not read at length from briefs, records, or authorities").

speaking your first words. Do this again whenever your voice falters. Make your lungs do the work, not your throat muscles. You will be surprised at how well your voice can carry. But if you already have a powerful voice, don't get carried away. A loud voice can make the bench uncomfortable.

Use the tone and volume of your voice to emphasize the more important things you say. Pause before or after your most important remarks.

Communicate tenacity with what one judge has called "disciplined earnestness": "a communicated sense of conviction that pushes a case to the limits of its strength but not beyond," using "words and body language, facial expression and eye contact, to radiate a sense of conviction without making every point a life-and-death issue."[5]

Avoid multitudes of detail when discussing cases and statutes. Focus on the big ideas. If your case is built on a synthesis of authority, describe it generally ("the majority of jurisdictions," "the recent trend of cases in other states," "seven of the federal circuits," "this court has previously held"). If you must quote—as you might with a crucial statute or holding—limit yourself to the half-dozen or so essential words that the court must interpret. Concentrate on the few most determinative facts. But you can also mention along the way a few facts that most bring the story to life. Some facts have little legal significance but help the judges "see" the story and put the case into a realistic perspective.

Don't distract the court with restless or anxious movement. Stand up straight. Don't play with a pen, shuffle your papers around frequently, put your hands in your pockets, or sway forward and back. Limit your gestures to those that naturally punctuate your argument. A visually busy lawyer radiates nervousness, rather than the confidence needed to establish psychological leadership. Stand at the lectern throughout your argument. Don't stroll out from behind it unless you need to find something in your briefcase to answer a question. And try not to let that happen. Wear conservative clothing that communicates professionalism.

§39.5 Formalities and Customs of the Courtroom

While a courtroom is in session, lawyers do not speak to each other. They speak only to the bench and—when the bench gives permission—to witnesses and juries. But because there are no witnesses or juries in appellate courts, you will speak only to the judges.

The dignity of the occasion will be demeaned if you speak in slang, in emotional rhetoric, or in terms that unnecessarily personalize the lawyers or judges. Even when discussing your adversary's arguments, refer to them as the party's, rather than as the lawyer's. There's a world of difference between "The plaintiff mistakenly relies . . ." and "Mr. Maggione mistakenly told you. . . ." Similarly, do

---

[5] Frank Morey Coffin, *The Ways of a Judge* 132 (Houghton Mifflin 1980).

not speak to the bench in flattering language. Judges are satisfied with respect. Obsequiousness makes them uncomfortable.

While your adversary argues, listen attentively and without facial expressions that could convey your opinion of what is transpiring. Write down whatever notes you will need to help you respond in your own argument (if you represent the appellee) or in rebuttal (if you represent the appellant). Don't interrupt your adversary's argument.

§39.6 Preparation for Oral Argument

Prepare two versions of the same presentation. One version would include the material that you *must* argue—the absolute core of your case. When delivered without interruption, it should fill no more than 30% or 35% of the time you're allowed. The other version would be an expanded development of the first. It would include the first version, as well as supplemental material that makes the core of your case more persuasive. If delivered without interruption, it should fill about 80% or 90% of the available time. You will know within the first two or three minutes of the argument whether the bench is hot or cold. If it's hot, you can deliver the core presentation and try to work the supplemental material into your answers. If the bench is cold, you can deliver the expanded argument.

There are many ways to prepare notes to use at the lectern. After you have argued several times, you will figure out which type and style of notes work best for you. But the consensus of experienced advocates is that you're better off with the fewest notes possible because you need them only to remind yourself of the subjects you intend to cover as well as a few key phrases that you intend to use.

If you're well prepared, you will know your case so well that a single page on a legal-size pad might be sufficient. If, in preparing the argument, you come up with an excellent phrasing for a difficult concept, you might write down those few words to remind yourself to use them. Otherwise, your notes should be only a list of subjects to cover. You can outline both versions of your argument on a single page divided by a vertical line, the core version on one side of the vertical line and the expanded version on the other side. Or you could take two pads to the podium, one for each version. But try to use only the top page on a pad. If you go to the second page, you might have too many notes. Some advocates take to the lectern notecards with synopses of the record and of the major relevant cases. You might or might not find that helpful. If you already know your case thoroughly, the cards might only get in your way.

Take the record and both briefs to the podium as well, in case you're asked about them.

Make a list of every weakness in your case and every question that you might ask if you were a judge. Prepare ways of overcoming the weaknesses and answering the questions. If you can't imagine hard questions a judge might ask, study your adversary's brief and the precedents that are contrary to your position.

Try also to predict any concessions you might be asked to make. Figure out which concessions you cannot afford to give up and which you might have to make to protect the reasonableness of the rest of your case. If you need to think about this for the first time at the podium when a judge asks you a question, you could make a serious and costly mistake.

Practice making your argument to a person who will ask you tough questions but who knows little about your theory of the appeal. If the person mooting you knows too much about your theory, the experience will be unrealistic.

Finally, update your research the day before you argue. The time between submission of the brief and oral argument might equal up to a month in law school and perhaps several months in the practice of law. Check to see whether controlling statutes have been amended or repealed, whether one of the key cases has been overruled, and whether any of the recent precedents has been reversed or affirmed. You don't need to check every citation in your brief, but it can be devastating to discover in the courtroom that some important texture of the law has changed.

Appendices

Sample Office Memorandum

Citation form in this memorandum conforms to local practice, which is permitted by both the ALWD Citation Manual and the Bluebook. The ALWD Citation Manual does so explicitly: "local custom sometimes dictates that local rules be used in other documents . . . , such as interoffice memoranda."[1] The Bluebook does so for documents submitted to a court (see the first page of the Bluebook's blue pages.[2] Clients need not be asked to pay for the extra effort it would take to cite differently in an office memo on the same issue.

---

[1] ALWD & Darby Dickerson, *ALWD Citation Manual* 8 (3d ed., 2006).
[2] *The Bluebook: A Uniform System of Citation* 3 (18th ed., 2005).

To: Verdetta Midori
From: Elizabeth Gastélum
Re: Chris Thorburn
Date: November 17, 2005

ISSUE

Is the City of Carbondale liable to a bicyclist injured on a public street and as a result of repairs the City performed?

BRIEF ANSWER

Probably not. A court would likely hold that the City is immunized from liability by the Illinois Local Governmental and Governmental Employees Tort Immunity Act.

FACTS

Chris Thorburn was riding her bike north on Oakland Street, at the intersection of Oakland and Whitney, when her front wheel wedged into a gap between two metal plates covering a hole. She was thrown forward and sustained a tendon injury to her thumb requiring medical treatment. Her insurance paid for the treatment, but the injury prevented her from working for five weeks.

Immediately before the incident, Ms. Thorburn saw construction on Oakland Street, but no workers were present at the work site. When Ms. Thorburn noticed two metal plates in the street, she looked to her left before attempting to move farther out into the street and pass them. But a Hummer on her left side prevented her from avoiding the plates. The city had been preparing the site to repair a broken water main.

On each side of Oakland Street are two signs facing in opposite directions immediately before and after the intersection of Grand and Oakland streets and approximately one block from the spot where Ms. Thorburn was injured. The signs are identical: yellow and diamond-shaped with a picture of a bicycle. One sign faces north and the other south. The south-facing sign, which could be seen by a cyclist traveling north (like Ms. Thorburn), is attached to a pole just above another sign that says "NO PARKING." The north-facing yellow bicycle sign, which a cyclist would see while traveling south, is above a sign attached separately to the pole that reads, "BIKE XING."

The yellow bicycle signs on Oakland Street are identical to yellow signs that appear on the cover the Carbondale Bikeway Map. These yellow

1

diamond shaped signs are also shown on the Illinois Secretary of State's website. The Secretary of State's website says yellow diamond-shaped signs warn of a hazard or potential hazard on or near the roadway. The back cover of the Carbondale Bikeway Map states that Carbondale has a "system of recommended bicycle routes," and that green signs are in place along those routes. No green "bike route" signs are posted on Oakland Street. The map inside the Carbondale Bikeway Map shows that Grand Street is a bike route and Oakland Street is not. The Bikeway Map is published by the City.

Yellow diamond-shaped signs depicting bicycles are common along Oakland Street, which is near Southern Illinois University. Students and faculty from Southern Illinois University have historically bicycled along Oakland Street because it connects an entrance to the campus with many intersecting residential side streets where students rent housing.

DISCUSSION

The City is probably not liable to Ms. Thorburn. A local government in Illinois cannot be liable for injuries sustained on city property unless the injured person was an "intended" and "permitted" user of the property under the Local Governmental and Governmental Employees Tort Immunity Act, 745 Ill. Comp. Stat. §10/3-102(a) (2007). Even if a local government has been negligent, this immunity is a complete defense because a local government owes a duty of care only to intended and permitted users of its property. *Id.*

The Tests for Determining When a Cyclist Is an Intended and Permitted User

The leading Illinois case on whether cyclists are intended and permitted users of a public street is *Boub v. Township of Wayne*, 183 Ill. 2d 520, 702 N.E.2d 535 (1998). The court held that under §10/3-102(a) a local government's intent can be determined by the nature of the property together with any presence or absence of "pavement markings, signs, or other physical manifestations." 183 Ill. 2d at 528, 702 N.E.2d at 539. The cyclist in *Boub* was injured when a tire became caught between two wooden planks on a bridge under repair. *Id.* He argued that he was an intended and permitted user because no sign suggested that bicycles were prohibited on the bridge, and because a bicycle, like any other vehicle, is permitted on a road unless prohibited. The court disagreed and held that for the purposes of §10/3-102(a) a cyclist is treated as a pedestrian, who is not intended or permitted in the street unless pavement markings or signs communicate otherwise. 183 Ill. 2d at 528, 702 N.E.2d at 539.

2

Cyclists have succeeded in lawsuits against local governments only where the government has marked a portion of a street for bicycle use. For example, a cyclist whose tire caught in a sewer grate prevailed because pavement markings demonstrated that the city had intended and permitted that cyclists travel exactly where the injury occurred. *Cole v. City of East Peoria*, 201 Ill. App. 3d 756, 559 N.E.2d 769 (1990). The fact that "the City ordered a white line painted a distance from the curb" indicated that the City intended for the area to be "used by others than those driving automobiles." 201 Ill. App. 3d at 761, 559 N.E.2d at 773.

Illinois courts are divided on whether a city is presumed to have intended and permitted use by cyclists when the city knew that cyclists have ridden on a particular street for a long time. The Appellate Court, Third District, held that "[h]istorical practice, when considered in conjunction with other factors," can show that a city has permitted and intended that use. *Brooks v. City of Peoria*, 305 Ill. App. 3d 806, 712 N.E.2d 387 (Ill. App. 3d Dist. 1999). In *Brooks*, a child bicycling on a sidewalk was held to be an intended user. 305 Ill. App. 3d at 810, 712 N.E.2d at 390. Among the other factors relied on by the *Brooks* court was the city's ability to foresee how the public would use the sidewalk. 305 Ill. App. 3d at 810-812, 712 N.E.2d at 390-392.

Brooks, however, will not control Ms. Thorburn's case. The *Boub* plaintiff argued that cyclists had traditionally used roads like the one where he was injured, but the state Supreme Court held that "historical practice alone" does not "make a particular use of public property an intended one." *Boub*, 183 Ill. 2d at 531, 702 N.E.2d at 541.

Moreover, Carbondale is in the Fifth District, where the Appellate Court came to the same conclusion the Supreme Court later did in *Boub*. *Deren v. City of Carbondale*, 13 Ill. App. 3d 473, 300 N.E.2d 550 (Ill. App. 5th Dist. 1973). The *Deren* plaintiff was injured near Southern Illinois University while walking in a street that students and others had long used as a walkway because of the absence of a sidewalk. *Id.* The court rejected a theory that this history and the city's apparent knowledge of it showed governmental intent and permission. "Plaintiff's complaint does not charge that the city took any *action* to convert a portion of the street to a sidewalk." 13 Ill. App. 3d 473, 477, 300 N.E.2d 550, 553 (italics added).

Even if the Illinois Supreme Court had not decided *Boub*, a trial court in Carbondale would still be bound by the similar holding in *Deren*. The Supreme Court has held that "when conflicts arise amongst the districts, the circuit court is bound by the decisions of the appellate court of the district in which it sits." *Alekson v. Village of Round Lake Park*, 176 Ill. 2d 82, 92, 679 N.E.2d 1224, 1229 (1997).

3

As a Cyclist, Ms. Thorburn Was Probably
Not an Intended and Permitted User.

Ms. Thorburn will probably not succeed in arguing that historical usage as well as signs on Oakland Street show that the City intended and permitted cyclists to use the street.

Both *Boub* and *Deren* held that historical usage could not show that the City intended and permitted cycling on Oakland Street. Thus, it is irrelevant that students and faculty from Southern Illinois University have historically bicycled along Oakland Street because it connects a campus entrance to many residential streets, especially those lined with affordable student housing. That is so even though the City could have foreseen this long-standing bicycle use for a long time.

The yellow signs on Oakland Street do depict bicycles. And anyone who has seen the city's Bikeway map would recognize the sign on its cover as similar to the signs on Oakland Street. Ms. Thorburn could point out that the signs facing her on the street indicated to motorists and other users on Oakland Street that bicycles travel on this road and that parking is prohibited. A reasonable inference from the locations of these two signs on the same pole is that parking is prohibited in order to allow for greater room along the street for cyclists.

But the City can more plausibly argue that it is unreasonable for cyclists to construe the signs to mark Oakland Street as a bike route. Motorists are expected to know that yellow diamond-shaped signs warn of hazards. In this case, the signs warn motorists to be alert for the sudden emergence of a bicycle crossing Oakland Street. In addition, under *Cole* the signs would create an intended and permitted use only if the City had also clearly marked a portion of the street as a bike lane, perhaps with painted white lines.

The City can also plausibly argue that the yellow sign on the front of the Carbondale Bikeway Map is irrelevant because there are no green "bike route" signs on Oakland Street. And the map inside the Carbondale Bikeway Map shows that Grand Street is a bike route and Oakland Street is not. A sign at Grand Street says "BIKE XING," which instead more logically marks a bicycle crossing for the established bike route on Grand Street that crosses Oakland Street. Thus the only intended and permitted use is to cross Oakland Street at Grand Street, which is not what Ms. Thorburn was doing when injured. Instead, she had been traveling on Oakland Street for some distance, and she was injured at Whitney Street.

4

CONCLUSION

The Local Governmental and Governmental Employees Tort Immunity Act immunizes a city against users that it has not "intended" and "permitted." While it would seem that cities permit and intend cyclists to use public streets, case law shows this intent to be difficult to prove. Under the case law, the street signs, the Bikeway Map, and historical usage of the street by cyclists probably do not show the City intended or permitted cycling on Oakland Street. Thus, Ms. Thorburn probably would not be able to obtain a judgment against the City.

5

Sample Client Advice Letter

A sample letter begins on the next page.

The client is Ada Warren of Lincoln Notch, Vermont. She's in her late fifties. When the Lincoln Creamery fell on hard times a few years ago, she lost her job as office manager and lived thereafter on savings. When her cousin Virgil died last year, she inherited his farm near Grafton, which she sold to a Boston developer for half a million dollars. She then booked a cruise on the *Pride of Seaside*, a six-cabin sailing yacht.

Huber & Stanislaw
Attorneys at Law
6 Front Street
Seaside ME 01203
(603) 555-1111

March 14, 2011

Ada Warren
22 Green Mountain Road
Lincoln Notch VT

Dear Ms. Warren:

As I promised when we met last week, I've researched your rights against Seaside Cruises and the state Marine Police. I think you probably would win a lawsuit against Seaside but lose against the police. In the second half of this letter, I'll explain why.

After you and I spoke last week, I examined the police logs and talked to some of the passengers, police, and crew. I was able to get some information (though not much) from the police officers and the captain of the *Pride of Seaside.* My advice later in this letter is based on my understanding of the facts, which are described in the next few paragraphs. If I've gotten any of the facts wrong, please tell me so that I can determine whether the law would treat the situation differently.

Facts

You boarded the *Pride of Seaside* at 8:30 in the evening. The boat left the dock at 9:00 p.m., and you went below at 9:30, drew your cabin curtains, and were asleep by about 10:15. At 10:40 p.m., the boat was boarded by Officers Magrane and Kroyer of the State Marine Police, who suspected that a sailor had marijuana hidden behind his bunk. They found what they were looking for, arrested the sailor, and ordered the captain to steam to the Marine Police dock. There, the boat was impounded and the sailor was taken away by the police. The other passengers and the rest of the crew were awakened by the ruckus and came on deck, where they were told by Officer Kroyer that they would have to leave the boat. Officer Magrane drove the passengers (except you) in a Marine Police van to a hotel, where they slept.

1

Neither the crew nor the police searched the boat to make sure no one else was aboard. The police officers did not ask for a list of passengers. The crew did not offer a passenger list to the police or compare the passengers on deck with the boat's passenger manifest. The police say they thought it was the crew's responsibility to get everyone off the boat. The captain says that he thought the police were doing that. You slept through the night. At 12:15 a.m., Officer Kroyer sealed the boat. He locked every outer door and hatch—including the door separating the main deck from the passageway on which the passengers' cabins are situated—removed the gangway, locked it in a shed, and went home. As a result, even though your cabin was unlocked, you would not have been able to get to the deck because all the doors and hatches were locked from the outside, and even if you had been able to get to the deck, you would not have been able to walk off the boat.

No one else was at the dock until Officer Tedescu arrived at about 6:30 the next morning. He found a note from Kroyer that the boat had been impounded but had not yet been searched, except for the sailor's bunk. He rolled out the gangway, walked on board, and at 6:45 unlocked doors and hatches. You were still asleep. You awoke at about 7:00, opened your cabin door, and found Officer Tedescu standing in the passageway. Officer Tedescu explained what had happened, and you felt light-headed and fell to the floor of the passageway. You revived in a moment or two, and he drove you to a hospital, where an emergency room physician decided that you needed no treatment.

You collapsed because of the shock and indignity of learning that you had spent the night locked up in a police boat yard rather than cruising at sea as you thought you had been. For you, this was the same as being locked up in a jail cell overnight because in both situations you would feel as though you were being treated as a criminal. Except for collapsing, you did not suffer physically from these events. Seaside Cruises has refused to refund the $3,500 that you paid for this two-week cruise. As I understand it, they have not provided any of the passengers with a refund.

Possible Lawsuits

I'll explain what I think would happen if you were to sue Seaside Cruises and the Marine Police.

Seaside Cruises: The law considers Seaside to be a common carrier. A common carrier is a business, like an airline, that transports anyone who pays the fare. Common carriers owe a very high degree of care to their passengers, including the duty to rescue a passenger from harm. Based on

2

the facts we have at this point, I think you would probably win on this claim. Seaside's employees should have made sure you were off the boat before it was locked up or at least told the police that you were aboard.

But it's harder to predict how much money a jury would award on this claim. It might be small because you were unaware at the time that you were locked in the boat. Or it might be larger if the jury can appreciate the depth of the indignity.

In addition, Seaside Cruises does owe you a refund of $3,500. You paid for transportation (a cruise), which Seaside did not provide. The law is clear that they are not entitled to keep the money, even though the cruise was prevented by police seizure of their boat.

You can bring both claims against Seaside—for the refund and for failing to get you off the boat—in a single lawsuit.

The Marine Police: I believe that you would not win a lawsuit against the state for false imprisonment. In this state, a false imprisonment claim can succeed only if the person confined knew of the confinement while it was occurring or was harmed by it. The law defines "harm" in this sense as economic loss or physical injury.

You did suffer an economic loss (the $3,500 that Seaside has not refunded), but not because you were locked in the boat. If the police had taken you to the hotel, Seaside would still have refused to refund the money since they have not provided a refund to any of the passengers who were taken to the hotel.

Because you learned of your confinement only after Officer Tedescu had unlocked the boat, we could succeed in a suit against the police only by showing that the confinement caused you physical injury. The only physical injury is your collapse when Officer Tedescu told you that you had been confined. Unfortunately, in a case called *Osborne v. Floyd*, our state supreme court recently decided that the physical injury must be caused by the confinement itself. It's not enough for the harm to be caused by knowledge of the confinement. In *Osborne*, a man was comatose and unaware he had been locked in a cellar. His medical condition did not deteriorate while he was locked in. But after he regained consciousness and learned what had happened, he experienced nightmares. The court held that the nightmares were not sufficient, and an injury would have to be physical for him to recover. I think the courts would treat your collapsing onto the floor the same way, especially because the emergency room physician decided that you needed no medical treatment. I wish this weren't so, but unfortunately, it is.

If, after thinking this over, you want to sue Seaside Cruises, I can explain what a lawsuit would cost so you can decide whether to go ahead. It might be

3

possible to reduce the expense of suing if other passengers join with you and sue together to get the refunds to which you each are entitled. Please call my office when it's convenient.

Sincerely,

Gary Stanislaw
Gary Stanislaw

4

Sample Motion Memorandum

UNITED STATES DISTRICT COURT FOR THE SOUTHERN
DISTRICT OF ILLINOIS

GEORGE VEDITZ,

       Plaintiff

    v.   2010-C-365

AMOS KENDALL,

       Defendant

MEMORANDUM IN SUPPORT OF PLAINTIFF'S MOTION FOR AN
ORDER COMPELLING MEDIATION

PRELIMINARY STATEMENT

Mr. Veditz has sued Mr. Kendall for failure to provide accommodations required by the Americans with Disabilities Act. Although Mr. Veditz has sued for an injunction and other relief, he prefers to mediate this dispute rather than go to trial. Mr. Kendall refuses to mediate. Mr. Veditz has now moved for an order compelling mediation.

STATEMENT OF THE CASE

The plaintiff, George Veditz, is deaf. Amos Kendall, the defendant and an attorney, represented Mr. Veditz in a divorce action. During that lawsuit, Mr. Veditz at times had difficulty understanding what was happening and why it was happening because the defendant failed to supply translation services that a deaf person in Mr. Veditz's situation could understand.

Last year, Mr. Veditz suffered a total hearing loss as a result of meningitis. (Aff. Amos Kendall ¶¶ 2 (July 22, 2008).) Since then, Mr. Veditz has learned some Signed Exact English (SEE), but the only way he can fully converse is through Computer Assisted Real-time Transcription (CART). (Pl.'s Cmpl. ¶ 6, 7 (June 1, 2008).) SEE is a sign language grammatically similar to English, and CART is frequently used for communication with deaf people. (Aff. Laurent Clerc. ¶ 4 (July 14, 2008.) A person who has

1

recently become deaf as an adult typically can communicate most effectively through SEE and CART. (*Id.* at ¶¶ 4, 5.)

At the settlement conference in Mr. Veditz's divorce case, both parties and their lawyers were present. (Pl.'s Compl. ¶ 9.) The lawyers and Mr. Veditz's former spouse talked continually for two hours. (*Id.*) Mr. Veditz could not understand most of what they said because the defendant had hired an uncertified interpreter who knew only American Sign Language (ASL)—and not SEE. (*Id.* at ¶¶ 9, 12-16.) Attempts at communicating in ASL, a language that Mr. Veditz does not know, confused him so much that he did not understand many of the details of the discussion and could not participate in it fully. (*Id.* at ¶ 10.) The defendant knew that Mr. Veditz was still learning to sign, but he failed to ask Mr. Veditz how to accommodate his needs. (*Id.* at ¶ 11.)

According to a communication specialist, Laurent Clerc, SEE is the appropriate method of signed communication for Mr. Veditz. (Aff. Clerc. ¶ 8.) Mr. Clerc, who regularly assesses the needs of deaf people, concluded that CART is the ideal means for a hearing person to communicate with Mr. Veditz. (*Id.* at ¶¶ 2, 9.) These services are widely used at a rate of $150 per hour. (*Id.* at ¶¶ 10-11.)

Mr. Veditz believes that the Defendant's failure to provide an adequate means of communication resulted in an unfair settlement because he was unable to participate in the discussions that led to the settlement. (Pl.'s Compl. ¶ 17.) Mr. Veditz will continue to have a maintenance obligation and will need continuing legal assistance from the defendant as a result of the defendant's failure to sufficiently accommodate Mr. Veditz pursuant to Title III of the American Disabilities Act (ADA). (*Id.* at. ¶ 18.) The defendant charged Mr. Veditz $100 per hour of service. (Aff. Kendall ¶¶ 2, 4.) The Defendant contends that "[t]he costs of CART are beyond what my practice can bear." (Aff. Kendall ¶ 14.)

Mediation has not yet taken place because Mr. Kendall has refused. (Aff. Kendall ¶ 4.) He claims that mediation will cost too much of his money and time. (*Id.*)

ARGUMENT

The Court Should Compel Mediation Between Mr. Veditz and Mr. Kendall.

A federal court has the authority to compel mediation in a lawsuit brought under the Americans with Disabilities Act. This authority derives from Rule 16(c)(2)(I) of the Federal Rules of Civil Procedure; Local Rule 16(a); the Americans with Disabilities Act, 42 U.S.C. §12212 (2006), and the court's inherent powers. Because of the relationship between the parties

2

and the nature of the dispute, the court should grant an order compelling mediation of this lawsuit.

A. The Relevant Court Rules and Statute Authorize and Encourage Mediation.

Rule 16(a) of the Federal Rules of Civil Procedure provides that "[i]n any action, the court may in its discretion direct [the parties to] appear before [the court] . . . before trial for such purposes as (1) expediting the disposition of the action . . . and (5) facilitating the settlement of the case." Federal Rule 16(c) provides that "the use of special procedures to assist in resolving the dispute, *when authorized by statute or local rule* . . . may facilitate the just, speedy, and inexpensive disposition of the action" (italics added). Rule 16 thus authorizes District Courts to order parties to participate in alternative dispute resolution. *Federal Reserve Bank v. Carey-Canada, Inc.*, 123 F.R.D. 603, 607 (D. Minn. 1988). "It is hard to imagine that the drafters of the 1983 amendments actually intended to strengthen courts' ability to manage their caseloads while at the same time intended to deny the court the power to compel participation by the parties to the litigation." *Id.*

Local Rule 16.2(a) of the Southern District of Illinois provides that a court may, "in its discretion, set any civil case for . . . [any] alternative method of dispute resolution which the court may deem proper," such as mediation. Local Rule 16.2(b)(3) provides that "any issue which, in the judge's opinion, may facilitate and expedite the trial . . . shall be discussed at the final pretrial conference and shall be included in the final pretrial order." Local Rule 16.3(a) further gives the court authorization to employ "alternative method[s] of dispute resolution which the court may deem proper," in order to "encourage and promote the use of alternative dispute resolution" so that "parties shall use an early neutral evaluation in the form of a settlement conference."

Mr. Veditz has sued under the Americans with Disabilities Act, 42 U.S.C. §§12101 et seq. (2007). Congress found that "communication barriers" are one of the ways in which "society has tended to isolate and segregate" the disabled. §12101(a)(1), (2), (5). The ADA prohibits discrimination on the basis of disability in a number of settings, including a lawyer's office. §12181(7)(F). The ADA also encourages mediation of complaints of discrimination. §12212.

B. Under Its Inherent Powers, the Court Can Order Mediation.

Even if no other law authorized a court to compel mediation, the court would still be able to do so through its inherent powers. Every federal court

3

has inherent powers "governed not by rule or statute but by the control necessarily vested in courts to manage their own affairs so as to achieve the orderly and expeditious disposition of cases." *Link v. Wabash R.R. Co.,* 370 U.S. 626, 630-631 (1962). Mediation in particular can accomplish an "expeditious disposition" of an appropriate case.

Both of the federal courts that have considered this question held that, despite a party's objection, inherent judicial powers can be used to compel mediation. *In re Atlantic Pipe Corp.,* 304 F.3d 135, 140 (1st Cir. 2002); *In re African-American Slave Descendants' Litig.,* 272 F. Supp. 2d 755, 759 (N.D. Ill. 2003). The *Atlantic Pipe* court reasoned that in cases especially difficult to resolve through trial, mediation can turn out to be much more effective than the objecting party imagined. 304 F.3d at 143. Unlike a trial, in which one party wins and the other loses, a mediation can lead to a solution that benefits both parties. *Id.* at 145.

The *African-American* court agreed in general but held that the unique nature of that particular lawsuit made mediation less satisfactory than trial. 272 F. Supp. 2d at 759-760. There, descendants of enslaved African-Americans sued several corporations for reparations on the ground that the defendants had profited from slavery. The defendants argued that they could not be legally liable to the plaintiffs, and that the only way to resolve the dispute would be through a trial, where liability could be determined. *Id.* at 760.

C. The Court Should Order Mediation in This Case.

Because Mr. Veditz will need the defendant's cooperation in the future with issues arising from Mr. Veditz's divorce, trial could not effectively resolve this dispute. Trial is a conflict in which one side wins and the other loses. Mediation seeks a resolution that both parties can accept as fair and reasonable.

In a case analogous to this one, a doctor refused to provide a deaf interpreter when meeting with a deaf patient. *Mayberry v. von Valtier,* 843 F. Supp. 1160 (E.D. Mich. 1994). The doctor argued that paying for an interpreter would prevent the doctor from making a profit from treatment of the patient. The patient was dependent on the doctor for medical care. Unable to pay for an interpreter herself, the patient sued under the ADA for an injunction requiring the doctor to treat the patient and to provide an interpreter at the doctor's expenses. The trial court held that the patient had made out a prima facie case of discrimination under the ADA.

4

313

CONCLUSION

Local Rule 16.3(a), Federal Rule 16, and the ADA authorize and encourage court-ordered mediation. Moreover, a court can order mediation through the court's inherent powers. Because the defendant is the plaintiff's former lawyer and will continue to play a role in Mr. Veditz's divorce representation, mediation is the most effective method of resolving this dispute. Therefore, this court should enter an order compelling mediation between the parties to this lawsuit.

Respectfully Submitted,

Nathan J. Bailey
Nathan J. Bailey
Attorney for Plaintiff

5

Sample Appellant's Brief

In some ways, the format of this brief does not follow practices in the Seventh Circuit, where the appeal is set. Instead, the brief's format blends practices in many courts so that it is somewhat representative nationally.

In the UNITED STATES COURT OF APPEALS
for the SEVENTH CIRCUIT
Docket No. 2011—Civ.—141

AMOS KENDALL
Appellant
v.
GEORGE VEDITZ,
Appellee

ON APPEAL FROM JUDGMENT OF THE DISTRICT COURT
FOR THE SOUTHERN DISTRICT OF ILLINOIS

BRIEF FOR THE APPELLANT

Joanne Olson
Caroline Borden
Attorneys for the Appellant

TABLE OF CONTENTS

Page

i

TABLE OF AUTHORITIES

---

* Authorities chiefly relied on are marked with an asterisk.

ii

iii

PROCEEDINGS BELOW

George Veditz, Appellee, is a former client of Amos Kendall, Appellant and a member of the Illinois bar. Veditz sued Kendall, alleging that Kendall failed to comply with Title III of the Americans with Disabilities Act and seeking an injunction and court-ordered mediation. (R. at 2, 11.) Kendall denied all the allegations in the complaint. (R. at 6). Both parties waived their rights to a trial by jury. (R. at 11.)

Over Kendall's objection, the District Court ordered both parties to submit to mediation, but stayed the execution of the order pending appeal. (R. at 11.) Mr. Kendall has now appealed to this Court. (R. at 28, 29.)

QUESTION PRESENTED

Mediation is a form of alternative dispute resolution through which disputing parties, with the assistance of a mediator, try to resolve their dispute. It is a collaborative alternative to an adversarial trial. Because mediation is collaborative rather than adversarial, it succeeds when parties discuss their dispute together and work with each other to resolve it. In this lawsuit, Kendall objects to mediation and is convinced that it will fail. He believes that his rights can be protected only through a trial because he provided Veditz with a deaf-signing translator at a settlement conference and because he otherwise communicated with Veditz through typing on a laptop, which Veditz himself uses in his own job to communicate reliably. On these facts: Did the District Court exceed its authority or abuse its discretion in ordering Kendall to mediate this lawsuit? Did the District err in determining that the accommodations provided by Kendall violate the Americans with Disabilities Act?

STATEMENT OF THE CASE

Amos Kendall, a seasoned attorney, is committed to providing clients with disabilities full and equal enjoyment of his legal services. His office is free from physical barriers, and he has represented many disabled clients. George Veditz, a client, has sued Kendall alleging that Kendall failed to provide a Signed Exact English (SEE) interpreter or a Computer Assisted Real Time Transcription (CART) even though Veditz did not request either of these accommodations.

Accommodations Provided to Veditz

While Kendall was representing Veditz in his divorce proceedings, Veditz became deaf due to viral meningitis. (R. at 13.) As a late-deafened adult, Veditz can communicate most accurately through writing, which he has

1

known and used all his life. (R. at 14.) At work, he communicates through writing. (R. at 14.) Veditz has never had formal training in any signed language. (R. at 4.) After the loss of his hearing, he has attempted to teach himself how to sign and now has a small vocabulary of signs. (R. at 14.) Veditz can understand some Signed Exact English (SEE), which has a grammar structure identical to English, but he is not fluent in SEE. (*Id.*) He has a difficult time understanding American Sign Language, which uses its own unique grammar. (R. at 4.) While Computer Assisted Real Time Transcription (CART) is an efficient method of written communication for late-deafened adults, handwritten or typed exchanges are also effective. (R. at 19.)

Initially, Kendall and Veditz communicated in part through written exchanges via a laptop (R. at 15). Kendall typed so that Veditz could read on the laptop screen. (*Id.*) Veditz communicated by speaking. (*Id.*) They also used email. (*Id.*) Veditz testified that although writing was not fast communication, he always understood what Kendall was telling him, and that he uses writing almost exclusively himself to communicate at work. (R. at 14-15.) Knowing that Veditz was learning signs, Kendall hired a sign language interpreter, Jane Fesenden, for the divorce settlement negotiations. (R. at 8.) Veditz did not ask Kendall to provide an interpreter or CART for the negotiation. (R. at 18, 24.)

The Divorce Negotiation

During the negotiation, Veditz told Fesenden he was unfamiliar with the grammar of ASL. (R. at 15.) Fesenden tried to use English grammar when signing to Veditz, but had to repeat herself and occasionally used ASL grammar. (R. at 16.) Regardless of the grammar Fesenden used, Veditz had trouble understanding her because he did not understand many of her signs. (*Id.*) Privately during the negotiation, Veditz told Kendall that he could not understand much of what Fesenden was translating. (R. at 16.) After learning that, Kendall typed accurate summaries of what each person said during the negotiation for Veditz to read. (R. at 16, 23.) Veditz testified that the typed summaries of the negotiation were "a way to be sure" he was understanding things correctly. (R. at 16.) Kendall testified that with the typed summaries Veditz was able to participate in the settlement. (R. at 23.) Veditz did not tell Kendall in any other way that the communication was ineffective, and he did not ask for CART services at that time. (R. at 18.) Moreover, Veditz did not ask that the negotiation be adjourned, and he did not ask that it be reopened later. (*Id.*) At the time of the negotiation, Veditz had never before used CART. (*Id.*)

Adequacy of Accommodations Balanced against Cost

Veditz alleged he was unable to fully participate in the negotiation and now needs continued legal counsel from Kendall to renegotiate the

2

maintenance settlement. (R. at 2, 16.) Veditz also alleged that the communication obstacle would be remedied by the use of CART. (R. at 17.) From these allegations, Veditz claimed that Kendall did not make sufficient accommodations. (R. at 2.) Veditz testified that he wanted Kendall to use CART if he represents him in the future. (R. at 17.)

Kendall has tried but cannot find a certified SEE interpreter in southern Illinois (R. at 8). Although CART is available, it costs $150 per hour, which Veditz wants Kendall to pay (R. at 23). Kendall bills only $100 per hour for his services. (*Id.*) Kendall has made sure his office has no physical barriers that would hinder clients with movement disabilities, of whom he has represented many. (R. at 8.) As far as Kendall knows, every other disabled client has been satisfied with Kendall's work and the disability accommodations that he has provided. (*Id.*)

SUMMARY OF THE ARGUMENT

The finding that Veditz requested CART services is clearly erroneous because it is contradicted and unsupported by the evidence. Even if Veditz had requested CART services, Kendall would not have to provide CART because CART is unnecessary and unreasonable. CART is unnecessary because Kendall provided Veditz with Veditz's own best method of communication, written English in typed summaries. As a late-deafened adult, Vedtiz has communication needs that are unique, and unlike most deaf people, he communicates best with written English. Finally, Kendall does not have to provide CART, which would be an unreasonable accommodation. Providing CART would be an undue burden because Kendall would lose $50 for every hour he supplies CART.

The District Court abused its discretion by ordering mediation over Kendall's objection. Even if the District Court has the power to order mediation in some cases, it should not have done so here because mediation would be pointless. Because Kendall objects to it and believes that only trial can protect his interests, mediation probably would not lead to a settlement.

ARGUMENT

I.
Kendall Should Not Be Required, Over
His Objection, to Mediate a Case That
He Could Reasonably Win at Trial.

Whether Veditz asked for CART services is a pure question of fact subject to the clearly erroneous standard of review. Fed. R. Civ. P. 52(a). A finding of fact is clearly erroneous if it leaves the court with "the definite and firm conviction that a mistake has been committed." *Anderson v. City of*

3

Bessemer City, 470 U.S. 564, 573 (1984). The Court of Appeals does not have to accept the District Court's findings of fact if they are not supported by the evidence. *Campana Corp. v. Harrison*, 114 F.2d 400, 405 (7th Cir. 1940).

The remaining ADA questions are mixed questions of law and fact. Whether Kendall provided an appropriate auxiliary aid that ensures effective communication is a mixed question requiring the court to apply legal rules to undisputed facts. The last issue under the ADA claim, the undue burden defense, is also a mixed question requiring a court to interpret and apply the undue burden test to the facts of the case. In the Seventh Circuit, a mixed question of law and fact is reviewed *de novo* when "there is a need for uniformity" and "the issue is so important that there is a felt need to authorize second-guessing of" the District Court. *Cook v. City of Chicago*, 192 F.3d 693, 697 (7th Cir. 1999). Both are true here because the court below took the extraordinary step of ordering Kendall, over his objection, to take part in mediation, a process that works only when the parties participate voluntarily.

A. *Veditz Did Not Request CART and Therefore Cannot Win at Trial Concerning That Accommodation.*

Veditz failed to request CART. Even if Veditz had made such a request, CART is unnecessary and unreasonable given the cost, and Kendall still could not be required to modify his practice of providing deaf clients with interpreters and written exchanges, which are generally effective.

When providing auxiliary aids to disabled people, a business subject to the ADA should ask what auxiliary aid will work best, but the business is not obligated to provide the stated preference. *Majocha v. Turner*, 166 F. Supp. 2d 316, 321 (W.D. Pa. 2001). In *Majocha*, the court held that if a business provided an auxiliary aid that ensured effective communication, a disabled person could not insist on a different auxiliary aid. *Id*. at 323. A business is not obliged to change its practices in order to provide a more technologically advanced auxiliary aid so long as the aid in current use ensures effective communication. 28 C.F.R. pt. 36, App. B (2004) (Attorney General's Report).

If a business provides ineffective auxiliary aids, disabled people can request that the business change its practice of providing such aids, and the business is obligated to change the practice if the modification is requested, reasonable and necessary. 42 U.S.C. §12182(b)(2)(A)(ii) (2000); *Dudley v. Hannaford Bros. Co.*, 333 F.3d 299, 307 (1st Cir. 2003). In determining whether a modification is reasonable, courts balance the effectiveness of the modification against the cost of making the modification. *Fortyune v. American Multi-Cinema*, 364 F.3d 1075 (9th Cir. 2004). A modification is necessary if a disabled person would be unable to use

4

the facilities, services or goods without it. *See PGA Tour, Inc. v. Martin,* 532 U.S. 661, 682 (2001).

Here, the District Court found that Veditz requested CART services and that Kendall failed to provide the requested service. (R. at 28.) At the time of the negotiation meeting, Veditz had never used CART. (R. at 18.) He admits that he never asked for CART services. (*Id.*) If Veditz did not ask for the services, the only request that the court could find would be an implied one. But an implied request does not give a business enough notice to change its policy. An explicit request is necessary because without it the business may not know how or why to change its practices. The District Court erred because no evidence in the record supports the District Court's findings.

The District Court's finding that Veditz requested CART is not supported by any evidence in the record and should be reversed.

B. Veditz Needed No Accommodation Because Kendall Provided Effective Communication.

The District Court erred in finding that Kendall did not provide effective communication. The typed summaries Kendall provided resulted in effective communication during the negotiation settlement because Veditz was able to understand and participate in the negotiation settlement.

The evidentiary record does not support the District Court's conclusion that the communication provided by Kendall was ineffective. (R. at 13.) Veditz testified that the typed written communication *was* effective during the office meetings with Kendall. (R. at 13.) During the negotiations, Veditz had trouble understanding the interpreter and he stopped the meeting, seeking to remedy this communication problem. (R. at 16.) He did not object after Kendall began typing summaries. (*Id.*) If the typed summaries were ineffective, Veditz could have easily stopped the meeting a second time. From these uncontroverted facts, the most reasonable inference is that Veditz let the meeting continue because he understood and participated in the negotiations.

The District Court's decision that Kendall failed to provide effective communication is clearly erroneous and should be reversed because Kendall provided Veditz with written English, his best way of communicating.

C. Kendall Probably Will Not Be Enjoined to Provide CART Services Because the Cost Would Impose an Undue Burden.

A business need not provide disabled persons with auxiliary aids if doing so would be an undue burden. 42 U.S.C. §12182(b)(2)(A)(iii) (2000).

5

Providing an auxiliary aid would be an undue burden if it is overly expensive or difficult to provide. 28 C.F.R. 5 §§36.104, 36.303 (2004). Because of their high costs, the District Court erred in finding that CART services were not an undue burden.

The case law provides examples of how to apply the factors listed in 28 C.F.R. §36.104 (2004). *Roberts v. Kindercare Learning Centers Inc.*, 86 F.3d 844 (8th Cir. 1996); *Mayberry v. Von Valtier*, 843 F. Supp. 1160 (R.D. Mich 1994). In *Mayberry*, the court determined that an auxiliary aid which costs $28.00 per hour would not be an undue burden for a doctor who charges $40.00 per hour. *Mayberry*, 843 F. Supp. at 1160. In *Roberts*, Kindercare did not have to provide a disabled person with a Personal Care Attendant when such an aid cost $200 per week and the cost of the child's weekly tuition is only $105. *Roberts*, 86 F.3d at 844.

The legislative history of the ADA provides the following example of the undue burden analysis which balances the costs of the auxiliary aid against the resources of the business:

> A small day-care center might not be required to expend more than a nominal sum, such as that necessary to equip a telephone for use by a secretary with impaired hearing, but a large school district might be required to make available a teacher's aide to a blind applicant for a teaching job.

H. R. Rpt. 101-485 pt 2. (May 15, 1990). In this example, it would be an undue burden for the small day care to provide an aide, but not for the large school. *Id.* Congress defined undue burden in this way because it was concerned about balancing the needs of disabled people with the high costs of accommodations. *Id.*, pt 3; 136 Cong. Rec. S9686 (daily ed. July 13, 1990). The legislative history shows that Congress intended to eliminate discrimination of disabled people in "a clear, balanced and reasonable manner." H. R. Rpt. 101-485 pt 2.

Here, providing CART would result in an undue financial burden. This case is factually similar to *Roberts,* and distinguishable from *Mayberry*. In *Mayberry*, the cost of providing an interpreter did not exceed the doctor's hourly charge, while in *Roberts*, the cost of providing a Personal Care Attendant did. The hourly cost of CART exceeds the amount of money that Kendall makes representing Veditz. (R. at 23.) If forced to provide CART, Kendall would lose money at a rate of $50 per hour. (*Id.*)

Veditz claims that CART is not an undue burden because Kendall will only have to provide CART when the parties are communicating face-to-face, or during group meetings at which Veditz is present. (R. at 20.) The fact remains, however, that Kendall would still lose money. For every hour that Kendall provides CART, he would not be paid for that hour of work,

6

and his next hour of regular work would be at half pay. Kendall's small private practice, as opposed to a large law firm, cannot absorb this loss. Forcing Kendall to provide CART may lead to substantial monetary loss, especially if future legal matters are long and complex. This evidence establishes that CART is a financial burden and does not support the District Court's findings.

The purpose of the ADA is to prevent discrimination against disabled people while limiting the severity of financial burden on small businesses. The undue burden exception applies differently to large companies and to small business owners. Kendall, as a small business owner, should only have to spend a small sum, such as the cost of an interpreter, and should not be required to pay for CART. The financial burden of CART negates Kendall's obligation to provide it. The District Court's finding that CART would not be an undue burden is clear error because Kendall loses substantial sums of money for every hour that CART is used. Written communication, the auxiliary aid that Kendall has provided, is the best auxiliary aid that Kendall can afford to offer Veditz.

II.

**The District Court Lacks the Power to
Order Parties to Mediate.**

This issue is one of law because it can be decided without reference to the facts of the case. Therefore, it is reviewed *de novo*, "that is, with no deference given to the finder of fact." *Reynolds v. City of Chicago*, 296 F.3d 524, 527 (7th Cir. 2002).

Veditz cites to several authorities, none of which explicitly provide a court with the power to order parties to mediate. In each instance, Veditz's arguments are based on strained interpretations of words that, read in context, mean something other than what Veditz claims they mean.

Rule 16(a)(5) of the Federal Rules of Civil Procedure allows a District Court to "direct" the litigants to "appear" at a pretrial conference, typically in a judge's chambers, for several purposes, among them "facilitating the settlement of the case." To facilitate means "to make easy or easier." *American Heritage Dictionary of the English Language* 653 (3d ed., 1992). It does not mean "order" or "compel." The plain wording of Rule 16 grants only the power to require parties to appear in a judge's chambers where, among other things, they might choose on their own to negotiate with each other. The words do not grant to a court the power to order parties to negotiate with each other, and they certainly do not grant the power to order parties to subject themselves to a mediation conducted by a mediator. The words "mediate," "mediation," and "mediator" do not appear anywhere in Rule 16.

7

This Circuit has held that Rule 16 does not grant powers others than those specifically mentioned in the Rule. *Strandell v. Jackson County*, 838 F.2d 884 (7th Cir.1987). There, a District Court ordered the parties to take part in a nonbinding jury trial, which is a form of alternative dispute resolution that (like mediation) is not mentioned in Rule 16. *Id.* at 884-886. This Circuit reversed, holding that Rule 16 does not justify "clubbing" the parties into a settlement procedure that one or both parties object to. *Id.* at 888.

Local Rule 16.2(b)(3) of the Southern District of Illinois also does not empower a District Court to order parties, against their will, to mediate. Instead, it provides that certain issues "shall be discussed at the final pretrial conference and shall be included in the final pretrial order," among them "any issue which, in the judge's opinion, may *facilitate and expedite the trial*." (italics added). Mediation does not facilitate or expedite trial. If successful, it settles the lawsuit and thus eliminates trial. The primary function of a pretrial conference is to coordinate getting ready for trial. Local Rule 16.2(b)(3) gives only one example of an issue that "may facilitate and expedite the trial." That is "the feasibility of presenting testimony [at trial] by a summary written statement." Local Rule 16.3(a) permits a District Court to order "summary jury trial or other alternative method of dispute resolution which the court may deem proper." None of these Rules mention mediation, and the example of summary jury trial suggests that the other permitted forms of alternative dispute resolution are limited to adversarial ones.

Although courts have many inherent powers in addition to those provided for in court rules, only one court has ever held that it had the inherent power to compel mediation. *In re Atlantic Pipe Corp.*, 304 F.3d 135, 140 (1st Cir. 2002). Another court recognized that it could have that power but declined to use it in part because parties objected. *In re African-American Slave Descendants' Litig.*, 272 F. Supp. 2d 755, 759 (N.D. Ill. 2003).

III.
Even if the District Court Had the Power to Order Mediation, It Abused Its Discretion in Doing So.

"To find an abuse of discretion, a court must have a definite and firm conviction that the district court committed a clear error in judgment." *Bell v. Johnson*, 404 F.3d 997, 1003 (6th Cir. 2005). Even if a court has the power to compel mediation, doing so over the objection of a party is a clear error in judgment. Mediation should not be compelled when one of the parties objects.

In exercising its inherent power, the court must use the power with restraint and discretion to enhance its processes. *In re African-American Slave Descendants' Litigation*, 272 F. Supp. 2d 755 (7th Cir. 2003). Voluntary participation is

8

the key to mediation's success and "when mediation is forced . . . it stands to reason that the likelihood of settlement is diminished." *Id.* Further, when settlement is unlikely, the investment of substantial time and money in mediation is inefficient and an undue burden on the objecting party. *Id.*

Mandatory mediation can be unfair, inefficient, or uneconomical. Mandatory mediation is overbearing when one party exerts its power over the other party, influencing the outcome of the mediation. Forced mediation also pressures parties to forgo trial and delays a party's day in court. Such a delay may effectively be a denial of justice. *G. Heileman Brewing Co., Inc., v. Joseph Oat Corp.*, 871 F.2d 648, 661 (7th Cir. 1987). Moreover, studies have shown that parties who mediate generally do not save time and money, and that courts do not reduce their caseloads, costs or delays. Holly A. Streeter-Schaefer, *A Look At Court Mandated Civil Mediation*, 28 Drake L. Rev. 367, 388 (2001).

In this case, mediation should not have been ordered because it would not produce a settlement. The likelihood that mediation will resolve this dispute is small because Kendall complied with the ADA and made accommodations for Veditz. Mediation, therefore, will not end the litigation, and the District Court will still have to resolve the case as an adversarial matter. Forcing the parties to mediation merely causes delay and adds to their expense.

CONCLUSION

For all these reasons the District Court erred in its findings and order, which should be reversed.

Respectfully Submitted,

Joanne Olson
Joanne Olson
Attorney for Appellant

Caroline Borden
Caroline Borden
Attorney for Appellant

9

Sample Appellee's Brief

In some ways, the format of this brief does not follow practices in the Seventh Circuit, where the appeal is set. Instead, the brief's format blends practices in many courts so that it is somewhat representative nationally.

In the UNITED STATES COURT OF APPEALS
for the SEVENTH CIRCUIT

Docket No. 2011–Civ.–141

———————————

AMOS KENDALL
Appellant

v.

GEORGE VEDITZ
Appellee

———————————

ON APPEAL FROM THE JUDGEMENT OF THE UNITED STATES
DISTRICT COURT FOR THE SOUTHERN DISTRICT
OF ILLINOIS

———————————

BRIEF FOR THE APPELLEE

———————————

Nathan J. Bailey
Attorney for the Appellee

TABLE OF CONTENTS

Page

i

ii

TABLE OF AUTHORITIES

Pages

Cases

---

* Authorities chiefly relied on are marked with an asterisk.

iii

Statutes

Regulations, Court Rules, and Legislative Histories

Other Authorities

iv

PROCEEDINGS BELOW

George Veditz is deaf. (R. at 8, 13.) Amos Kendall, a lawyer, represented Mr. Veditz in a divorce case. (R. at 3.) Mr. Veditz complained to Mr. Kendall that he could not understand Mr. Kendall's advice or even what was happening during a settlement negotiation. (R. at 2-16, 23.) Despite this, Mr. Kendall refused to provide an effective means through which he and others involved in the divorce case could communicate with Mr. Veditz. (R. at 18.)

Mr. Veditz, the appellee here, brought an action under the Americans with Disabilities Act against Mr. Kendall, the appellant. (R. at 1.) Mr. Veditz sought an injunction requiring Mr. Kendall to provide legal services in the future in compliance with the Act as well as attorney's fees, costs, and court-ordered mediation. (R. at 2.) Mr. Veditz also moved for an order compelling the parties to mediate their dispute. In granting that motion, the District Court found that Veditz had promptly asked for a type of disability accommodation called Computer Assisted Real Time Transcription (CART), that Mr. Kendall's failure to provide CART had prevented adequate communication between the parties while Mr. Kendall represented Mr. Veditz, and that providing CART would not be an undue burden on Mr. Kendall. (R. at 27.)

This appeal followed. (R. at 28, 29.)

QUESTIONS PRESENTED

1. Did the District Court have the authority under relevant court rules and statutes and through its inherent powers to order a lawyer to mediate a dispute with a deaf client where the client will continue to need the lawyer's services to resolve remaining issues from a prior representation?

2. Did the District Court properly determine that the deaf client had timely requested a method of communication appropriate to his deafness, that the lawyer had failed to provide a communications accommodation and thus prevented communication with his own client, and that a communications accommodation would not cause an undue burden on the lawyer?

STATEMENT OF THE CASE

George Veditz, who is deaf, was represented by Amos Kendall, an attorney, in a divorce action. During that lawsuit, Mr. Veditz at times had difficulty understanding what was happening and why it was happening because the defendant failed to supply translation services that a deaf person in Mr. Veditz's situation could understand.

1

Accommodations Needed to Overcome Mr. Veditz's Deafness

While represented by Mr. Kendall, Mr. Veditz suffered total hearing loss as a result of viral meningitis. (R. at 8, 13.) Mr. Veditz is a forty-three-year-old self-employed architect who specialized in historic preservation projects. (R. at 13.) Mr. Veditz can communicate fully with the aid of Computer Assisted Real-time Transcription (CART), and he can understand some Signed Exact English (SEE). (R. at 1.)

A highly trained deaf specialist, Laurent Marie Clerc, testified that SEE would be an effective method of signed communication for Mr. Veditz. (R. at 4.) Mr. Clerc, who regularly assesses the needs of deaf people, further stated that CART would be the best means to communicate with Mr. Veditz in meetings with multiple participants. (R. at 4, 19.) These services are easily obtainable at a rate of $150.00 per hour. (R. at 4, 19-20.) The District Court itself used CART services during the District Court proceedings. (R. at 12.).

Communication Failures During
the Divorce Settlement Negotiation

During a divorce settlement conference involving both lawyers and their clients, the lawyers and Mr. Veditz's former spouse talked continually for two hours. (R. at 5.) For this meeting, Mr. Kendall did not provide CART services or an SEE translator. Instead, he hired an uncertified interpreter who knew only American Sign Language (ASL). (R. at 4, 25.) The uncertified interpreter is a college student. (*Id.*) Mr. Veditz first met the interpreter immediately prior to the settlement conference. Mr. Veditz does not know ASL, and the interpreter's attempts at communicating in ASL only confused Mr. Veditz during the negotiation. (R. at 2, 15-16.) Mr. Veditz had to ask the interpreter to repeat herself many times because he did not understand all that she was signing. (R. at 16.)

Consequently, for Mr. Veditz the settlement conference was mostly a discussion he could not fully understand. Mr. Veditz privately informed Mr. Kendall that the student interpreter could not translate what was happening. (R. at 16.) After this, Mr. Kendall supplemented the sign language with summaries of the proceedings typed into his laptop. *Id.* Mr. Veditz testified that typing summaries on a laptop gave him only a rough idea of what was taking place and turned him into an observer instead of a participant at the conference. (R. at 14, 16.) Mr. Veditz believes that he missed opportunities to make his needs known at the conference, which lasted two hours and resulted in a written agreement between Mr. Veditz and his wife. (R. at 16, 23.)

Failure to Provide Communications Accommodations

Mr. Kendall knew that Mr. Veditz was still learning to sign but failed to ask Mr. Veditz how his communication needs could be accommodated.

2

(R. at 8.) Mr. Veditz believed that he could trust Mr. Kendall to do his best to obtain effective communication, and hence did not request CART specifically at the conference. (R. at 18.)

Although Mr. Veditz communicates mostly in writing while at work, his communication needs there do not need to be quick. In a law office, however, time is measured by money. Mr. Kendall charges $100 per hour. (R. at 3, 23.) Like many lawyers, he bills in 12-minute increments, which means that every 12 minutes of Mr. Kendall's work cost Mr. Veditz an additional $20. Mr. Veditz paid Mr. Kendall a total of $2,000 for his services. (R. at 24.)

Because Mr. Kendall failed to accommodate Mr. Veditz, Mr. Veditz will continue to have a maintenance obligation and need further legal assistance to resolve it. (R. at 16.)

SUMMARY OF THE ARGUMENT

The District Court correctly mandated mediation pursuant to the Federal Rules of Civil Procedure, the Court's local rules, the Alternative Dispute Resolution Act (ADR Act), and the Civil Justice Reform Act. The District Court also properly used its inherent powers to ensure the speedy disposition of cases. Furthermore, in light of public policy, the Court should compel mediation.

Mr. Veditz thus was denied the opportunity to have full legal representation because he is deaf. The District Court properly found that Mr. Veditz requested CART services, even though he is not required to request effective communication. The District Court also properly found that ineffective communication at Mr. Veditz's negotiation meetings was the result of Mr. Kendall's failure to provide reasonable accommodations. Lastly, the District Court correctly found that Mr. Kendall could comply with the ADA by providing CART services, which do not impose an undue burden on him.

ARGUMENT

I.
The District Court's Order Compelling Mediation Should Be Affirmed Because This Dispute Can Be Resolved More Effectively Through Mediation Than Through Trial.

Whether the District Court has the power to compel mediation is a question of law, to be reviewed *de novo*. *United States v. Weaver,* 234 F.3d 42, 46 (D.C. Cir. 2000); *United States v. Cuffie,* 80 F.3d 514, 517 (D.C. Cir. 1996). A District Court's authority to compel arbitration derives from several sources of law: the Federal Rules of Civil Procedure, the local rules of the Southern District of Illinois, and the court's inherent powers.

3

A. Rule 16 of the Federal Rules of Civil Procedure Authorizes a District Court to Order Mediation.

Rule 16(a) of the Federal Rules of Civil Procedure provides that "[i]n any action, the court may in its discretion direct [the parties to] appear before [the court] . . . before trial for such purposes as (1) expediting the disposition of the action . . . and (5) facilitating the settlement of the case." Federal Rule 16(c) provides that "the use of special procedures to assist in resolving the dispute, when authorized by statute or local rule . . . may facilitate the just, speedy, and inexpensive disposition of the action." This Circuit has held that "[t]he spirit, intent, and purpose of [Rule 16] allow[s] courts to actively manage the preparation of cases for trial," while broadening judges' ability to "manage their affairs as an independent constitutional branch of government." *G. Heileman Brewing Co. v. Joseph Oat Corp.*, 871 F.2d 648, 650 (7th Cir. 1989).

When the Federal Rules of Civil Procedure were amended in 1983, the Advisory Committee noted that the goal of the amendments was the use of settlements as a valuable tool in the promotion of case management. *Federal Reserve Bank v. Carey-Canada, Inc.*, 123 F.R.D. 603, 607 (D. Minn. 1988). Rule 16 thus authorizes district courts to order parties to participate in alternative dispute resolution. *Id.* "It is hard to imagine that the drafters of the 1983 amendments actually intended to strengthen courts' ability to manage their caseloads while at the same time intended to deny the court the power to compel participation by the parties to the litigation." *Id.*

On the other hand, in *Strandell v. Jackson County*, this Court ruled out an argument made regarding the 1984 advisory committee comments. 838 F.2d 884, 888 (7th Cir. 1987). In *Strandell*, an attorney was ordered by the District Court to participate in a nonbinding jury trial, and this Court ruled that the District Court did not have the power to compel parties to participate in summary jury trials pursuant to Federal Rule 16. *Id.* The *Strandell* court held that the rule was not designed as a means of "clubbing" the parties into an involuntary settlement. *Id.*

Soon after *Strandell*, however, district courts in three other circuits expressly rejected this Court's analysis and enforced court-ordered alternative dispute mechanisms as authorized by Federal Rule 16. *Federal Reserve Bank*, 123 F.R.D. 603 (concluding that a court's inherent power and Federal Rule 1 & 16 authorize the court to order alternative dispute mechanisms); *McKay v. Ashland Oil*, 120 F.R.D. 43, 47-48 (E.D. Ky. 1988) (holding that both Federal Rule 16 and the District Court's inherent power authorize a local rule for mandatory alternative dispute mechanisms); *Arabian American Oil Co. v. Scarfone*, 119 F.R.D. 448, 449 (M.D. Fla. 1988) (holding that Federal Rule 16 authorizes courts to order parties to engage in pretrial settlements).

4

In addition, soon after these three circuits rejected *Strandell*, Federal Rule 16(c) was amended, resulting in its current wording. The Advisory Committee noted that:

> The primary purposes of the changes in subdivision (c) are ... to eliminate questions that have occasionally been raised regarding the authority of the court to make appropriate orders designed either to facilitate settlement or to provide for an efficient and economical trial. The prefatory language of this subdivision is revised to clarify the court's power to enter appropriate orders at a conference *notwithstanding the objection of a party.*

Fed R. Civ. P. n. (1993) (Advisory Committee). (Italics added). The committee further noted that the amendments to the "rule acknowledge the presence of statutes and local rules ... that may authorize use of some of these procedures even when not agreed to by the parties." 28 U.S.C. §§473(a)(6), 473(b)(4).

> B. *Local Rule 16 of the Southern District of Illinois*
> *Authorizes the District Court to Order Mediation.*

Even if Federal Rule 16 were held not to authorize court-ordered mediation, the District Court still has the power to do so under the Southern District's Local Rule 16 which is broader than Federal Rule 16. Local Rule 16.2(b)(3) provides that "any issue which, in the judge's opinion, may facilitate and expedite the trial ... shall be discussed at the final pretrial conference and shall be included in the final pretrial order." Southern District Local Rule 16.3(a) further gives the court authorization to employ "alternative method[s] of dispute resolution which the court may deem proper," in order to "encourage and promote the use of alternative dispute resolution" so that "parties shall use an early neutral evaluation in the form of a settlement conference."

Local Rule 16.3 was written after *Strandell*. In *McKay v. Ashland Oil, Inc.*, the court distinguished *Strandell* by noting that Eastern and Western Kentucky Joint Local Rule 23—which is identical to Local Rule 16, except that "court" is replaced by "judge"—provides a District Court with the power to compel alternative dispute mechanisms. 120 F.R.D. at 48. In *McKay*, the judge was in an excellent position to determine the intent of Local Rule 23, because he was, in fact, the drafter of that rule. *Id.* The judge held that this language was written for the express authorization of compelled alternative dispute resolution. *Id.* The adoption of Southern District of Illinois Local Rule 16.3 after *Strandell* and the ruling in *McKay*, therefore, shows that compelled mediation is authorized by the local rules.

5

C. A District Court's Inherent Powers Include the Power to Order Mediation.

"Even apart from positive law, District Courts have substantial inherent power to manage and control their calendars." *In re Atlantic Pipe Corp.*, 304 F.3d 140, 143 (1st Cir. 2002). A court's "ability to take action in a procedural context," therefore, is governed by the "control necessarily vested in courts to manage their own affairs so as to achieve the orderly and expeditious disposition of cases." *G. Heileman Brewing Co.*, 871 F.2d at 650. The Supreme Court held that federal courts have inherent powers that are not dependent upon any express statutes or rules. *Link v. Wabash*, 370 U.S. 626 (1962).

"The exigencies of modern dockets demand the adoption of novel and imaginative means lest the courts, inundated by a tidal wave of cases, fail in their duty to provide a just and speedy disposition of every case." *Lockhart v. Patel*, 115 F.R.D. 44, 47 (E.D. Ky. 1987). While parties are often reluctant to participate in procedures outside the traditional norm, the need to compel the parties to mediation (and other forms of ADR) is an integral aspect of the court's ability to manage its docket. *Federal Reserve Bank*, 123 F.R.D. at 604.

Empirical evidence shows that cases compelled to mediation settle at about the same rate as those voluntarily mediated, and thus compulsion does not impede the effectiveness of mediation. *See* McEwen & Maiman, *Small Claims Mediation in Maine: An Empirical Assessment*, 33 Me. L. Rev. 237, 254 (1981). Even if mediation does not result in a settlement, it may cause a clarification of the issues, which reduce the length and cost of a later trial. *Federal Reserve Bank*, 123 F.R.D. at 605 (D. Minn. 1988).

The overall benefit of mediation is overwhelming. Mediation does not deprive a party of the right to litigate in court. Even when compelled, mediation only provides an alternative to trial, and trial can still occur if mediation fails. Mediation is also less costly and a more efficient method to resolve a dispute.

It is, therefore, within the court's inherent powers to compel mediation in this case. The District Court has already made the decision to order mediation and this Court should uphold that decision. The District Court's use of the "Standard Pre-trial Order" form, instructing that "the parties must mediate their dispute," makes it apparent that the court wishes to compel mediation in situations it deems necessary. Even though Mr. Kendall claims that mediation would impose additional costs on him, the cost of trial would be greater.

6

II.
The District Court Properly Found That Mr. Veditz Requested Cart Services, That the Parties Could Not Adequately Communicate Without Them, and That They Would Not Unduly Burden Mr. Kendall.

Determinations made by a District Court involving the ADA are findings of fact, reviewed for substantial evidence on the record. *See Melendez v. United States Department of Justice*, 927 F.2d 211, 216-219 (2d Cir. 1991).

The ADA provides that "[n]o individual shall be discriminated against on the basis of disability in the full and equal enjoyment of the . . . services . . . of any place of public accommodation by any person who . . . operates a place of public accommodation." 42 U.S.C. §12182 (2000). The ADA defines discrimination to include "a failure to take such steps as may be necessary to ensure that no individual with a disability is excluded, denied services . . . or otherwise treated differently than other individuals because of the absence of auxiliary aids and services, unless the entity can demonstrate that taking such steps . . . would result in an undue burden." *Id.*

A. Mr. Veditz Requested Better Communication and Is Not Required to Request CART Services Specifically.

A business subject to the ADA, like Mr. Kendall's law practice, is ultimately responsible for selecting the appropriate auxiliary aid, provided that the method chosen causes effective communication. 42 U.S.C. §§12102 *et seq.*; *Proctor v. Prince George's Hosp. Ctr.*, 32 F. Supp. 2d 820 (D. Md. 1998). The Supreme Court has held that the basic requirement of the ADA entails "that the need of a disabled person be evaluated on an individual basis." *PGA Tour, Inc. v. Martin*, 532 U.S. 661, 690 (2001). Based upon a careful review of the ADA legislative history, the Department of Justice found "that strongly encouraging consulta-tion with persons with disabilities [concerning their needs] . . . is consistent with congressional intent." *Majocha v. Turner*, 166 F. Supp. 2d 316, 321-322 (D. Pa. 2001), citing, 56 Fed. Reg. 35565-35567 (July 26, 1991). In effect, "the best way to serve hearing impaired clients is to plan in advance" by consulting with the client and researching all possible alternatives. Roy Miller & Sheila Simon, *Lawyers, Hearing Impaired Clients, and the Americans with Disabilities Act*, 81 Ill. B.J. 153, 154 (1993).

In determining whether Mr. Veditz requested CART services, this Court should defer to the District Court's finding of facts. The facts indicate that Mr. Veditz's request for further help should have prompted Mr. Kendall to integrate Mr. Veditz fully into the settlement negotiations. The ADA does

7

not require Mr. Veditz to specifically request CART services. Rather, it requires Mr. Kendall, a practicing attorney, to know the law and insure that he follows it to communicate with his client.

B. *The Inadequate Communications Accommodations Mr. Kendall Provided Violated the ADA.*

Title III of the ADA, along with the regulations implementing the Act, provide that a business furnish appropriate auxiliary aids and services where necessary to ensure effective communication with disabled persons. 28 C.F.R. §36.303(c) (2004); 42 U.S.C. §§12102 (2000), *et seq.* The ADA term "auxiliary aids and services" includes "qualified interpreters or other effective methods of making aurally delivered materials available to individuals with hearing impairments." 42 U.S.C. §12102 (2000). The main requirement of the communication method, therefore, is effective communication. *Id.*

While there are no national standards for interpreters, state law can provide useful guidelines for determining whether or not an interpreter is qualified. Under Illinois Law,

> No person may represent himself or herself as an interpreter for the deaf, work as a professional interpreter for the deaf, or use the title "interpreter for the deaf" . . . unless he or she can show proof of: (1) a certificate issued by the Registry of Interpreters for the Deaf (RID); (2) a satisfactory evaluation by the National Association of the Deaf; (3) a satisfactory Interpreter Skills Assessment Screening (ISAS) evaluation; or (4) licensure or certification or a satisfactory evaluation or screening in another state.

225 Ill. Comp. Stat. §442/5(a) (2007). The record contains no evidence that the novice ASL interpreter provided by Mr. Kendall has these qualifications. (R. at 25.) The uncertified interpreter did not know SEE, the language Mr. Veditz was familiar with, and admitted to not being able to communicate effectively. (R. at 16.) Instead, the interpreter knew ASL, a language that Mr. Veditz was not familiar with. *Id.*

Furthermore, the summaries typed on a laptop, in lieu of verbatim dialogue, are hardly sufficient. While the laptop may have been previously helpful between the parties, it cannot be adequate in negotiations or in a situation where more than two people are communicating back and forth. The participants will inevitably speak far more quickly than Mr. Kendall could have typed. And if he was typing, he could not have been using his time fully to argue for his client. The expert witness at trial testified that the laptop method was not effective for meetings with multiple participants, and that, in these instances, CART would be ideal. (R. at 19.)

8

C. Providing CART Services Would Not Impose an Undue Burden on Mr. Kendall.

An accommodation under the ADA is not required if it would impose an undue burden on the business involved by requiring "significant difficulty or expense." 42 U.S.C. §§12111(10)(A), 12182 (2000); 28 C.F.R. 36.104 (2004). Mr. Kendall argues that he would suffer an undue burden because he would lose money if he were to pay $150 an hour for CART services while charging Mr. Veditz $100 an hour. That is not true, either factually or legally.

A business the size of Mr. Kendall's law practice is entitled to a disabled access tax credit for part of the cost of providing accommodations to the disabled, including "provid[ing] qualified interpreters or other effective methods of making aurally delivered materials available to individuals with hearing impairments" 26 U.S.C. §44(a) & (c)(2)(B) (2000). The credit equals fifty percent of the costs greater than those that add up to more than $250 for the taxable year, not exceeding $10,250. §44(a). This is not a deduction reducing taxable income. It is a credit that directly reduces Mr. Kendall's federal income tax by half of every dollar he spends on accommodating the disabled over $250 for the taxable year.

Mr. Kendall testified that he billed $2,000 to Mr. Veditz at a rate of $100 per hour for 20 hours of legal services. (R. at 23-24.) Only two of these 20 hours would have required the CART services that Mr. Kendall says would be too expensive. (R. at 23.) At $150 an hour, CART services would have cost $300. If Mr. Kendall spent no other money on disability accommodations during the taxable year, the tax credit would have reduced that to $275 (50 percent of the amount over $250). But if Mr. Kendall spent at least $250 on other forms of accommodations, the tax credit would have reduced the CART expense to $150. Thus, of the $2,000 Mr. Kendall charged Mr. Veditz, either $275 or $150 would have gone to CART services. That effectively would have lowered his hourly billing rate concerning Mr. Veditz from $100 to either $86.25 or $91.25.

Thus, it is misleading to compare the $150 hourly cost of CART services with Mr. Kendall's hourly rate of $100. The practice of law is filled with similar expenses that seem large when compared with a lawyer's hourly rate but do not make representing a client unprofitable when compared to the total paid by the client to the lawyer over the course of the representation. An example is the cost charged by Lexis and Westlaw for computer-assisted legal research.

Concerning the cost of accommodations under the ADA, Dr. I King Jordan, President of Gallaudet University, testified before the Senate that "it needs to be made clear to people that the accommodations are not nearly as large as some people would lead us to believe." 135 Cong. Rec. S10765 (1989). That same day, Senator Leahy stated that "In this country, equality

9

for all Americans is not a matter of cost. It is a matter of justice." *Id.* Under the ADA, therefore, one is "legally required to provide effective communication, and meeting that obligation is simply a cost of doing business" Miller & Simon, 81 Ill. B.J. at 154. In fact, in some instances "the financial benefits of accessibility may outweigh the costs." *Id.*

CONCLUSION

Mr. Kendall can be compelled to mediate and should be required to do so. The order of the District Court should therefore be affirmed.

Respectfully Submitted,

Nathan J. Bailey
Nathan J. Bailey,
Attorney for Appellee

10

Troublesome Punctuation

This is not a comprehensive guide to punctuation. It hits only the persistent issues.

1. Apostrophes, Fingernails, and Chalkboards

For many readers, apostrophe mistakes are like hearing fingernails scraping a chalkboard.

Start by distinguishing among plurals (more than one); possessives (which show ownership or something similar); and contractions (two words mushed together). In a formal memo or brief, don't use contractions, although they're fine in an informal client letter.

NOUNS: A plural noun usually ends in an *s* with no apostrophe ("six plaintiffs"). A singular, possessive noun usually ends in an *s* preceded by an apostrophe ("the plaintiff's complaint").

> **wrong:** Both the legislature and the *court's* have refused to modify the rule.

This concerns more than one court. "Court's" should be plural, but the apostrophe makes it possessive instead.

> **also wrong:** The defendant appealed the *courts* decision.

Troublesome Punctuation

This is the opposite problem. The court owns the decision and should be possessive. But without an apostrophe, it is plural instead.

PRONOUNS: Pronouns follow different rules. That's where the trouble usually starts. Don't confuse a contraction with a possessive. And be careful with *it, who,* and *they.*

it—

contraction:	*it's* = *it is* or *it has* ("It's election day tomorrow.")
possessive:	*its* means that *it* possesses whatever follows ("The state reelected its attorney general.")
fingernails on chalkboard:	writing *it's* when you mean that *it* possesses something (write *its* instead)

who—

contraction:	*who's* = *who is* or *who has* ("Who's going to lunch?")
possessive:	*whose* means that *who* possesses whatever follows ("Whose sandwich is this?")
fingernails on chalkboard:	writing *who's* when you mean that *who* possesses something (write *whose* instead)

they—

contraction:	*they're* = *they are* ("They're late.")
possessive:	*their* means that *they* possess whatever follows ("Their papers were time-stamped too late.")
fingernails on chalkboard:	writing *they're* when you mean that *they* possess something (write *their* instead)

What's wrong with these sentences?

The courts have limited this precedent to it's facts.

The courts can impose sanctions on a party who's complaint lacks a basis in law or fact.

The courts have streamlined they're procedures by adopting a new set of rules.

Here's the basic principle: *Because a pronoun's contraction is formed with an apostrophe, its possessive cannot have an apostrophe.* Otherwise, the contraction and the possessive would look exactly the same.

This box might also help you remember:

the contraction	the possessive
it's ("it is")	its
who's ("who is")	whose
they're ("they are")	their

2. Commas and Introductory Words, Phrases, and Clauses

An introductory phrase or clause is usually set off from the sentence by a comma. Without a comma after "computer," the first example is confusing:

wrong: Frustrated with all the spyware and viruses on his computer the mouse potato threw it out the window.

correct: Frustrated with all the spyware and viruses on his computer, the mouse potato threw it out the window.

If the introductory word or phrase could have been moved elsewhere in the sentence and would not have needed a comma there, a comma is not usually required to set it off at the beginning of the sentence. But you might want to use a comma anyway for stylistic reasons.

correct: Unfortunately he then sat in front of the television and became a couch potato.

placed elsewhere: He then sat in front of the television and unfortunately became a couch potato.

also correct: Unfortunately, he then sat in front of the television and became a couch potato.

To prevent confusion, set off a *long* introductory phrase with a comma, even if it's not required.

3. Commas Both Before and After an Interruption

If a word, phrase, or clause should be set off with commas because of the way it interrupts a sentence, one comma should precede it and a second comma should follow. You need both the "before" comma and the "after" comma. Don't leave one of them out.

> **wrong:**   Joe who has been granted parole, will be released.

Where does the interruption begin? The one comma above tells the reader only where it ends.

> **wrong:**   Joe, who has been granted parole will be released.

Now we know where the interruption begins. But will the reader be able to tell— without rereading the sentence—where the interruption ends?

> **correct:**   Joe, who has been granted parole, will be released.

4. Commas and Independent Clauses

Two independent clauses can be joined together into one sentence with a conjunction (*and, but, or*). When you do that, put a comma before the conjunction.

> **wrong:**   The T-Rex in *Jurassic Park* ate a lawyer and audiences cheered.

This sentence has two independent clauses. Each has a subject ("The T-Rex" and "audiences"). And each has a verb ("ate" and "cheered"). Each clause could be a separate sentence. That's why they're independent. The conjunction "and" is not enough to join them together. It needs a comma as well:

> **correct:**   The T-Rex in *Jurassic Park* ate a lawyer, and audiences cheered.

If what comes after the conjunction doesn't have a separate subject of its own, don't add a comma:

> **wrong:**   The T-Rex in *Jurassic Park* ate a lawyer, and got indigestion.

"The T-Rex in *Jurassic Park*" is the subject for both "ate a lawyer" and "got indigestion." In a list of two (here, two verbs), no comma separates them. The conjunction "and" does the job.

> **correct:**   The T-Rex in *Jurassic Park* ate a lawyer and got indigestion.

5. Commas and Breathing

Don't add a comma just because a person reading the sentence aloud would run out of breath. No rule of grammar justifies the comma in this sentence:

> **wrong:** The argument that Napster did not infringe Metallica's copyrights when distributing the band's music over the Internet, is undermined by case law.

If reading the sentence aloud would cause a breathing problem, something is probably wrong with the way the sentence is structured. Try moving the big, complicated part of the sentence to the end:

> **restructured:** Case law undermines the argument that Napster did not infringe Metallica's copyrights when distributing the band's music over the Internet.

6. Commas and Missing Words

Don't add a comma just because you've left out a word. No rule of grammar justifies the comma in this sentence:

> **wrong:** The court held, abduction by aliens does not excuse failure to attend one's own deposition.

Take out the comma and insert the missing word:

> **correct:** The court held that abduction by aliens does not excuse failure to attend one's own deposition.

7. Punctuation at the End of a Quotation

If you need punctuation at the end of a quotation, does it go inside the quotation marks or outside? A comma or a period goes *inside* the quote marks, even if it's your own comma or period and did not appear in the original quotation. But if you add a colon, semicolon, dash, or question mark, put it *outside* the quote marks.

> **correct:** The defendant may have called the plaintiff "the worst Elvis impersonator in the state," but that is hardly defamatory.

Did the defendant use the comma? Or was it added by the writer? It doesn't matter. Either way, it goes inside the quote marks.

also correct:	In fact, it would be futile to try to find defamatory meaning in "the worst Elvis impersonator in the state": our state is so richly endowed with excellent Elvis impersonators that our least talented practitioner might be considered brilliant elsewhere.

Here it does matter where the colon came from. If it was added by the writer, it goes outside the quote marks.

8. Simple and Complicated Lists—Commas and Semicolons

Legal writing is full of lists. Lawyers have to be able to express lists in ways that are crystal-clear to the reader. With a simple and easily understood list, separate the items with commas. Use semicolons instead if the list is so complicated that commas won't clearly show where one item ends and the next begins.

correct:	The plaintiff sued, went to trial, and lost.
also correct:	The court ordered the corporation dissolved; placed the property under the control of a receiver; and enjoined the defendants from conducting business by interstate telephone, wire, or delivery service.

The second example has a list within a list:

- ordered the corporation dissolved;
- placed the property under the control of a receiver; and
- enjoined the defendants from conducting business by
  - interstate telephone,
  - wire, or
  - delivery service.

Using semicolons for the big list allows you to use commas for the little list inside the third item in the big list.

9. Parentheses and Enumeration

Enumeration is the numbering of items in a list. When lawyers and judges state a rule of law, they often enumerate the elements. When you do that, enclose each number completely in parentheses.

wrong: At common law, a person committed burglary by 1) breaking
and 2) entering. . . .

correct: At common law, a person committed burglary by (1) breaking
and (2) entering. . . .

Troublesome Words

AND/OR is both ambiguous and awkward. Instead, find a solution like this:

needs rewriting: Under Rule 11, sanctions can be imposed on the attorney and/or on the client.

much better: Under Rule 11, sanctions can be imposed on the attorney, the client, or both.

APPLY does not communicate a precise meaning. For example: "The Freedom of Information Act applies to this case." Does the Act require that the document at issue be published in the Federal Register? Does it require that the document be given to anyone who asks for a copy? Does it require that the document be available for photocopying, but not at government expense? Or does it give the government permission to refuse to do any of these things? Replace *applies* with a verb that communicates exactly what the Act does.

ARGUE: Lawyers argue; courts don't. Argument is intended to persuade others. You argue when you lack the power to decide, and you argue to those who have that power. A court therefore *decides, holds, finds, rules, concludes, determines,* and so on. A dissenting judge, however, did not decide the case and can accurately be said to "argue" in the dissent.

DEAL WITH does not communicate a precise meaning. For example: "The court dealt with common law larceny." What exactly did the court do to larceny? Define it? Define only one of the elements? Clarify the difference between larceny and false pretenses? Decide that the legislature impliedly abolished the crime of larceny when it enacted a theft statute? Delete *dealt with* and insert a verb that tells exactly what the court actually did.

GUILTY and INNOCENT: Despite what you hear on the evening news, criminal defendants do not plead "innocent." And juries do not find them "innocent." *Innocent* and *not guilty* do not mean the same thing. *Innocent* means the defendant did not commit a crime. *Not guilty* means the prosecution did not prove beyond a reasonable doubt that the defendant committed a crime. What if the defendant committed a crime but the prosecution didn't prove it beyond a reasonable doubt? The defendant is *not guilty*. In a criminal case, the issue is not whether the defendant is innocent. The issue is whether the prosecution can prove guilt beyond a reasonable doubt. *Not guilty* means the prosecution did not do that.

GUILTY and LIABLE: A *guilty* defendant has been convicted, in a criminal prosecution, of committing a crime. In a civil case, a losing defendant might be *liable* to the plaintiff. Some civil cases do not involve liability. But in a civil case there's no guilt. And in a criminal case there's no liability.

INDICATE does not communicate a precise meaning. For example: "The defendant indicated that he was interested in buying hashish." How did he do that? By nodding affirmatively when asked if that was his desire? By asking, "Is hashish sold in this neighborhood?" By saying, "I want to buy some hash"? The law might treat these possibilities differently, and the reader needs to know exactly what happened.

INVOLVE does not communicate a precise meaning. For example: "Section 452(a) involves the Rule Against Perpetuities." That says only that §452(a) has some connection with the Rule Against Perpetuities. Has §452(a) codified the Rule? Modified it? Abolished it? Delete *involves* and insert a verb that specifies exactly §452(a) and the Rule Against Perpetuities have to do with each other.

JUDGMENT: Lawyers always spell *judgment* with only one *e*. Other people might spell it with two *e*'s *(judgement)*, but lawyers never do.

MOTION: A motion is a request for a court order or a judgment. To get an order or judgment, a lawyer *moves* or *makes a motion*. A lawyer does not "motion for an order." (Like everybody else, a lawyer "motions" by making a physical gesture, such as waving or pointing at something.) And a lawyer does not "move *the court* for an order." In that phrase and others like it, "the court" is understood—and need not be stated—because only courts and administrative tribunals can grant orders. And to many readers, adding "the court" looks silly because it evokes other meanings. For example: "The judge wiped away a tear, and it was clear that the witness's story had moved the court."

OVERRULE and REVERSE mean different things. An appellate court *overrules* a precedent when it decides that the precedent is no longer good law. (Only an appellate court has the power to do that.) An appellate court *reverses* when it determines that a lower court decided incorrectly. (In another context, *overrule* has an entirely different meaning. When a trial judge rejects an attorney's objection to something the opposing attorney has done, the objection is *overruled*.)

SAY: Statutes do not *say* things, and courts *say* things only in dicta. Statutes are called *Acts* because the legislature did something by enacting. In statutes legislatures *provide, create, abolish, prohibit, penalize, define*, and more. When a court *holds* or *finds*, it is doing and not merely talking. *Hold* and *find* have synonyms—*conclude, determine, decide, reason, define*, etc.—but *say* is not one of them. On the other hand, a judge writing a concurrence or dissent does not act for the court, and therefore can accurately be considered to *say* things. (See **Argue.**)

THE is sometimes omitted by lawyers, but only before *plaintiff, defendant, appellant, appellee, petitioner, respondent,* and similar party designations. But much of the time your writing will seem less artificial if you say *the* even before party designations. It's fine to title a document "Memorandum of Law in Support of Defendant's Motion for Summary Judgment," but inside the memorandum you're better off writing "The defendant is entitled to summary judgment because the plaintiff has adduced no evidence that could show . . . ."

VERBAL: If you want to be precise, don't write *verbal* when you mean *oral. Verbal* means having to do with words, spoken or written. A verbal communication is one that was made in words and not through gestures or shrieks. An oral communication is spoken rather than written. "The misuse of *verbal* for *oral* has a long history and is still common."[1] But the law needs clear ways of differentiating between the written and the spoken word and between communication through words and communication through other means. For example, in contract law the statute of frauds makes certain *oral* contracts unenforceable. A lawyer who tells a judge that the parties made a "verbal" contract is apt to be interrupted with a question like "Counselor, do you mean they made an oral contract? Or do you mean that this contract is expressed in words as opposed to an implied contract created by the parties' conduct?" Use *oral* for spoken communication and *verbal* for communication in words.

---

[1] Bryan Garner, *A Dictionary of Modern Legal Usage* 911 (2d ed. 1995).

Document Design

Designing a document is deciding how it should look on the page. Design has nothing to do with the content (your words expressing your ideas). Instead, design creates a visual personality for the document—an attractive appearance that's easy to read. Some documents are unfriendly and hard to read just because of the way they look. Others appear good on a page, seem inviting, and are a pleasure to read.

Layout and typeface are the primary elements of document design. Layout is the arrangement of type on the page so that your organization is clear and the reader is not overwhelmed with text.

Typeface is what the letters and numbers look like: type size, font, and features like *italics* and **bold**. Type size is how big the letters and numbers are, usually measured in points. A font is a group of letters and numbers with a common design (which will become more clear in a moment).

Good document design can help persuade a reader. Here's what the Seventh Circuit tells its lawyers:

> Judges of this court hear six cases on most argument days and nine cases on others. The briefs, opinions of the district courts, essential parts of the appendices, and other required reading add up to about 1,000 pages per argument session. Reading that much is a chore; remembering it is even harder. You can improve your chances by making your briefs typographically superior. It won't make your arguments better, but it will ensure that judges grasp and retain your points with less struggle. That's a valuable advantage, which you should seize.[1]

---

[1] *Requirements and Suggestions for Typography in Briefs and Other Papers*, at 4, http://www.ca7.uscourts.gov/Rules/type.pdf. *See also* Derek H. Kiernan-Johnson, *Telling Through Type: Typography and Narrative in Legal Briefs*, 7 J. ALWD 87 (2010); Ruth Anne Robbins, *Painting with Print: Incorporating Concepts of Typographic and Layout Design into the Text of Legal Writing Documents*, 2 J. ALWD 108 (2004).

Judge Frank Easterbrook of the same circuit speaks more pointedly: "Why should lawyers think that their [briefs] can be physically ugly and hard to read, yet still go over well?"[2]

If you're running out of time before an assignment is due, *please stop reading this appendix now*. Write the document. Don't spend your limited time trying to enhance its appearance on the page. *Just write it*. Content does matter more than document design.

Part 1. Simple Document Design

Your word processor is the software in your computer with which you write documents. It is probably either Word or WordPerfect. What we say here applies to both.

Default font and type size: Your word processor probably defaults either to Times New Roman or Calibri (fonts) and 11- or 12-point (type sizes). The fonts look like this:

Times New Roman

Calibri

Later versions of Word default to Calibri. Earlier versions default to Times New Roman, as does WordPerfect. You can change these default settings. Unless they are changed, your word processor will automatically produce one or the other of these fonts every time you start a new document.

For the most part, fonts are either *serif* or *sans serif*. In a serif font (like Times New Roman) most letters have little transverse lines called *serifs*. A sans serif font (like Calibri) has no serifs. (In *sans*; the second *s* is silent. *Sans* is French and means *without*—without serifs. *Serif* is pronounced "SAIR-if"—not "se-REEF.")

Look closely as the Times New Roman and the Calibri examples above. Calibri looks streamlined because it has no serifs. Later versions of Word default to Calibri because it looks good on a computer screen. On computer and television screens, on signs, and in advertisements, a sans serif font is usually easier to read than a serif font.

But in a long document printed on paper a serif font is easier to read. The serifs actually help the reader's eyes travel through extended text. Books are usually printed in serif fonts, although in some (including this one) the headings are sans serif. In law practice, memos and briefs are printed in serif fonts.

Courts with typeface rules usually require that the text of submitted documents be printed in a serif font. You will not be able to use Calibri for most

---

[2] Frank H. Easterbrook, Speech, *Challenges in Reading Statutes*, at 16 (Chi., Ill., Sept. 28, 2007) at http://lawyersclubchicago.org/docs/Challenges.pdf.

documents you write in a law office. If it's the default font in your word processing software now, you might consider changing it. The easiest choice would be Times New Roman, just because it's commonly used and is the default font in other versions of Word and in WordPerfect. Lawyers use it regularly, and although it's problematic, you'll see it in many of the documents that come out of law offices. If you want to consider other fonts, see Part 3 of this appendix.

Near the top of your Word or WordPerfect screen is a small window that tells you which font the word processor is using. Next to it is an even smaller window that tells you the size of the type (a number). In Word 2007 those windows are on the top left, near the Home button. In earlier versions of Word, they're to the right of the top center of your screen. In WordPerfect, they're on the top left.

From each of those windows, a drop-down menu lets you change the font or the point size. To open the menu, click on the little down-arrow next to it. Click on the font you want; then click on the point size you want. If you are switching from Calibri to Times New Roman, be sure the point size is 12 points (not 11).

When you create a new document in either Word or WordPerfect, you can set its font and point size by placing the cursor at the very beginning of the document and clicking on the font and point size you want. In Word, you may have to do this before you type anything. To change an existing document's font and point size in Word, you may have to block the entire document and click on a font in the drop-down menu. In WordPerfect, just put the cursor at the beginning of the document and click on a font and a point size from the drop-down menus, and the whole document should change.

It's more complicated to reset your word processor's defaults so that *all* new documents will be in the same font and point size. But if you'll be using the same font often in the future, it'll take less effort in the long run to change the default once rather than choose the font every time you start a new document. Search your word processor's help function for instructions about changing the default font and the default point size.

Default justification: Justification determines where lines of type begin and end. If your documents are left-justified, the left side of your text forms a straight vertical line, and the right side is ragged because the text lines do not all end in the same place. If a document is fully justified, however, both the left and the right sides of the text form straight vertical lines. Most books are fully justified. The default setting on your word processor is probably left justification. That's fine. Nobody will criticize you for using it, and many readers will prefer it in the documents you produce.

White space: Too much type on a page can make a document difficult and unpleasant to read. Creating white space opens up the page and makes it less crowded and easier on the eye. Your word processor's default margins are probably one inch on each side. You can create white space by moving the left and right margins each a quarter inch toward the center of the page so that each has become 1.25 inches.

You can also create white space by the way you handle headings. In a single-spaced document, many writers will skip a line above a heading and skip another line below it. Instead, skip two lines above the heading. That will make your organization more visually obvious. The heading will more clearly belong to the text below it because twice as much white space will appear above as below. If your document is double-spaced, you can get similar results by pressing the Enter key twice above the heading and once below it. With double spacing, a line is skipped automatically every time you press Enter.

Don't go overboard. Too much white space reduces the amount of text on each page. You don't want to add so much white space that the reader has to turn pages constantly and can't easily back up to review what you said a paragraph or two earlier.

Adding white space also might increase the number of pages in your document. If your teacher has imposed a word or character limit on document size, increasing the number of pages won't matter. But if you're subject to a page limit, adding white space might put you over that limit.

Part 2. More Advanced Document Design

Headings: Each component of a memo or brief gets a heading, and the component headings are usually the largest in the document.

Office memo components include the Issue, Brief Answer, Facts, Discussion, and Conclusion. Sometimes you'll want to break up the Facts or Discussion with additional headings. They should be smaller than the component headings and can be italicized to set them off from the text. Here's a reasonable way of sizing the headings and text—but it's not the only way:

component headings:	TIMES NEW ROMAN 14-point
lesser headings:	*Times New Roman 13-point*
text:	Times New Roman 12-point

(If your text size is 11-point, reduce the component headings to 13-point and the lesser headings to 12-point.)

Lawyers have traditionally underlined lesser headings because that's all a typewriter could do. With a word processor, however, you can use italics instead, and italics are easier on the eye than underlining. In the Appendix A office memorandum, the component headings are in all-caps, and the lesser headings are italicized (as above).

In a persuasive document submitted to a court, such as a trial court memo or an appellate brief, the components would include—among others—the Statement of the Case and the Argument. The Argument is divided by point headings and might further be divided by lesser headings called *subheadings* (see Chapter 33).

The Statement of the Case might also be divided by lesser headings similar in size to the Argument subheadings. Here is a reasonable—*but not the only*—way of sizing the headings and text:

component headings:	TIMES NEW ROMAN 14-point
Argument point headings:	**Times New Roman 13-point in bold**
lesser headings:	*Times New Roman 13-point*
text:	Times New Roman 12-point

(If your text size is 11-point, reduce the component headings size to 13-point and the point headings and lesser headings to 12-point.)

Lawyers typically place the component headings centered on the page. They do the same thing with point headings in persuasive documents. Legal documents have looked that way for generations, and your readers will expect it. Some document design specialists say that if you left-justify the text, you should probably left-justify headings as well (move them to the left margin, like the section headings in this book). Lawyers, however, almost always center the component headings and the point headings. Some center lesser headings as well, but some move them to the left margin.

Lawyers traditionally all-cap the component headings. That's fine. Component headings are short, usually one to four words, and all-capping them causes no problems. See the memos in Appendices A and C and the briefs in Appendices D and E.

In persuasive documents submitted to courts, lawyers have traditionally all-capped point headings as well. You'll see that in most trial court memos and appellate briefs. In the typewriter era, all-capping was the only way to make a point heading stand out. Today an increasing number of lawyers use bold print instead of all-caps, which has been done in the Appendix C motion memo and the Appendices D and E appellate briefs.

Because point headings have more words than component headings, they're harder to read when all-capped. Compare two versions of the first point heading in Exercise I at the end of Chapter 33:

all caps, Times New Roman, 13-point:	THE DETAINEE ACT DOES NOT STRIP THE COURT OF JURISDICTION OVER THIS CASE.
bold, Times New Roman, 13-point:	**The Detainee Act Does Not Strip the Court of Jurisdiction Over This Case.**

All-capping makes the first example hard to read. The second example stands out well because it's in bold, and it takes up less space and is more readable because it's not all-capped.

But the second example is not as readable as it could be. That's not the fault of bolding. It's a font problem. The rest of this appendix explains why.

Part 3. The Truth About Fonts

One of the oldest traditions of the bar seems to be that legal documents should always *look* boring. Many readers of legal documents intensely dislike this tradition.

Legal documents should look *professional*. That's not the same as looking boring. Judges spend enormous amounts of time reading briefs and other lawyer-submitted documents, and nearly all the judges who have stated their views on this subject would like to read attractive and readable fonts that reflect good taste.

Should you use a font other than Times New Roman for legal documents? An advantage of using Times New Roman is that you don't need to think about it. And in law school you have more important things to do than playing around with fonts to find the one you like best. Unless you really do have the spare time to choose a new font, skip the rest of this appendix.

Times New Roman can be tiring to read. When you compare it with another commonly used font, you can see how its letters are cramped and tightly packed:

Times New Roman 12-point

Century Schoolbook 12-point

The Seventh Circuit has run out of patience with Times New Roman and implores lawyers to use some other font. This is on the Circuit's website: "Typographic decisions should be made for a purpose. The *Times of London* [a newspaper] chose the typeface Times New Roman to serve an audience looking for a quick read. Lawyers don't want their audience to read fast and throw the document away; they want to maximize retention."[3]

Times New Roman is a newspaper font. Its letters are crammed close together so they can fit into narrow newspaper columns, on the assumption that most readers won't read much more than the first few paragraphs anyway. It was not designed or intended for long documents like memos and briefs. Even newspapers have been switching to other fonts.

The Supreme Court will reject any brief printed in Times New Roman. It insists on fonts in the Century family, such as Century Schoolbook.[4] "The Justices are tired of bad typography," says Judge Easterbrook of the Seventh Circuit.[5] Many other fonts look professional, and you might like one of them better.

---

[3] *Requirements and Suggestions, supra* note 1, at 3.
[4] Supreme Court Rules 24.1 and 33.1(b).
[5] Easterbrook, *supra* note 2, at 15.

How to choose a replacement font: Choosing a new serif font is not a substitute for studying or for doing a writing assignment. It's a study-break activity.

You'll want a font that looks professional, is easy to read, and pleases the eye. Eye appeal is not the same as readability. An attractive font makes a good impression visually by inviting a reader warmly into the document and helping the reader feel comfortable—all by being pleasant to look at. Lawyers might think it odd to consider the reader's pleasure, but the Seventh Circuit recommends doing exactly that.

A safe choice might be Century Schoolbook. If the Supreme Court insists on a Century-family font, you can safely assume that it's readable, attractive, and professional.

But in case you'd like more choices, below are some professional-looking fonts, with Century Schoolbook for comparison. In the text of a memo or brief, you could use these point sizes or one point smaller (for example, Century Schoolbook in 11-point).

Bell MT 13-point

Book Antiqua 12-point

Calisto MT 12-point

Century Schoolbook 12-point

Goudy Old Style 12-point

If you like any of these, take a document you've already written, change its font, and see how it looks. If you're not happy with the result, change it again until you find the font you're most happy with. (Part 1 of this appendix explains how to change fonts.)

Be careful about the point size recommendations in Part 2 of this appendix. If you select a font other than Times New Roman, you should experiment to find the point sizes that work best in headings.

The most attractive fonts were created by artistic people, and some fonts are considered art. In *The Elements of Typographic Style*, Robert Bringhurst wrote that letters on the page "have a life and dignity of their own. . . . Well-chosen words deserve well-chosen letters. . . ."[6]

---

[6] Robert Bringhurst, *The Elements of Typographic Style* 18 (1992, 2002) (italics omitted).

Index

References are to sections (§), chapters (Ch.), and appendices (App.).

Index

Index